EDUCATION AND SOCIETY

An Introduction to the Sociology of Education

by

A. K. C. OTTAWAY
Senior Lecturer in Education
The University of Leeds

With an introduction by
W. O. LESTER SMITH

LONDON
ROUTLEDGE & KEGAN PAUL

First published in 1953
by Routledge and Kegan Paul Ltd.
Broadway House, 68-74 Carter Lane
London EC4V 5EL
Reprinted three times
Second edition (revised) 1962
Reprinted 1964, 1966, 1968, 1970, 1976

Printed in Great Britain by
Redwood Burn Limited
Trowbridge & Esher

ISBN 0 7100 4662 6 (p)
ISBN 0 7100 3316 8 (c)

Contents

CONTENTS

Introduction

by

PROFESSOR W. O. LESTER SMITH
Professor of the Sociology of Education in the University of London

We are all sociologists now in the sense that we recognize that it is impossible to think purposefully about many contemporary problems without thinking also about society. Such an approach is certainly not new, for none have used it more effectively than did Plato and Aristotle. But in modern times the study of society has acquired a new name for itself—not a remarkably euphonious one—and has become a discipline in its own right. As such it has been set on its ever widening course by pioneers in various countries—Durkheim in France, Max Weber in Germany, Hobhouse in England—and to-day as a study it flourishes nowhere more profusely or profoundly than in the United States. Like other studies, it has various specialisms: statistical, demographic and so on. But in spite of the widening scope of sociological literature, teachers in this country are not well provided for if they wish to examine its special application to educational principles and practice. For them, and for students preparing for the teaching profession, there is not, so far as I am aware, any book which can serve specifically as an introduction to the sociology of education and furnishing an appropriate bibliography. Yet there is a growing demand for such an introduction, one that illuminates social and political issues that affect education, relates them to our own contemporary problems, and does this with an understanding of British ways of thought and life.

What I have found in my experience to be a particular need is a book of this kind, which adheres fairly closely to the sociological tradition so well set in motion in this country by Hobhouse and Graham Wallas and so wisely developed in our generation by Professor Ginsberg and others. One happy feature of this tradition is that it presents the problems of society in English undefiled by the jargon which some schools of thought affect, and does not clutter our vocabulary with such verbal infelicities as 'acculturization', 'sociatric', and the like. It can say with William of Wykeham that 'manners maketh man', without finding it necessary to debase this into 'a certain configuration of behaviour situations determines the dynamic orientation of the male character structure'. How refreshing it is to turn from one of these needlessly obscure treatises to Wallas's *The Great Society* or to such transatlantic models of plain English as the writings of Professor MacIver or the Harvard Report on 'General Education in a Free Society'.

Karl Mannheim did, perhaps, more than anyone to arouse the interest of the teaching profession here in sociological thinking, and his all too brief spell of service in the University of London already stands out as a landmark in the recent history of the training of teachers in this country. His *Diagnosis of Our Time* and his *Man and Society* have had a far-reaching influence, creating among teachers a growing demand for literature and lectures on the relationship of social and political thought to school problems. Sir Fred Clarke, by the influence of his personality, his inspiring quality as a lecturer to teacher audiences, and his stimulating little book *Education and Social Change* fostered and furthered this interest in the study of society during the post-war years. For this and other reasons—not least the implications of the Education Act of 1944—the necessity for a book on educational sociology for English readers has become increasingly urgent. Mr. Ottaway is, therefore, much to be congratulated on being the first to make a serious attempt to fill this important gap, and he is well fitted for the difficult pioneer task that he has undertaken. After taking his first degree in science, and teaching biology and chemistry for some years at Abbotsholme School, he took up full-time study and research for the M.A. degree in education at the University of London Institute of Education, enjoying the unique advantage of coming under the direct influence there of Fred Clarke and later Karl Mannheim. For the last five years he has lectured and tutored at the University of Leeds Department of Education, and this book has been forged on the anvil of that valuable experience. It is not for me to commend it; it will, I am confident, commend itself and soon gain recognition as a thoughtful and useful introduction to the general study of educational sociology.

In a recent appreciative survey of Karl Mannheim's writings, *The Times Literary Supplement* commented on his contact with wide circles of men and women interested in social and political thought. 'The most remarkable of his concrete achievements', it observed, 'was to found and edit that unique series of volumes known as 'The International Library of Sociology and Social Reconstruction'. Having regard to Mannheim's active interest in the training of teachers, it is surely appropriate that one volume in that series should aim at providing teachers with an introduction to aspects of education which Mannheim deemed to be of first importance. Certainly all, who, as teachers in university training departments and training colleges, seek to expound the social significance of education will be glad that the series now provides an introductory study of this kind—a volume that students preparing for the teaching vocation can be confidently recommended to read and digest. There is a paragraph in the McNair Report on the Training of Teachers, much quoted when the Report was first published in 1947, which says: 'It is a truism to say that every teacher, in however humble a capacity he or she may be serving, is directly and vocationally involved in moulding the shape of things to come.' If that truism be true, it is important that as part of his education every teacher should, when at college, be made clearly aware of the field of study which Mr. Ottaway maps out so attractively in this book. The unsettled times in which our young citizens are going to live their lives make it necessary that those who aspire to teach should have thought and should continue to think about the problems of society with all the intelligence at their command.

'Where a social tradition is firm and effective', Dr. J. H. Oldham once observed, 'no great harm is done if schools confine themselves in the main to teaching the distinctively school subjects. The influences which touch the deeper springs of character are supplied in other ways. Religion, tradition, the home, prevailing custom and the institutions of the national life all exert their influence on mind and heart. It is far otherwise when the social tradition is in a process of dissolution. It then becomes imperative that the school should assume wider functions and definitely set itself to the task of creating and fostering the sense of social obligation and loyalty to the community.' When he wrote these words he was not thinking particularly of this country, and few would maintain that here the social tradition is in process of dissolution; but most will agree that our society is passing through a phase of rapid change and fundamental reconstruction and that the outcome is uncertain. Whether the reconstruction will be for good or ill depends not a little on our schools and on the wisdom of those who teach in them: and on their appreciation of the various issues that are at stake. Teachers in the United States and many other countries are confronted with similar problems, but though similar they are not quite the same as ours; for that reason some of the admirable American literature on educational sociology has a background which makes it often inappropriate and irrelevant as a guide to teachers in this country about the social problems that are their daily concern.

Mr. Ottaway has in this volume made it his primary concern to illustrate some of the relations between our own educational system and our own society, and he has done this in such a stimulating way that his readers will be encouraged to go forward to more specialized studies and also find themselves wanting to explore comparatively the sociological literature of other countries. For while it is true that the social problems of every country differ, it is no less true that they are fundamentally the same. For example, it is impossible to read Margaret Mead's delightful lectures on 'The School in American Culture' without feeling that much of her detail is quite inapplicable to the English social landscape, but when she generalizes she speaks for us all. Indeed there are several passages in these lectures which might have been written to preface just such a book as Mr. Ottaway has given us. For her theme is that teachers to-day cannot succeed unless they are able to adjust, adapt and rethink their methods to meet the changing demands of a changing world. 'In a very stable, very slowly changing society', she remarks, 'teachers as they grow older may easily grow gentler and wiser by simply watching generations of youngsters who pass through their hands . . . but in a changing society, age brings not wisdom, but confusion, unless provision is made for the teachers to change as the children change.' Certainly this book of Mr. Ottaway's will help many perplexed teachers to think things out for themselves, and enable them to serve more effectively children growing up in this bewildering age.

Preface

FIRST I would like to thank Professor Lester Smith for writing the Introduction to this book. Not only has he expressed so clearly my aims and intentions in undertaking this work, but by his appreciation of the importance of its subject matter he has encouraged me in my hopes that it will prove useful. The Introduction having explained my purpose, and given some details of my experience in the field of education, there remain only a few points I wish to add in this preface.

The reader will soon find that I have interpreted the scope of sociology very broadly, and have made use of contributions from any of the relevant social sciences. The study of education as a function of society is bound to require the collaboration of workers in many different subject disciplines. I have therefore taken account of some recent discoveries in anthropology and social psychology as well as in general sociology.

I have tried, in general, to make a scientific approach to social problems, and to separate fact from speculation. A primary difficulty in this approach is the distinction between sociology and social philosophy. The sociologist can describe what appears to him to be happening in a given society, and can look historically at the social factors which have operated in the past, but it is strictly outside his province, as a scientist, to say what the values of a society ought to be. However I have written mainly of education in a democratic society, and therefore admit that in many contexts I have assumed that our democratic values in England are worth while, and have, in Chapter IX in particular, given my own interpretation of their possible application in school life. I have been careful to point out in the text the assumptions which are being made. In order to clarify some of my reasons for accepting a democratic philosophy I have added Chapter XI, and in calling it 'Beyond Sociology' have, I hope, made my intention clear.

PREFACE

My thanks are due to Professor R. N. Armfelt and Professor W. R. Niblett both of whom were kind enough to read my manuscript with great care and made many valuable suggestions. I am also indebted to my friend Professor J. A. Lauwerys for stimulating my thoughts on sociological topics (among many others) over a period of many years.

A. K. C. OTTAWAY

Acknowledgment

Thanks are due to the editors of *Researches and Studies*, published by the University of Leeds Institute of Education, for permission to include in Chapter IX many passages adapted from an article by the author in the May 1951 issue of this journal, and also some passages in Chapter VII from an article in the June 1957 issue.

Preface to the Revised Edition

Since the publication of this book there have been further advances in the study of the sociology of education. During the 1950's several workers in this country carried out researches on the relation of education to social mobility and the occupational structure. Investigations were also made of the influence of social factors on educational achievement, and their bearing on selection for secondary and higher education. Two influential reports of a marked sociological character were put before the Government by the Central Advisory Council, namely those on *Early Leaving* and *15 to 18* (*The Crowther Report*). As a result of all this work we have become more aware not only of the growing connection of education to the success of the national economy, but also of the reserves of undeveloped ability which still remain in our population, and the need for a new concept of educational opportunity which these facts reveal. I have summarized our new knowledge of all these matters in two additional chapters which now form Chapters VI and VII in this edition.

Chapter V on the educational needs of our future society has also been partly re-written in the light of the new developments in science and technology which we see around us, and their consequences for our cultural life. Because of the growing importance of the teaching profession I have added a note on the roles of the teacher.

The small additions made in other places, and the complete revision of the bibliography have all been undertaken with the intention of keeping the student up to date in a rapidly developing subject. The reader will find some references in the general bibliography to the increasing literature on the sociology of education in other countries, but

PREFACE

I have been unable to find room for comparative studies, and by a deliberate policy have only discussed developments in the educational and social structure of England and Wales.

A. K. C. OTTAWAY

Leeds 1962

CHAPTER I

The Sociology of Education

A Definition of Society—The Scope of Education—The Relations between Education and Society—The Study of Education as a Social Science

EDUCATION can be studied from many different points of view. What is here called the sociology of education is a fairly new name for an aspect of education which has always been the concern of the educator in some form or another.[1] Education is an activity which goes on in a society, and its aims and methods depend on the nature of the society in which it takes place.

Sociology, as a separate discipline of social science, is the study of society, but not the whole of that study. The distinction between the different fields of study in the social sciences is sometimes difficult to make. It is to be expected that they will overlap, since they all have the behaviour of human beings in society as their subject matter. The extent to which the different functions of mankind can be isolated for study is the justification for the different disciplines of sociology, anthropology, psychology, economics, political science, and so on. Yet at the same time one is aware that man's activities in practical life are interrelated. What distinguishes the social sciences from each other is the particular aspect of human activities that each selects to focus upon. The central concern of sociology is the social relationships of mankind. It includes such topics as social structure and organization; the interaction of social groups; the means of social control and the processes of social change.

The sociology of education may be defined briefly as a study of the

[1] See Bibliography, Part I, p. 216, for a list of works on the social aspects of education, arranged in chronological order and annotated.

relations between education and society. It is thus a social study, and, in so far as its method is scientific, it is a branch of social science. It is concerned with educational aims, methods, institutions, administration, and curricula, in relation to the economic, political, religious, social and cultural forces of the society in which they function. In the education of the individual it concerns the influence of social life and social relationships on the development of personality.

The main object of this chapter is to give a general description of a sociological approach to education, and to introduce the major topics which will be treated further in subsequent chapters. This will involve a certain amount of descriptive definition of terminology, since another difficulty in the present stage of the social sciences is that the definitions of terms vary with different writers.

A DEFINITION OF SOCIETY

People living together are said to live in a society or a community, and these two words are often used in almost the same sense. The difference between them depends on the type and degree of organization in the group, and the extent to which the people are conscious of their social mode of life. Both imply having something in common, such as a certain geographic territory, and a feeling of belonging to the same kind of group.

'Community' is here taken to be the more general word, and 'a society' to be a particular type of community. Confusion arises between the use of the word 'society' in a general sense meaning the whole range of social relationships, and the use of the term 'a society' which refers to a definite population living somewhere.[1] It will be observed that 'a community' also refers to a definite population living somewhere and the point at issue is the difference between the two. To some extent, in ordinary speech, it does not matter very much. But when a distinction is needed, and for certain purposes it is important, a useful one is made by R. G. Collingwood.[2] The following definitions are based on his views. A community is everybody, adults and children, social and non-

[1] It might refer to a society of insects, but that is another usage. Compare also the meaning of 'a society' as an association of people with a common interest, e.g. a Dramatic Society, The Society for Nautical Research, etc.

[2] In *The New Leviathan*, Chaps. XIX, XX, XXI.

social persons, living in a certain territory where all share a mode of life, but not all are conscious of its organization or purpose. A society is a kind of community (or a part of a community), whose members have become socially conscious of their mode of life, and are united by a common set of aims and values.

For education this is a useful distinction because children are members of the community, but cannot be said to be members of the society until they are conscious of the way their society functions, and of their rights and duties in it as full citizens. They are potential members of society, and it is one of the tasks of education to prepare them for full membership. While they are in the process of being educated for social life they are a part of what Collingwood calls 'the non-social community'. It can be said that society is the fully social part of a community, and the special nature of a society is judged by the behaviour of those members with full social consciousness.

That all societies have some set of aims and values is a matter of fact, and such facts can be studied by the sociologist. It is necessary, however, to draw a distinction between sociology and social philosophy. The sociologist, as a scientist, can describe what the aims and values of a given society appear to him to be, but he cannot say what they *ought* to be without entering the province of philosophy or religion.[1] The social fact that a society has a set of aims, which means that its members are to some extent conscious of the direction in which they wish it to change, is very important. A society is never static, but is a collection of people who look towards the future. They may be uncertain of their aims, but to the extent to which they are socially conscious they are attempting to live together in some kind of organized way. The members of any society have a set of techniques for bringing up and educating their children.

THE SCOPE OF EDUCATION

The educator, in accordance with the aims he accepts, attempts to develop the personality of the child and to prepare him for member-

[1] It is true that many sociologists have also written on social philosophy, but in doing so they have left the sphere of pure sociology. I have tried to clarify this problem in Chapter IX. Throughout this book when writing of education in our particular democratic society I cannot claim to be free from the assumptions of what we in England think worth while at the present time.

ship of his society. This dual function of education corresponds to the double role of a person has to play in life, both as an individual and as a member of society. These functions can, quite reasonably, be distinguished and up to a point discussed separately. But it is the same person who plays the double role, and he or she has to play several other roles as a member of different groups, associations or communities, and while achieving or having achieved full membership of the wider society which includes them all. Hence the sociological approach stresses that the development of the child should be thought of in relation to his society and culture. It is not only that the individual cannot, in fact, grow up separated from his social group, but that he becomes the kind of person he is, at any stage of his development, by means of interaction between himself and his social and physical environment.

That education is concerned with the development of personality is a normal assumption in our society to-day. Personality is one of those concepts for which there is a number of definitions. It is usually regarded as an organized whole and all-inclusive, comprising the physical, mental, emotional and spiritual characteristics of a person. It includes character and temperament, which are parts of personality. Put quite simply personality means the kind of person someone is. We have just said above that the kind of person someone is depends on the interaction between the individual and his social and physical environment. The individual does not come into the world a blank, but with inborn constitutional factors and qualities. So the growth of personality depends partly on innate factors, and partly on environment. The influence of the environment in this combination will clearly depend on the way of life of the society in which the person grows up. The most important part of this environment is the human environment, namely the other people of all kinds and ages who are around him and influence him during his period of growth and learning. The sociology of education is specially concerned with the influence of the social environment on the growing child, but this should not allow us to forget that it is always an *individual* with his own unique gifts and qualities who is being educated.

One of the difficulties which arises from considering education in this wider sense of the development of personality is that it may be confused with the influence of the whole of life. Personality, it will be said, is developed by living. It appears necessary to distinguish more clearly the function of education in relation to the whole social *milieu*. The clarification of this problem may, at the same time, make our ideas clearer over certain other related problems.

(i) Consider the *activity* of education. This is partly a set of practical techniques for the instruction given in schools, colleges, and any institutions established for the purpose of what we call formal education. From our point of view we cannot restrict the term 'education' to this narrow use and make it equivalent to 'schooling' or the teaching of a certain body of subject matter. In fact, schools and all educational institutions in our society attend to the development of character and personality by means of their social life, games, participation in drama, music, and the visual arts, religious observances, and all kinds of out-of-class activities, all of which they consider a part of their programme of education.

(ii) Consider the *intentions* of the educator. A great deal of his time the teacher is making a deliberate and conscious attempt not only to teach his pupils a certain body of knowledge but also to change their behaviour, and to change it in desired directions. These intentions of the teacher are concerned with the development of personality, and thus may touch on any aspect of life. But observe that teachers in schools and colleges are not the only people who teach. Much of human behaviour has to be deliberately taught, and the process begins in the cradle. The parents consciously begin the teaching of language—one of the most important instruments of culture—they teach feeding, dressing, good manners, and an enormous range of things which are intended to change the behaviour of their children in desired directions. Children teach each other, the clergy teach, youth leaders teach, the policeman teaches, the B.B.C. teach, the educational film maker teaches, the government official teaches through his information services. Society is full of educators all deliberately and consciously carrying on the process of education in the wider sense of the full development of personality as well as in the narrower sense of instruction. Adults as well as the young are also subjected to similar educative influences.

(iii) Granted that society is full of educators, and that any experience *may* be educative, yet all experiences provided by society are not of equal value, and some are harmful to the educator's purpose. As an illustration let us consider the situation of a teacher in a school. Let us assume that the teacher knows, by and large, what he is trying to do. He may not succeed very well; he may use wrong or inappropriate methods; but he knows fairly clearly what he is aiming at. Now suppose certain influences in the outside world conflict with his conscious aims. For example his pupils may be acquiring ideals of competition and money making, while the teacher is encouraging co-operation and the ideals of service to the community. Or the television and the comics may, in his view, be condoning habits of violence and lawlessness while he is teaching restraint and obedience to the law. What is his reaction to these potentially educative influences of society? Clearly he will not accept them as a part of education, except to call them mis-education or bad education. Nevertheless he is *concerned* with all such influences, so that he can evaluate them, and when possible exert a corrective influence on what he considers a bad experience. So it is suggested that all educators, in practice, judge the experiences of life in relation to their own educational aims. All experiences which conflict with the educator's intentions are rejected as not being of educational value, and not even worthy to be given the name of education. From the point of view of the learner he will accept or reject experiences also, and his powers of selection will be determined by the kind of education he has already received, and his reaction to it. *We conclude that the difference between education and life is determined by what the educator and the learner are trying to do.* In learning how to live we both select our experiences and have them selected for us. The educator has his views on how to live which determine his aims of education, which, in turn, help determine his pupil's views on how to live.

(iv) There is a further matter bearing on this problem which must be settled. We have been speaking of education as a conscious process. Yet it is well known that everybody learns a great deal unconsciously. In particular the habits of social living are partly learnt by unconscious imitation of the behaviour of others. The growing child learns by the mere fact of growth itself, or in day-to-day adjustments to accidental situations. An older child may acquire an attitude towards knowledge, a feeling of belonging to a certain way of life, or a deep sense of belief in certain values without being fully aware of what has happened to him. The results may become conscious while the means of learning were unconscious. In so far as the growth of his personality in society is modified in this unconscious way should it not be called a part of his education? Again consider the teacher, whatever his intentions, he cannot always be aware of the influence he is exerting. Are we then faced with accepting two modes of the educational process; conscious and unconscious? The facts are inescapable, but they are facts about how learning and teaching take place. The educator has to watch for the evidence of unconscious learning in his pupils, and his own unconscious teaching, and try to become more aware of the results of such influences in the development of personality. For only from the resulting behaviour can it be judged whether the unconscious processes are of value for his purpose. He still has his deliberate and conscious aims in education with which to check upon the results of all experiences, conscious or unconscious.[1]

THE RELATIONS BETWEEN EDUCATION AND SOCIETY

So far we have undertaken some discussion on the nature of society and of education. Both, when defined from the point of view of purpose, are attempts of human beings to do something, and the sociology of education is a study of the relations between them. It is now proposed to outline the major areas of study within this field, which are treated in detail in later chapters.

(i) *The relation of education to culture*

The parents are the first educators of the child, and they still maintain an educative function throughout the child's upbringing. In some societies, but not in all, the parents send their children to school. The school may be regarded as a social invention to serve a social need. It is a device provided by the members of a society for the specialized teaching of the young. Schools arose as a result of the increasing division of labour in civilized societies. But the school and the home are still only two of the many agencies of education. When education is defined in the wider sense as the development of personality, it is something which goes on outside, as well as inside the home and the school. 'Education, properly understood, is an activity of the whole community', is the point of view of a recent writer. In fact he goes further and writes: 'Education is in fact nothing other than the whole life of a community viewed from the particular standpoint of learning to live that life.'[2]

[1] The next chapter deals with the cultural patterns of society, which are acquired partly unconsciously by the mere fact of growing up in a particular society.

[2] M. C. V. Jeffreys: *Glaucon*, p. 3 and p. 71.

A single word to express 'the whole life of a community' is a special use of the word 'culture', which has been developed by the social anthropologists. Culture is a word used in many senses.[1] With reference to education it is usually taken to mean a high level of intellectual and artistic excellence in a person or group. This is culture as 'the best that has been thought and known' of Matthew Arnold in his *Culture and Anarchy*, where he defines culture as 'a study of perfection'. This is the culture of a highly educated, or specially cultivated section of society, not the culture of the whole society. The meaning of the phrase 'culture of a society' as it is now used in the social sciences is the total way of life of a society. This would include the way of eating food, wearing clothes, using language, making love, getting married, getting buried or playing football. It would also include reading literature, listening to music, looking at the works of painters or sculptors, or the other activities which we may think of as representing culture in the narrower sense. The concept of culture in this total sense throws so much light on the problems of education that it is worth while considering its meaning in some detail. This topic is therefore developed in Chapter II.

We shall examine the extent to which education is influenced by the culture of the society in which it takes place. The child and his social environment are thus considered together in the process of education, and are thought of as influencing each other. Recent studies in anthropology and social psychology have shown the extreme flexibility of human behaviour, and have stressed the extent to which the individual personality is determined by the culture in which he is brought up. This point of view is sometimes criticized on the grounds that it neglects the uniqueness of the individual with his own powers of self-development, and regards him merely as a creature moulded by the environment. This type of criticism may be justified when the supporters of environmental determinism over-stress their case, but it may also be due to a misunderstanding of the culture concept. It is true that man makes himself, for he also makes his culture. Culture is not an impersonal force existing outside the minds and actions of human beings. The outside forces of society are also human forces, and are exercised by individuals or groups of individuals. So man is both influenced by and influences his environment, and it is only by the concept of the continuous inter-

[1] T. S. Eliot compares three main uses in his *Notes towards the Definition of Culture*, 1948.

action of the person and his society that the development of personality can be properly understood.

(ii) *Education as the transmission of culture*

One of the tasks of education is to hand on the cultural values and behaviour patterns of the society to its young and potential members. By this means society achieves a basic social conformity, and ensures that its traditional modes of life are preserved. This has been called the conservative function of education. But a modern society also needs critical and creative individuals, able to make new inventions and discoveries, and willing to initiate social change. To provide for change is the creative function of education.[1] Handing on tradition is bound at times to be in conflict with a desire to initiate change. When a society is changing slowly the new elements of its culture can be more easily absorbed, but the rapid changes in the industrial societies of the twentieth century have led to much conflict between old and new habits of life and thought. Here then are two contradictory functions of education which are both necessary, and it can be shown that there are conditions of society under which they can be reconciled. But first let us examine a little further the conservative function of the transmission of culture, since this is basic to the continued life of a society.[2] Sir Fred Clarke has drawn attention to the need for what he calls an 'educative society'. The first sentence of his book on this subject[3] reads: 'An educative society is understood here to mean one which accepts as its overmastering purpose the production of a given type of citizen.' To the believer in the freedom of the individual the production of citizens to type will at first sight suggest a rigid authoritarianism. Sir Fred

[1] The conservative and creative functions were often stressed by Sir Percy Nunn. See his *Education: its Data and First Principles*, Chapters 3 and 4. While he was strongly in favour of encouraging the creative power of the individual there was little reference in his time to any social criticism, or the need to prepare for new forms of society.

[2] On this the *Spens Report* speaks in some detail. See especially pp. 147–8, the passage beginning: 'Speaking broadly the interest of the State is to see that the schools provide the means by which the nation's life may be maintained in its integrity from generation to generation;' . . . and ending 'there is the unformulated but very real demand of the community that the young shall grow up in conformity with the national *ethos*.' Also pp. 151–3.

[3] F. Clarke, *Freedom in the Educative Society*, 1948.

Clarke's argument is that a general knowledge and acceptance of the ideals and aims of our society is essential for all its citizens, and it must be achieved through education, but in a form which makes it compatible with freedom. So he reconciles the double purpose by saying: 'Admittedly the purpose of the educative society may be to make men conformable. But overmastering that must be the purpose to make men free . . .' then—quoting Professor W. E. Hocking—'the educational purpose is to communicate the type and provide for growth beyond the type'.

We can agree with Sir Fred Clarke that a society needs a stable set of values and a unified purpose. However the need for conformity and the need for change can be reconciled another way. When used as a means of social control education can modify the behaviour of the young to fit society. Under an authoritarian regime the range of behaviour would be strictly limited, and criticism forbidden. But in a democratic society 'fitting' it means also able and ready to change it. The apparently opposed functions of handing on traditional values and developing critical individuals tend to become more and more part of the same function. There are three reasons for this. (a) The tradition of democracy allows the maximum of freedom of thought and expression, and favours criticism and change. (b) The values of democracy include looking towards and believing in the possibility of an improvement in democracy itself, and (c) the social forces directing change are subject to the control of the government and operate by common consent. The more fully democracy spreads the greater checks can be given to the abuse of power by a ruling group.

In short this means that fitting the society and changing it both become the duty of the person in a democratic society. To be a fully developed person in such a society implies full membership of it, and also *creative* membership of it with powers to change it. This is not true of a totalitarian society. If the community is ruled by a dictator or a single party the unquestioning conformity by the mass of the people is the most desired state of affairs, and education will become propaganda and be used as a powerful means of social control.

Nevertheless a warning must be given that too rapid change tends to break up a society, especially when there is not a sufficiently stable core of attitudes and values transmitted to coming generations, and widespread uncertainty develops over the society's aims. Many writers think that we are approaching this danger point in our western civilized societies.[1] It is said that there is a 'crisis in valuation' and that we have 'no settled views, especially in our democratic societies, concerning the right patterns of human behaviour and conduct'.[2] The young as they grow up are presented with too great a choice of alternative forms of behaviour and belief. The stress and strain of adolescence in our society is partly due to this, and does not occur in primitive societies where the young are initiated into established patterns of living.[3] All this makes it even more important for a society in transition to be certain of its core of values, for then it is able to stand the disintegrating power of change. The transmission of culture still remains a vital function, and is not to be dismissed as merely conservative in the sense of being old-fashioned. Our children, although potentially the society of the future, still belong to the non-social community, and education in this respect can be regarded as a socialization of the young. Helping in the socialization of the younger generation is part of the role of being a mature adult. This is expressed by the definition of Emile Durkheim: 'Education is the action exercised by the generations of adults on those which are not yet ready for social life.'

(iii) *The Social Determinants of Education*

If it is true that education depends on the total way of life of a society, then the kind of education provided will be different in different kinds of society. The study of these differences is the field of comparative education. Not only will educational systems and institutions be different, but each society has its own ideal types of men, or cultural heroes, for the young to emulate, so that the development of personality will also vary from one culture to another.

It will also follow that the education provided within any given society will change from time to time as the society changes. The record of such changes is the subject matter of the history of education. The causes of social and educational change are a matter of social dynamics which can

[1] Ralph Linton, *The Study of Man*, Chapter XVI writes: 'We are rapidly approaching the point where there will no longer be enough items on which all members of the society agree to provide the culture with form and pattern.' . . . 'In modern civilizations . . . the core of culture is being progressively reduced.'

[2] Karl Mannheim: *Diagnosis of Our Time*, p. 12.

[3] Margaret Mead, *Coming of Age in Samoa*, see her oft-quoted passage on p. 119, with regard to the many choices facing an adolescent. Penguin edn.

be studied both historically and sociologically. It is sometimes suggested that education is one of the causes of social change. The opposite is more true. Educational change tends to follow other social changes, rather than initiate them. Ideas of change originate in the minds of men; often in the mind of a single man. Exceptional individuals invent new techniques and propound new values for their society. These ideas arise from the impact of man on his culture, but do not change the culture until they are shared and transmitted by a social group. Education cannot be changed until the culture changes—except by a few pioneers who are ahead of their time and are trying to educate society. Educators may also themselves, as citizens, act as a force for change, and the great educationist may influence change more directly in a similar way to other exceptional men, but this is to anticipate the argument of a later chapter. The statement that education tends to follow social change is explained and supported by the theory of social change put forward in Chapter III. Some examples of how education has been socially determined in England are given in Chapter IV, and some of our future educational needs, based on the same point of view, are discussed in Chapter V.

The concept of causation in the social sciences is dangerous and difficult. There are always a large number of variables interacting together. That is why education is rejected as a cause; it is rather a dependent variable. That education has an important role to play in social change is undoubted, but its influence is secondary and not primary. Education is a technique which is used by people with a deliberate and conscious aim. When the aim changes the education changes, but the aim has to change first. The people who provide education are the directing social force; and social forces are always exercised by groups of people. For example in Nazi Germany education was used with the intention of causing rapid changes in the attitudes of a generation of young people. That it succeeded showed the power of education as propaganda, but the ends it served were already decided by the people who directed it. In a democratic society, as we have already seen, education, used in a particular way, can *prepare* for changes in society, and that is part of its creative function. It prepares children for change by encouraging permissive and critical attitudes, but it can only do this because these are already sufficiently accepted values of the society. These values were established by the action of social forces in the past.

(iv) *Education and the Social Structure*

The concept of social structure is central to modern sociology. The use of the word structure implies an ordered arrangement of parts linked together into a whole. What are the parts of a society which are thus structurally inter-related? Writers have differed in the emphasis they have placed on individuals or groups as the components of a social structure. Actual social relationships are between individuals even when the individual is acting for, or representing, a group. Any concept of a social structure or system is thus an abstraction from a set of living, personal interactions. If we think of society as made up of a multiplicity of groups such as families, schools, occupational groups, political parties, trade unions, etc., we soon realize that these are all institutional groups, which exhibit established, organized, fairly stable and commonly accepted ways of behaviour. The groups, in fact, are distinguished by the sort of roles their members play, and the individual persons thus take part in the social structure by reason of their membership of institutional groups. A social structure can be defined as the network of social institutions within which personal relationships take place.

Education is the process of preparing people to fit into this complex social structure, and to play particular social roles as members of more than one institutional group. Children have to learn to be fathers or mothers, school-teachers or civil-servants, shopkeepers or priests. They have to learn to keep the law, to understand how they are governed, and to be prepared to try and change the social *mores* when they see that they can be improved. There is no one way in which a society is structured. The principal social institutions are concerned with regulating the economic, political, familial, educational, and religious aspects of human life. All social institutions define the pattern of relationships and behaviour expected of the persons who belong to them; and they grow and change in response to basic human needs. Thus the need of any society to bring up and educate its children leads to the institution of the family and to a whole set of educational institutions, which are inter-related with the rest of the social structure.

From what has already been said about the culture of a society it can be seen that it is through the functions of people in their institutional relations that the patterns of culture are maintained. Looked at only from the point of view of structure a social system may seem to exist in a static framework. From the point of view of function the society springs into the dynamic and changing life that we all experience. The culture can be likened to the flavour of the pie, and the structure to what holds its parts together; the two being at least partly interdependent. The structure of institutions can be described in terms of status positions, rules, rights and duties, and chains of authority; but the culture of institutions results from the manifest activities of their living participants, in terms of attitudes, feelings and sentiments, social and cultural habits, recreations, ceremonies and rituals. The function of education both in the maintenance and renewal of the social structure, and in the transmission and development of culture may be looked upon as the central core of studies for the educational sociologist.[1]

In an advanced industrial society like our own the educational system has had to adapt itself more and more to meet the demands for recruitment and training for the whole range of a complex and varied occupational hierarchy. However we interpret the meaning of a non-vocational education, and whatever we think of the value of acquiring 'knowledge for its own sake' we must accept that education is also concerned with the preparation of the child for his future occupation in life. This is its main economic function in the interests of the national community, as well as for the benefit of the individual. A growing technology demands the fullest possible use of skilled man-power at all levels. Hence the search for talent, the need to discover and eliminate any wastage of ability, and to ensure the equality of educational opportunity. The demands to prolong the period and to extend the scope of education will increase as the stage of industrialism becomes more intense.[2]

The problem turns out to be not only a question of the provision of schools and universities, and the allocation of resources in money and materials, but also a question of the different attitudes, assumptions and expectations with regard to education which are associated with the differences of social status in our class-stratified society. All these matters are discussed in Chapters VI and VII, and an attempt is also made to assess the place of sociological research in the determination of future educational and social policy.

[1] See also A. K. C. Ottaway: 'The Aims and Scope of Educational Sociology', *Educational Review*, Vol. 12, No. 3, June 1960.

[2] A collection of papers referring to the relations of education to the growth of advanced industrial and technological societies is given in A. H. Halsey, Jean Floud and C. Arnold Anderson: *Education, Economy and Society*, 1961.

(v) *Social Interaction*

Social interaction is the name given to any relation between persons and groups which changes the behaviour of the participants. It is by social interaction that children acquire the culture of their group. Any social interaction can be a part of education provided it changes behaviour in the direction desired by the educator. The responsible educator need not always be present, even in the school, and indirect control may be more effective than direct control. Human beings respond to the situation they are in. So a large part of modern education consists in arranging suitable situations in which learning can take place; in which the learners are, in a sense, also the teachers, in so far as they teach each other or teach themselves.

But the child takes part in group learning situations long before he reaches school. The most fundamental and earliest group is of course the family. From the point of view of the child growth involves ever-widening circles of social contacts. He begins to learn his role in different groups, and this is part of the development of his personality. When at school he also belongs to other organized groups in the locality, which may be connected with a church, with clubs, with his leisure activities, as well as the more transitory relations with groups or gangs of friends. On leaving school a fresh circle of relationships begins, connected with his work and further exploration of the local community. So throughout life we are all simultaneously members of many different groups, both large and small, and with different degrees of solidarity and organization.

Hence the study of group behaviour is of great importance to the educationist, and is a major field in the sociology of education. These topics are discussed in Chapter VIII. There is also a new and developing field of research and study known as 'group dynamics'[1] to which reference is made elsewhere and especially in Chapter X. Group dynamics is an excellent example of a subject which overlaps with sociology and psychology. It is perhaps best described as a branch of social psychology, but it is an integral part of a comprehensive science of human behaviour.

Social interaction can also be said to include the means of communication on a large scale, such as the press, the cinema, and the radio.

[1] Note the foundation of The Research Centre for Group Dynamics, Ann Arbour, Mich., U.S.A. in 1945, and The Tavistock Institute of Human Relations, London, which between them publish the Journal *Human Relations*.

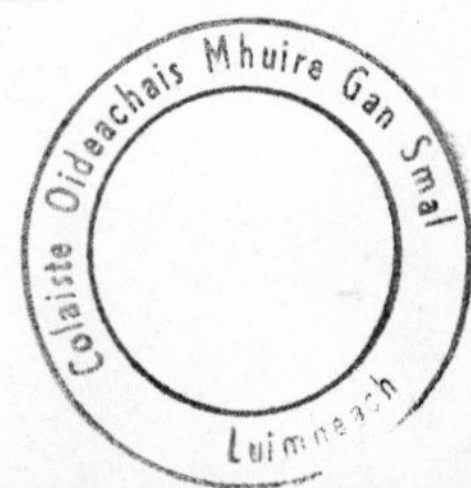

These are sometimes called *mass media* of communication, and are also known as *social techniques* for influencing the behaviour of people in the mass. Their use is familiar as a means of propaganda as well as of education. They are cultural influences outside the individual and his immediate circle but which act upon him most powerfully, and reflect in considerable measure the nature of our society. Are the cinema and the radio educative influences or not? The answer is that it depends on their results, and how far these are acceptable to our aims of education.

The wider definition of education which we shall maintain throughout provides another difficulty beside that of having to decide what are the proper limits of education. When everything in society may be an educative factor one is bound to reconsider the function of the school. The school is a social unit within the wider society, and until recently has been a very isolated unit. Clearly one consequence of our point of view is to bring the school in closer relation with the other social groups in the community. Hence the emphasis that is now put on home and school co-operation, and parent-teacher relations. Further than this schools are trying to turn their activities outwards into the community, as well as bringing the impact of the community into the school. The school is being thought of more as a transitional society, of a special kind, between the family and the greater society outside. Yet another aspect of the school life is receiving considerable attention. This is the social relations within the school itself, not only among the pupils, but among the staff, and between pupils and staff. We need to study the kind of community a school is in its normal functioning. All these topics are considered in Chapter IX which deals with the school as a social unit.

THE STUDY OF EDUCATION AS A SOCIAL SCIENCE

If the activity of education has such close relationships with the activity of society, some of which have already been outlined in the preceding pages, it is necessary to consider the limits of the study of education as a social science. This involves a brief examination of what this 'subject' called 'education' really is. First it is a help to distinguish education in practice and in theory. The practice of education is exercised by a collection of techniques. There are techniques of teaching, of class management, of bringing up children, of arranging situations in which people learn, of testing knowledge, of the relation between teacher and learner, of applying discipline, of multi-sensory learning aids, and so on, over the whole range of both formal and informal teaching method, character training, and personality development. Such techniques are mostly applied to the young, that is to those not yet ready for full membership of society, but we must also reckon with the process of adult education at any age. These techniques can be applied to the learning of any aspect of life, and such learning is called education when it is in accord with the deliberate and conscious aim of the educator, even though some of the learning may take place unconsciously. The practice of education is presumably both an art and a science. Teaching is generally considered to be an art, but teaching method can be based on scientific principles. How far it is an art and how far a science need not be discussed for the present argument.

The theory of education, as distinct from the practice, must concern the study of the whole process. (There will be a theory of teaching, but that is only a part of the whole theory of education.) The whole process of education is the interaction of individuals and social groups, with certain ends in view (called the aims of education) for the development of the individuals. The whole process has a past, hence the need for studying the history of education. The whole process can be studied from the point of view of the individual. Hence the need for studying the psychology of education. Psychology is also a social science but normally it starts from, or has its focus on, the behaviour of the individual, but with respect to the behaviour of other individuals and groups. The psychology of education centres on how the individual reacts, changes, experiences and develops as part of a social process.[1] Education when studied from the sociological point of view is a study of social relationships. But the whole process of education is made up of social relationships. The relation of education and society is the relation of one social process with a larger social process. The sociology of education focuses upon the social forces through which the individual

[1] At one time, quite recently, psychology was called the study of the mind, and educational psychology is still largely concerned with individual abilities, aptitudes, drives, goals, responses, learning methods, etc. However the present trend is to treat child development and mal-adjustment in relation to the social group, and treat imitation, interest, motivation, learning and such topics as a part of social psychology. In the recent work of what is called personality psychology, while the emphasis is on the *person*, and how the *person* reacts, changes and builds new habits, the person is always seen in the setting of the social group.

is developed, and the social relations by which the individual gains experience. It is as incomplete to study the sociology of the group without considering the individuals which compose it, as to study the psychology of the individual without considering the group to which he belongs. Hence looked at in any of the ways we have just considered the theory of education is the study of a social process which has an historical, a psychological, and a sociological aspect.

It may be asked what room is left for the principles of education? Here again a distinction can be made between theory and practice even though they are closely related. The principles of teaching consist of rules for the carrying out of certain techniques, but the principles of education are concerned with the purpose of those techniques in their relation to life. Can it be said that there are any principles of education outside the principles of the society in which the education takes place?[1] This is a philosophical question. If there are such principles, and if by 'outside' is meant outside any particular time and place, then it might be suggested that they belong to the study of metaphysics, not education. But what of the philosophy of education? Is there not such an activity? Possibly, but it is difficult to distinguish between a philosophy of education and a philosophy of life. You can reflect upon the whole process of education, but then you are reflecting upon the whole of life from a certain point of view. Those who are being educated are learning to live, are acquiring some conscious purpose, are developing some philosophy of life. Education touches life at every point.

If philosophy is the clarification of thought, can we not use it to clarify our thoughts about education? Yes, certainly, as much as we can about anything else; but this is the use of philosophy as a technique of clear thinking or analysis. Or consider the function of philosophy as criticism. Can we not examine the methods of education, and criticize their presuppositions and assumptions? Yes, there might be a philosophy of the science of education, and this would be a part of the philosophy of science. Similarly there might be a philosophy of the art of education

[1] It has been widely thought so. Theorists who believe that there is one ideal form of human nature, under whatever different historic and social conditions, will aim at its perfection, and accept at least some principles of education which can be applied to all human beings at any time. There are, of course, universal principles common to all societies, which are based on observed needs common to all mankind, but these are empirical principles and not absolutes.

as part of the philosophy of art. Methods of learning and teaching, as we have said, have principles. There are laws of learning, theories of motivation, tests of achievement, all based on the science of psychology. Such principles can be criticized, evaluated, and their logical validity and fitness of their purpose examined. This activity, in so far as it goes beyond science, can be called a philosophy of educational method.

When it comes to the aims of education are they not dependent upon the educator's philosophy of life? The question 'What is education for?' can only be answered by also answering the question 'What is life for?' It is, from this point of view, not necessary to consider the philosophy of education as a separate discipline. It always reflects the philosophy of the educators. If you are an idealist you will think one way about education, and if you are a dialectical materialist you will think another. Whether education is thought of as the development of the individual or as the preparation for citizenship, its ends will be determined by the aims and values of the society in which it takes place.

As education is also concerned with the bringing up of children with standards of right and wrong it will involve the study of ethics and religion. Similarly if you would have education create an appreciation of beautiful things you will get help from the study of aesthetics.

It can be concluded that education is intimately bound up with philosophy, and that there is no more important study for the educator. To be effective in pursuing his deliberate and conscious aims he has to submit them to philosophical tests, and then apply them to education. If education is 'philosophy in action' then what we do as educators depends on our general philosophy of life. To find a philosophy of life and apply it to education is the way of showing that there is a philosophy of education.

The need for a stable core of values in our own changing society has been stressed earlier (p. 11) and this means that educators need a social philosophy for education. To go any further and state the nature of such a philosophy is to go beyond sociology, and beyond the scope of this book.[1]

With regard to the study of education in general, whether in its social or other aspects, we should perhaps beware of making it too much of a separate 'subject', and of trying to isolate its principles. Might it not be

[1] I admit to assuming that for us in Great Britain it will be a philosophy compatible with the aims of a democratic society. See however Chapter XI.

best to study history, psychology, and sociology as a part of a comprehensive science of human nature, and then apply the results of our study to the practice of education? The problems of education cannot be solved by a group of specialists of any one kind. They require the collaboration of experts in different 'subjects' and in the borderland between 'subjects'. This is what we would call the combined approach, and in this approach the social sciences have the largest part to play.

CHAPTER II

The Culture Concept

The Definition of Culture—Culture Patterns and Personality—The Influence of Heredity—Civilized Societies and Sub-Cultures—Education and Culture

It was said in Chapter I that we should need to examine the extent to which education is influenced by the culture of the society in which it takes place. The use of the word culture, in its sociological sense, to mean the whole way of life of a community was introduced. We shall now consider the meaning of this concept of culture in some detail, and describe its relation to the growth of the individual by the study of some illustrations from the work of social anthropologists. We shall then be in a position to draw some conclusions on the importance of these observations for the theory and practice of education.

THE DEFINITION OF CULTURE

A thorough definition of culture has been given by Ralph Linton as follows: 'A culture is the configuration of learned behaviour, and the results of behaviour, whose component elements are shared and transmitted by the members of a particular society.'[1] This definition requires a little explanation. The word configuration suggests a sort of pattern. The term *culture pattern* has come into common use in the years since Ruth Benedict wrote her well-known book called *Patterns of Culture* in 1935. A *culture pattern* can be taken to mean the ways of behaviour associated with any permanent need or function in the social life. For example the method of bringing up children in a given society follows

[1] Ralph Linton: *The Cultural Background of Personality*, 1947, p. 21.

a certain culture pattern. It will be a complex of ways of behaviour associated with the universal needs of reproduction and the care of the young. The bringing up of children is a permanent need of all societies, and the particular way in which it is done is a culture pattern of that society.[1] Other examples of culture patterns would be: religious practices, methods of doing business and trade, ways of eating and drinking, or ideals of life, all of which may differ from one society to another. The whole culture is a configuration of all its interacting culture patterns.

The word behaviour refers, of course, to thinking as well as doing, and all such forms of behaviour have to be learned. 'Culture is the learned portion of human behaviour', is another definition. This distinguishes cultural behaviour from inborn instincts or other inherited traits. As contrasted with biological heredity culture may be called the *social heredity*; it is passed on by the social group.

A culture is also represented by material objects which are included under the *results of behaviour* in the definition quoted above. The creations of man, whether buildings, works of art, tools or machines are all part of the material culture. A great deal can be learned about a people by looking at the things they make. It is often the task of the archaeologist to reconstruct the ways of life of now extinct societies from a few discoveries of material relics left behind. Behaviour can also have results which remain in the mind as attitudes or beliefs, and which may be passed on from one generation to another, though becoming changed in the process. Thus the aims and values of a society are also a part of its culture. Patriotism, love of sport, belief in ghosts, or kindness to animals are attitudes which are learnt from repeated behaviour or the imitation of others; as also are the most profound religious beliefs.

The next important point to be noted from the definition is the need to share and transmit the elements of culture. Behaviour only becomes a part of culture when it is accepted by the members of a society and passed on. The passing on of the cultural patterns is often stated as one of the functions of education. Let us take an example from the social habits in our own society. That women should wear trousers, under certain circumstances, has become accepted, yet it is by no means a

[1] Indeed within a large and complex society there may be ways of bringing up children sufficiently different to constitute separate culture patterns typical of different sub-cultures. For the concept of sub-cultures see pp. 32–4.

universal habit nor universally approved. A new habit or custom becomes at first an alternative[1] way of behaviour, not universal for the whole society. The changing position of women during this century provides many examples of changes in our culture patterns. The custom of women being employed in commerce and industry has vastly increased, whereas to-day hardly any women become domestic servants, which at the beginning of the century was their largest occupational group. Women have gained access to many professions formerly occupied only by men, but it is still unusual to find women in the church, the law, Parliament, or in engineering and other technological occupations. It has also become common for women to continue in paid employment after marriage, and with the tendency to marry earlier and have fewer children, more women than formerly regard it as a normal expectation to return to their careers when their children have reached school age. Young women now enjoy a much greater freedom from parental supervision, and this change is particularly marked in the middle-class. Thus the opportunities for getting to know the opposite sex have led to changing attitudes to sexual ethics, which, in the absence of a firmly established code of behaviour, cause concern to society as a whole. All such changes have important consequences for the educator.

The problem of how changes in culture come about will be considered in the next chapter. Exceptional individuals who become inventors or creators in any sphere play a great part in cultural change. But the matter is not simple since some new ideas are more readily accepted than others, and it is the sharing and transmission of learned behaviour which must take place before it can be considered a part of the society's culture.[2]

CULTURE PATTERNS AND PERSONALITY

The comparative study of the culture of human societies is the proper sphere of the subject of cultural anthropology. The results of such studies have many implications for the student of education. To show

[1] See Ralph Linton on universals, specialities, and alternatives, in *The Study of Man*, Chapter XVI.

[2] For full details on the culture concept see the works of Ralph Linton, op. cit., also Clyde Klukholn: *Mirror for Man*, Chapter 2. Ruth Benedict: *Patterns of Culture*, and in any work of modern anthropology.

the importance of the culture concept for education we shall examine some statements which would be accepted by anthropologists as true, giving illustrations from observational research, and later suggest what light they can throw on the bringing up of children in our own society.

(1) *Different societies have different cultures*

This statement is self-evident from the definition of culture, but it is important to realize the extreme diversity of cultures in the world, including the differences between civilized societies. The Cross-Cultural Index at Yale University lists the characteristics of all known societies, whose cultures are analysed according to different categories of behaviour and custom. Some of these categories of behaviour will be common to all societies, while others will only be found in a few. It will be found, for example, that all societies have some form of marriage and family life, but only some permit polygamy; all societies have some customs and taboos with regard to eating, but only a few practise cannibalism, and so on. While in fact a large number of categories of behaviour are represented in every single one of the cultures analysed, the *form* of the behaviour varies from society to society. This is the essence of the culture concept. The behaviour is in response to certain universal needs of human beings. A culture is distinguished by the type of response to the same problems which all human beings must solve. To take one more example, all men get hungry and must eat or die, but what a man eats is partly due to culture as well as to geography. What he selects when there is choice, how it is obtained, how it is cooked, how he eats it, and how often and where, differ with the habits of his social group. Frogs, birds' nests, rotten seal, sago grubs, mushrooms, are all prized items of food to some people but not to others. Moslems won't eat pork nor will Hindus eat beef, and the Chinese dislike milk. Kluckholn tells a story[1] of a woman in Arizona who served to her guests delicious sandwiches filled with meat which they described as chicken or tuna fish. After they had eaten she told them the sandwiches were filled with the flesh of freshly killed rattlesnakes. On hearing this they were all very ill, and their sickness was a cultural reaction which would not have occurred to anyone for whom rattlesnakes were a great delicacy.

[1] *Mirror for Man*, p. 27.

(2) *Children grow up to fit their society, that is, personality is partly determined by the culture in which it grows*

Children who are born and grow up in New Guinea, instead of England, quite clearly grow up differently. They acquire a different culture. But those who are born and grow up in France, or in Russia, equally acquire different cultures. Let us first consider a few examples from the lives of primitive peoples. The following is an extract from a newspaper report:

Bombay,
15*th August* 1951.

India has been shocked to learn that head-hunting has become the fashion again in Nagaland. The Nagas have been smarting for some time at the Government's attitude to this old and popular tribal sport. They use the trophies as necklaces, ornaments for mantelpieces, or garden fences, and even the most educated Naga finds nothing in head-hunting that goes against the teachings of his schoolmasters.

When I went recently into the Naga hills an English-speaking trousered Naga, very familiar with the operation of electric generators since he helps to run a hydro-electric station, explained that a man's virility was formerly reckoned in terms of heads, and to this day no woman can resist a man of whom it is said that he has the head of a child or two to his credit. Looking at his worsted trousers and fingering his tie, my informant asked, wistfully: 'How can these compete with a small skull?'[1]

Notice from the above account that the teaching received by the young is quite consistent with head-hunting, and that good little Nagas will grow up to follow the tribal custom, so long as they don't lose their own heads first. Note also that the culture of the British can be acquired with regard to electric generators and clothing, but still without affecting the attitudes acquired at home in another category of behaviour.

Interesting studies of the way children grow up in primitive societies have been made by Margaret Mead. Her two books, *Coming of Age in Samoa*, 1928, and *Growing Up in New Guinea*, 1930, first drew attention to the education of children in these simple societies, and made a direct comparison with the educational problems of the United States of America. The value of the comparison lies partly in the clarity with which the responses of the growing child to the cultural environment can be seen in a simple society, free from the complex factors of our

[1] *The Manchester Guardian.*

urban civilization, and partly from the possibility of comparing a particular feature of the development of a human child under two very different environmental circumstances. Assuming a similar basic biological heredity in the Samoan child (and they all pass through the same processes of physical development), then a comparison of their personalities with those of our own children is a kind of experiment to test the variability of human behaviour. Some of the most important evidence provided by Margaret Mead's work in Samoa showed that the so-called storm and stress of adolescence, so typical of our society both here and in the United States, appears to be culturally determined. There are no adolescent conflicts of this kind in Samoa, nor in New Guinea, nor in many primitive societies. One therefore concludes that it is not in the nature of the human boy or girl to undergo this difficult period of growth, but due to his or her society. Our society causes the maximum of conflict because of the varying standards of conduct and belief, and the confusing number of choices of behaviour which are put before the young. Margaret Mead's suggestions on what can be done to help our adolescents can best be discovered by reading the relevant chapters in her book.[1]

The above is only one of numerous examples which could be quoted from the work of anthropologists to illustrate how the social climate is, for the child, as important as the air it breathes. The social group to which he belongs determines to a large extent his future behaviour and character. The same conclusion is reached by Ruth Benedict in her *Patterns of Culture*. In this book there is a comparison of the ways of life of North American Indian tribes which are biologically of one race, and many of them linguistically related. Consider for instance the contrast between the Pueblo Indians of New Mexico in the south-west, and the Plains Indians of the west. Benedict compares the differences as those between an Apollonian and a Dionysian way of living. A typical Apollonian society is the Zuni, who show moderation, restraint and sobriety in their lives. Their ceremonies and dances are formal, repetitive, compulsive, but showing no excess. The Plains Indians on the other hand (and this is common to several culture areas) are lovers of excess, orgy and violence. They hold drunken and frenzied ceremonies and seek visions through the wild exaltation and ecstasy of the Diony-

[1] *Coming of Age in Samoa*, Chap. XIII, Our Educational Problems in the light of Samoan Contrasts, and Chap. XIV, Education for Choice.

sian dance. It is interesting to compare the personality type admired by these different tribes, since their children will obviously be brought up to follow the behaviour to which the adults assign the highest value.

In the Zuni the ideal man has dignity, is sociable and generous, and does not try to lead. He even avoids office, and when he takes it, after it is thrust upon him, he must always appear unwilling. A man who thirsts for power or position receives nothing but censure, and is apt to be persecuted for sorcery. The individual thus tends to sink himself in the group, which is the functioning unit. The individual seeks no personal authority and is never violent. What is normal in the Plains Indians on the other hand is emphasis on self-assertion in the individual, who constantly tries to justify his greatness and the inferiority of all his rivals. The self-reliant man who easily gains authority, the warrior, the daredevil and the super-individual are the models set before youth. Preparation for the warpath, and for violence and fighting is the normal training of the young North American Indian, and the curious thing, at first sight, is that the Pueblos of the south-west should detach themselves from this culture and live such a peaceful and non-assertive life. Ruth Benedict rejects any suggestion that the distinction is racial or physiological. She maintains it is a question of acquired culture. Certain potentialities of human beings have been selected and given value by the community, and then cultivated by the high prestige and rewards attached to the selected types of behaviour.

THE INFLUENCE OF HEREDITY

Culture is entirely dependent, by definition, on the interaction of individuals with the social environment, and has to be learnt from the social group. Personality, however, also depends on biological inheritance. The theory here put forward stresses the importance of the environment. Clearly there is always an interaction between inborn and cultural factors, and any complete determinism is unlikely to be true. Anthropologists tend to point out the extent to which personality differences are due to a modification, by training and living, of the same *general* biological and psychic needs and capacities, most of which are considered inborn, and *not* to *specific* inherited differences. Biological needs are such obvious things as air, water, food, sleep, protection for the young, escape from pain, and sexual activity. All human beings have these needs as animals, but *how* they satisfy their needs for food, sleep or sex depends, as has been said, on their culture. Three psychic needs common to all human beings have been given by Linton[1] as follows:

(i) The need for emotional response from other individuals. This is so strong and necessary that it is often regarded as instinctive in the sense of being inborn, but it is certainly strengthened during infancy when a child's survival depends on some amount of emotional response.

(ii) The need for security, both in the future as well as the present.

(iii) The need for novelty of experience or adventure. This again might be explained by early conditioning, and is not necessarily inborn. To these we would add a fourth related to the first, namely (iv) the feeling of belonging to a group. This is a universal need which is associated with the need for emotional response since the individual cannot live alone, and merely being among other people is not enough, because he requires the approval of his group. The approval of adults is the most fundamental type of reward which fixes the child's behaviour in the cultural patterns of his community. These biological and psychic needs, even if inborn, are very generalized and easily influenced by the environment.

It may be asked whether there are no specific inherited factors which have a more direct influence on the future personality, and are relatively independent of the environment. Opinions differ very much among recognized authorities on the question of which qualities are innate and which are not, and to what extent. There is no doubt that physical characters like the colour of the eyes, the shape of the face, and the structure of the body are inherited. These characters follow the already known genetic mechanisms. It is generally supposed that some factor called by psychologists general intelligence is inherited, at least to some considerable extent. There is perhaps more doubt over temperamental qualities, but there is evidence that differences in the physiology of the body, such as the functioning of the ductless glands, account for different temperaments, and that the physiological bases of these are inherited. The factors of intelligence and learning may also have a physiological basis which would increase the probability of their forming part of the machinery of inheritance. That there are widespread and considerable psychological differences between people is a fact which is

[1] *The Cultural Background of Personality*, Chap. I.

easily observed. That some of the causative factors are innate is generally accepted by psychologists. How *much* of any particular ability is due to inheritance it is impossible to say with any accuracy at the present stage of our knowledge. The old opposition of nature and nurture is the wrong approach since both are necessary and inevitably interact.

The assumption of innate qualities makes no essential difference to the culture concept. It is a question of what weight is attached to different factors, all of which go to make up personality. In any case the innate qualities will be conditioned by environmental factors which will decide for what purpose, and maybe to what extent, an individual uses his abilities. Heredity will affect the capacity for response to the environment, and may determine much of a person's abilities, and sometimes his genius, but it is always under the influence of socially transmitted culture patterns. The large part which culture plays, and its dominance in certain respects, is what is being claimed. The exceptional individuals will play their part in influencing and sometimes changing the culture. Any concept like that of a basic personality type for a group is a norm, from which there will be many individual variations. To say that the Zuni are unaggressive does not mean that there are no aggressive individuals to be found among them. Similarly there will be peaceful and non-violent people among the Plains Indians. This would follow if the inherited constitution in the tribes were similar, and aggressive behaviour diminished in the one case and encouraged in the other by the way the young are brought up. What seems unlikely to the upholders of the culture concept is that the two peoples should be born with different quantities of some innate instinct of aggression or pugnacity. In brief the aggressive or non-aggressive personality type has been determined mainly by the environment.

It is of course conceivable that a small primitive society, if isolated for a long time, might by inbreeding develop hereditary changes which would determine a change in its basic ways of life. There is no clear evidence of this in any scientific study, and it could not possibly be the case in large modern societies where large cultural differences are also found. This brings us to the next stage of the argument.

CIVILIZED SOCIETIES AND SUB-CULTURES

The third statement to be examined may be expressed as follows:

(3) *There are variations of culture between civilized societies, and between sub-cultures within the same society*

In recent years anthropologists, whose field of study has usually been primitive peoples, have turned their attention to the study of complex civilized societies. Social and cultural surveys within their own countries have become an activity of social scientists of all kinds. These are not always personality studies, but they often include details on social habits and customs, attitudes to social class status and so on. Such surveys are, as a rule, cross sections of culture in a particular city, town, or village.[1] There are also studies of particular sub-cultures which will be referred to later. One of the first attempts at an anthropological study of personality types in the total society of a modern nation was Margaret Mead's work on *The American Character.*[2] A similar study was made a few years later by Geoffrey Gorer called *The Americans.* It is from this latter work that we take as an example a typical American culture pattern as described by Gorer. A brief summary of his views on the status of the mother and father in the United States, will illustrate a norm of family life in many respects different from the norm in this country.

The outstanding fact is that in the United States the mother tends to take over the role of the father in the European family. The female Statue of Liberty is a more acceptable symbol than Uncle Sam. As a result of the rejection of father the mother takes the lead in raising the family, and implants a feminine conscience in the child. This has two obvious results. First that mother love is respected and idealized to a high degree, and second that a great fear of being too feminine is developed in the boys, with a consequent great assertion of masculinity. The clinging mother over there is as much a menace as the bossy father over here. The dominating authority of the father in the family is a European pattern, which appears to have been thrown over along with the traditions of the fatherland, when the next generation grew up from the

[1] See for example the studies of Michael Young and Peter Willmott: *Family and Kinship in East London*, 1957 and *Family and Class in a London Suburb*, 1960. Also W. M. Williams: *The Sociology of an English Village: Gosforth.* Also N. Dennis, F. Henriques, and C. Slaughter: *Coal is Our Life*, 1956, J. B. Mays; *Growing Up in a City*, 1954.

[2] Published Penguin Books, 1944. There have been many books on the English people, but not by anthropologists. Typical examples are: D. W. Brogan: *The English People*, 1942. Ernest Barker (Ed.): *The Character of England*, 1947. George Orwell: *The English People*, 1947. See also Geoffrey Gorer: *Exploring English Character*, 1955.

original immigrants. The dominance of the mother in the U.S.A. is reinforced for the child by the majority of teachers being women. Now the mother is a full supporter of the 'success system' because to 'make good' and be a success is another culture complex very powerful with all Americans. Mother's child therefore must not be a failure and must compete at all ages. From infancy on nothing is too good for the children, who must be bigger and better than ever before, and hence the importance of food, and the latest methods of child rearing and psychology and so on. Above all he must not be a 'sissy', and nor must *she* either for this applies to both sexes, and means *not* to show dependence, fear, lack of push, shyness, or passivity. Thus the pace is set for the freedom and independence of children. Americans hate to restrict the freedom of children who tend to dominate their parents. So off goes the little boy to show his initiative, and back he comes to tell the tale, and to get approval for it whenever he triumphs. Hence the importance of talk, and big talk, too.

Condensing a lot of material into this shortened summary may appear to give a distorted picture, but it is certain that Gorer makes a case which requires a good deal of study, and is of fundamental importance since it concerns the roles of male and female. The roles assumed by growing individuals are chosen from those choices offered by the culture, and nothing could be more important in the bringing up of children than the ways in which the functions of father and mother are interpreted.

The American custom of 'dating' links on to the bringing up of children and is worth a little description, since Gorer gives it the full flavour of the anthropologist at work. It is pre-courtship behaviour which, he says, 'is a highly patterned activity comparable both to a formal dance . . . and a competitive game'. It continues from about the age of twelve until the age of betrothal. The competition of the 'success system' continues and 'Am I a success?' becomes the equivalent of 'Am I loved?' or rather the aim is to prove yourself worthy of love. It *appears* to be love-making, but its object is far more to gain self-esteem and success than sex pleasure. Success for the boy is to put over a good 'line' of talk; to get the girl to show that he is lovable; to do better than his rivals by getting as many favours as possible; and to 'date' the most popular girls. Success for the girl is to get as many 'dates' as possible; to get a lot of money spent on her, and the best show of flowers, and the smartest car; not to give way to the boy's advances too much, but enough to keep him interested; to parry his 'line' and in fact to make the result a draw.

Added together with all the other aspects of the American way of life the final result is a set of culture patterns very different from any European nation though sharing common elements with several. We must also notice that there is more and more a diffusion of American cultural habits to Europe, and we are apt to see an imitation of their attitudes from their motion pictures, as well as from direct mixing with their citizens. This process is likely to continue in many parts of the world because of the growing dominance of the United States as a world power.

With regard to sub-cultures within the same country a little thought will show that such contrasts must exist in any large society with a complex division of labour and marked inequalities of income. This means that any composite picture of national character is to some extent unreliable, since the culture of a nation is not homogeneous. Thus some of the habits of the Americans as described by Gorer or Mead would not be typical of all Americans, and some would have to be modified according to the place of living and social status of the inhabitants. England is a suitable country for studying sub-cultures since they are closely linked with social class distinctions. There is no standard definition, but it may be said that the people making up a sub-culture have grown so accustomed to a sufficiently distinctive set of attitudes and habits of life, that any one of them would be out of place and unable to feel 'at home' if suddenly transferred to another sub-culture. The consciousness of belonging to a particular group, which is different from other groups, is a feature of social class membership. Hence in class stratified societies each social class tends to develop a sub-culture of its own, while also sharing common traits with the national culture. A social class has been defined by Ginsberg as 'Groups of individuals who, through common descent, similarity of occupation, wealth and education, have come to have a similar mode of life, a similar stock of ideas, feelings, attitudes, and forms of behaviour, and who . . . meet one another on equal terms, and regard themselves . . . as belonging to one group.'[1] This definition shows the similarity in the ideas of social class and sub-culture. In spite of the breaking down of traditional class barriers and the levelling of incomes, the fact is that we are all conscious of different cultural groups, but find it extremely difficult to define their limits or their characteristics

[1] *Encyclopedia of Social Science*, Vol. XI.

with any degree of exactness. A large number of factors have to be considered to make an estimate of social grouping. The reader can think for himself how people in his home town differ in the following respects, and see whether any obvious cultural groups emerge.

(a) *Miscellaneous factors:* income, occupation, education, language habits (speech, accent and vocabulary), type of residence, spending habits.

(b) *Living habits:* clothes and dress, eating and diet, physical habits and means of keeping healthy, attitudes to marriage and sex, techniques of bringing up children, patterns of family life.

(c) *Leisure pursuits:* reading (including newspapers), radio and television programmes preferred, sports (played and watched), entertainments favoured, means of artistic expression, ways of spending holidays.

(d) *Belief and value systems:* moral attitudes and standards, religious belief, political views, social ambitions, aims in life.

To describe a person in terms of all the above factors is to give a fairly good indication of the culture to which he belongs.

Another approach is suggested by T. S. Eliot when he considers how much is embraced by the term 'culture'. 'It includes all the characteristic activities and interests of a people:' he writes, 'Derby Day, Henley Regatta, Cowes, the twelfth of August, a cup final, the dog races, the pin table, the dart board, Wensleydale cheese, boiled cabbage cut into sections, beetroot in vinegar, nineteenth-century Gothic churches, and the music of Elgar. The reader can make his own list.'[1] Here one has to ask the question for what kind of people are these characteristic activities and interests? Let us add a list of our own: The Eton and Harrow Match, Blackpool, *The Times*, The *Daily Mirror*, *Punch*, Fortnum and Mason, the Co-op., The Athenaeum, garden parties, Mecca dance-halls, The Old Kent Road, football pools, fish and chips, suburbia, back-to-back houses, pin-stripe suiting, seaside boarding-houses, The Music Hall, mowing the lawn. All, one must admit, referring to something typically English; but not all for the same kind of English people.

From such exercises as the above it will be found that the concepts of social class and sub-culture are closely linked together, and yet they are not the same. The class concept implies a vertical stratification; one class is invariably spoken of as 'higher' or 'lower' than another. Yet people who were unmistakably of the same class might be out of place and unable to feel 'at home' with each other (the criterion we have

[1] *Notes Towards the Definition of Culture*, p. 31.

chosen), because of cultural differences. This is noticeable even on moving from one region of England to another, before adaptation to the new environment has taken place. It can also be seen in the culture areas within a large city. Sociologists still write in terms of a class structure, although recent studies stress the overlap, and attempts have been made to give descriptive accounts of typical ways of life in cultural and ideological terms.[1] Children are born with the sub-culture of their family and home environment. They become influenced also by the elements of the national culture which are common to all groups and classes of the community. But the sub-culture of the family is the dominant influence unless, and until, the child is able to move out of it. To-day children do move out of the family circle much more easily than in the past. While the best indication of a person's class used to be to inquire about his family this ceases to be true with the increasing social mobility due largely to the greater opportunity for education. A person's occupation is now becoming a surer guide to his social standing, and broadly speaking the way to a better job is to get a better education. Education gives the opportunity for the clever child to change his class or cultural group if he has the need to do so. For an account of the relations of education, social class and social mobility see Chapters VI and VII.

Confusion over the meaning of the word 'culture' has caused a good deal of trouble, and is likely to cause more, in spite of the amount of writing on the subject. There has been much discussion of the growing gulf of mutual incomprehension between the literary intellectuals and the physical scientists in our society. This is reflected in school and university by the gap of understanding between the arts and science students. Another more widespread division is between those who have had a prolonged education until the age of eighteen or beyond, and those who have not. The works of Raymond Williams[2] among other writers on literature and the arts, have drawn attention to the need for a more integrated and commonly accepted culture. He sees the problem partly in terms of the differing values of the traditional middle-class and the rising, socially conscious working-class. Contributions to culture

[1] Roy Lewis and Angus Maude: *The English Middle Classes*, 1949. C. Wright Mills: *White Collar*, 1951. T. H. Pear: *English Social Differences*, 1955. F. Zweig: *The Worker in an Affluent Society*, 1962.

[2] *Culture and Society*, 1958 and *The Long Revolution*, 1961.

come increasingly from all levels of the social scale. But what kind of culture are we speaking of, and in what sense can a common culture be said to be emerging? We have already distinguished two main aspects of culture (see p. 8). This first is the level of intellectual and artistic excellence in the society. To understand, accept, share and transmit this 'high' culture (as it may in brief be called) in any of its branches can only be within the capacity of a minority, even when, by the spread of education and the increase of communication, it is made accessible to all. It is difficult to see, with all the opportunity in the world, in what sense the culture of the creative artists, writers and thinkers in the humanities or the sciences could become a 'common culture'. Yet it might become what would be more rightly called a 'communal' culture, in the sense that participation in it was widely diffused throughout society, and not dependent on belonging to any particular *élite*; except where entrance to the *élite* has been genuinely and freely open to all.

The other aspect of culture is the everyday way of life of a social group. It is related to the intellectual life, but may be discussed separately since it is more dependent on class traditions, social habits and occupational function. Whereas participation in high culture is minimal for the majority of the population, yet everyone lives in accordance with *some* set of culture patterns. And yet, in social habits, how much do we have in common with a different sub-culture? The major obstacle here is the tenacious persistence of our social class structure. Money cannot be the social solvent; it will merely change the basis of differentiation. The new professional and managerial class will have much in common—the same cars, the same houses and furniture, the same clothes, the same parties and the same drinks. They will share the way of life that money can buy, and will be the model for the ambitious just below, who will seek to partake in the new culture of their betters. And yet the idealistic educator can still hope that it is possible for our future society to build patterns of culture which give a high priority to other values in life as well as money making and social advancement.

EDUCATION AND CULTURE

What can be concluded of importance to education from these statements on the culture concept? There are two general conclusions:

(1) *That the behaviour of human beings is very flexible, and will adapt itself to the cultural environment.*

One is tempted to say that human nature can be changed, but such a statement is liable to different interpretation according to the meaning attached to the term 'human nature'. Human nature in the sense of the manifest behaviour of human beings can certainly be changed. But there is a sense in which the nature of man is assumed to be the same in all cultures, races, or historical periods, and in this usage it is unchangeable by definition. Or again human nature could be empirically described as the sum of all the characteristics which distinguish mankind from the other animals. This would include all the behaviour which is common to human beings everywhere, and therefore independent of environment, though presumably it will have changed in history with the evolution of the species of man.[1] 'Man has no nature; he has history', said Ortega y Gasset. There are, nevertheless, many generalized needs, beliefs, and goals which are common to all mankind. The striking thing is that the ways in which different societies interpret and use their 'human nature' are so varied the world over. From the point of the sociologist 'human nature' is not a very useful concept if it is regarded as being independent of time and place, and the use of the term 'human behaviour' is preferable to avoid confusion. The evidence we have presented indicates quite definitely that human behaviour can be changed by the social environment.

This is not to say that one form of behaviour is as good as another. That different societies have different standards of right and wrong, and different ideals of behaviour, is known as the principle of cultural relativity. This principle has been misunderstood by people who have advocated a form of behaviour in their own society on the grounds that it is acceptable in another society. Others have gone further and suggested that since behaviour is relative to the culture it is not necessary to have any fixed standards. Both these conclusions are false. It is as if we should say that because polygyny is successful among the Tanala of Madagascar it would be successful in England. In the first place a culture pattern is related to the total culture, and cannot, except under

[1] But since the evolution of *homo sapiens* took place at different rates in different parts of the world this use of the term only makes sense as a norm for the species in a certain territory during a given time.

exceptional conditions, be isolated and transferred to another culture. Secondly the ethical values of our society at the present time would reject it. Each society has its own code of what is right and wrong, and these are the facts which the anthropologist reports. We have to judge what is good for our society not by what *is* but what we think *ought* to be. If our standards are so flexible that we cannot judge, then our society is in danger of breakdown because a stable core of values is not being maintained. (See p. 11.) Nevertheless standards can and do change, and modification of behaviour by means of the environment offers us renewed hope of effecting improvements.

The culture concept impresses upon us more strongly than ever the importance of the way children are brought up. The child grows up to fit his society, and the possible resulting personalities are as varied as the possible kinds of society. The society of the child begins with his mother and father, and the children and adults in his home, and extends through enlarging circles of human relationships. Through the development of psychoanalysis and psychiatry more and more stress has been laid on the importance of the early years of childhood in conditioning the future personality.[1] We are still extremely ignorant of the influence of different methods of child rearing on the future development of character, but enough is known to state with certainty that basic psychological processes and states are initiated in the first few years which are of significance to the individual through life. A study of psychology is essential to an understanding of social life. Psychology, and in particular what is known as personality psychology, studies how and why individuals change in response to the forces operating upon them both from within themselves and from the environment. It is thus an essential part of a comprehensive science of human behaviour. Most human problems require a multi-disciplined approach, which means a combined operation of social scientists of all kinds. Psychology plays its part along with anthropology and sociology in the interpretation of culture. The study and practice of education, touching life as it does at all points, must move side by side with the study of society. This leads us to the second general conclusion arising from this chapter:

[1] Very important works on this subject are those by D. W. Winnicott: *The Child and the Family*, 1957, and *The Child and the Outside World*, 1957, or Ian D. Suttie: *The Origins of Love and Hate*, 1935, edition by Penguin Books 1960.

(2) *That education depends on the whole culture of a society*

We have seen how personality is partly determined by the culture in which it grows. It therefore follows that education, being concerned with the growth of personality, is also dependent on the culture of the society in which it takes place. It should have become very clear by now that the school is only one educative agency, and that society is full of educators making their various attempts on the growing child.[1] Most subtle of all are the unconscious moulding influences of the culture patterns we all take for granted. We must not forget that the individual being educated also selects his own experiences, so far as it is within his power. He hits back on his environment. Man is moulded by society, but society is also moulded by man. How does he do this? The individual has aims too, even the small child. It is true that he gets them from his culture, but he combines them with something unique in himself. We are told by psychoanalysts that basic attitudes are acquired in early childhood. Examples of such attitudes are the child's feelings of security or anxiety, his degree of curiosity or his lack of initiative. The curious and secure child selects a different environment from the anxious and apathetic child. There is no doubt over the different attitudes, it is the cause of them which often eludes us. The individual responds to the situation he is in, and he responds with something which is within himself. However far back you take the situation, *some* of the response was born with the individual. The result of the education of a person, up to the point in life he has reached, is the result of the educative experiences of all kinds, self-chosen and imposed upon the self, plus the individual's adjustment to those experiences. This includes unconscious adjustment as well as conscious.

Having said this one immediately thinks of the different sets of experiences different children can have within the same complex society. So that in England education depends on the sub-culture of the child's

[1] Cf. T. S. Eliot, op. cit., p. 106: 'If we include as education all the influences of family and environment, we are going far beyond what professional educators can control though their sway may extend very far indeed; but if we mean that culture is what is passed on by our primary and secondary schools or our preparatory and public schools, then we are asserting that an organ is the whole organism. For the schools can transmit only a part, and they can only transmit this part effectively, if the outside influences, not only of family and environment, but of work, play, of newsprint and spectacles and entertainment and sport are in harmony with them.'

home and environment, as well as on the elements of the total culture common to all homes and environments. The earlier references to sub-cultures in England should help to make this point clear. With these ideas in mind we realize that we cannot generalize about 'the Child' but must ask from which cultural class he comes.[1] It has been found that children from different social groups have different attitudes towards the solving of mental problems. This even leads to a source of error in intelligence tests if they are not adapted to the cultural background.[2] There is thus evidence that the individual learns to think in the way his group defines thinking. The recognition of the existence of sub-cultures makes it necessary for the teacher to know about the environment of his pupils. He also needs to understand the cultural motivation of their parents, which is most clearly shown by what the parents expect of education. It might be thought that all the people in the same society would agree about the aims of education. This state of affairs has been nearest to realization only in small societies in a relatively stable phase of development, where, in spite of different educational procedures according to future function and status in the society, all were agreed on the social purpose and the methods employed. In a large, complex, and changing society like England during this century there are considerable differences of opinion over the aims of education, which reflect differences over objectives in life. The administrators and staffs of different schools are faced with different problems depending on such factors as the length of the period of school education, the future occupations of the pupils, the wishes of the parents, and the cultural background from which the pupils come. In the light of the culture concept educators

[1] J. B. Conant: *Education in a Divided World*, 1948, writes the following on this point: 'Education is a social process, our schools and colleges neither operate in empty space nor serve identical communities. Before you judge a school analyse the families from which it draws its students and the opportunities presented to its pupils. What may be a satisfactory curriculum for one group of pupils may be highly unsuitable for another. And the difference is often due not to discrepancies in the intellectual capacities of the students, but to the social situation in which the boys and girls are placed.'

[2] This case is well argued by Allison Davis: *Social Class Influences on Learning*, 1951. He considers the following factors affect an intelligence test: H—Hereditary; C—Cultural, covering experience with the content and symbols employed; C1—Training at school or at home; C2—Cultural motivation, e.g. drive or incentive to solve the problem; S—Phenomenon of 'speed' if a time test. Another work is by F. K. Eels, *et al.*: *Intelligence and Cultural Differences*, 1951.

must ask themselves such questions as the following: Are there not differences in aim as well as content between the education given by a Public School, a Technical College, a Secondary Modern School, and a Private 'Progressive' School? (To quote a few examples of our diverse schools.) And do not these schools to some cxtent, symbolize sub-cultures within our society? That all our schools have a set of objectives and values in common is no doubt true, but what are these values, and how important do we regard them?

CHAPTER III

Social Forces and Cultural Change

The Interaction of Techniques and Values—The Nature of Social Forces —Social Needs and Cultural Change—Power and the Body Politic— Education and Social Change

If, as has been maintained in the last chapter, education depends on the whole culture of a society it becomes valuable to have a workable theory of how to describe or explain the culture of a society at a given time, and the causes of cultural change. The culture of a society during a given period is influenced by the interaction of two classes of factors (a) the stage of technical invention and scientific discovery it has reached, and (b) the dominant aims and values of the society. This statement can be shortened into: culture can be described in terms of

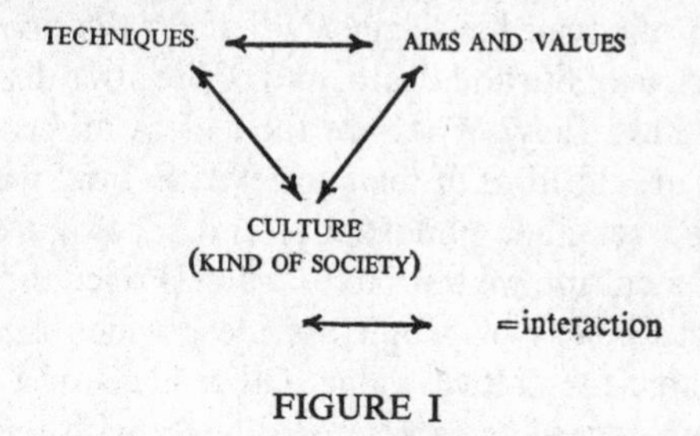

FIGURE I

the interaction of techniques and values. The relation can be represented diagrammatically as in Fig. I where the double arrows represent a dynamic interaction, or a two-way process.

First the use of the term 'techniques' requires some explanation. Some of the first questions a person would ask about an unknown society would be: 'How do they get food? What kind of houses do they live in? What kind of tools or machines do they use? What language do they speak and how is it written?' All of these would be inquiries about techniques, which are the means by which the members of the society satisfy their basic human needs for food, shelter, reproduction, communication, artistic expression, social organization, and in general the preservation and continuance of the race. The development of such techniques in the history of mankind has depended on discoveries and inventions such as: simple hand tools, the use of fire, cooking, agriculture, the domestication of animals, the wheel, the use of metals, mathematics, the development of machines, and the harnessing of power by use of wind, water, steam, oil, electricity or atomic energy.

There has also been a correlated development of social techniques by means of social inventions to satisfy the needs of living together in a group. Under this heading would be included spoken and written language, forms of family life, money, trade, methods of government, education and propaganda. Here also would perhaps come the techniques of the arts and crafts, unless they are placed in another category. But all types and classes of techniques operate together. Warfare may be regarded as a social invention. It is a method people adopt when they cannot solve their problems in any other way.

However, a society can be described only partially in terms of its techniques. Questions regarding values would also arise immediately the investigation of social life begins. 'What do the people believe in? What are their ideas of life and death, and of life after death? What kind of God or gods have they? What are their ideas of beauty, truth and goodness? What are the aims of their society?' In brief we need to know something of the religion, philosophy, and ideology of the people. These aspects of a culture we refer to as 'values' since the guiding social aims and religious beliefs of people are ideas which they think worth while, and to which they attach value. Other ideas of a purely neutral or logical kind we regard as associated directly with techniques. They are a part of the scientific thinking necessary to carry out the technical activities which the society need, or which they value and hence desire. R. M. MacIver has used the term 'myth' where we use the term 'value'. In his usage 'myths' are 'value-impregnated beliefs and notions that men hold, that they live by or live for'.[1] He says that every society is held together by a myth-system, and that 'all social relations are myth-born and myth-sustained'. 'Myth' includes 'the most penetrating philosophies of life, the most profound intimations of religion. . . .' This seems to be using the word 'myth' rather far from its normal use, since it is usually understood to mean a fictitious story or belief. A myth suggests a popular idea which is not in fact true, and one hesitates to apply this term indiscriminately to the philosophies and religions of mankind. Hence the use here of the word 'values' for the ideas men live for.

THE INTERACTION OF TECHNIQUES AND VALUES

There is no doubt that both techniques and values change, and it is their interaction which characterizes the nature of a society at a given time. It is of little use to describe social change either in terms of technical progress or in terms of a change in values, when the one is considered independently of the other. The state of society depends on both, and they are inseparable. Nor is it at all easy to say which influence is dominant, or takes the lead, in any particular social change. It is frequently said, and with some truth, that new inventions are a primary cause of social change. But the invention *alone* is not a sufficient explanation. Its use will depend on the prevailing set of values in the society. The aims and values of a community determine how its techniques will be used. The same technical invention can be used in a different way in different societies, or indeed its use may be delayed if the state of society is unfavourable for its development. On the other hand those who think that value-systems, ideas and aspirations are dominant in changing society, must reckon with the force of technology which by changing habits of work and life also changes habits of thought and belief. In dealing with the problems of social change we are presented with a number of variables each of which is influencing each other.

The theory of social change which is here put forward accepts the comprehensive definition of culture as the whole way of life of a society. Thus it differs slightly in terminology from some of the sociological writing on this subject. For instance, R. M. MacIver and C. H. Page, in their standard work on *Society* distinguish between the technological factors and the cultural factors in social change. For these two sets of

[1] R. M. MacIver: *The Web of Government*, 1947, p. 4.

factors we have used the terms techniques and values. We are here following those who take the anthropological view of culture, and therefore include technological factors (techniques) as a part of culture. We are in complete agreement with MacIver and Page over the interaction between the two sets of factors, but wish to avoid all theories which place the technical and the cultural in opposition to each other, and stress the dominance of the one or the other in determining change. This was the difficulty with W. F. Ogburn's original hypothesis[1] where he used the terms material culture and non-material culture, and spoke of a 'cultural lag' when values did not adapt and respond at the same rate as changes in material conditions. He also assumed that material change comes first, is more rapid, and more effective, and the main determinant of other social changes. The extremes of economic-technological determinism had, of course, already been held by Marx and Engels and their followers, as the basis of their economic interpretation of history. Thorstein Veblen, the American sociologist, has also developed in a brilliant way the thesis that the kind of work which men do determines their habits of thought which in turn determines the social structure. While he rightly stresses the powerful effect of habituation and adjustment to a changing technique, he neglects, from our point of view, the selective and critical response of individuals according to their aims and values.

We hold the view that changes in techniques and values, which correspond to the material and non-material aspects of culture, are both simultaneously involved in any social change, and that neither is necessarily dominant. The relative importance of the one or the other will be different on different occasions, and in relation to other variables and social forces at work. To make an issue of material versus non-material, or technological versus cultural, is as unprofitable as the discussion of nature versus nurture, if carried on in the sense that one or the other is, in every case, more important. The original hypothesis of 'cultural lag', while still popular among those who complain that man's values have not kept pace with his technical development, has not stood up well to criticism.[2] It is however a useful conception, since it is true that the

[1] W. F. Ogburn: *Social Change*, 1922.

[2] In Ogburn's later work it has been modified. One of the most valuable treatments of social change is in W. F. Ogburn and M. E. Nimkoff: *A Handbook of Sociology*, 1947, Part VII.

various components of culture may change at different times, and when any two variables can be validly correlated, the different rates of change can have predictable effects on society. The doubtful proposition is that it is always the non-material aspects which are 'adaptive' and lag behind the material. We have always to decide what lags behind what. In a case quoted by Ogburn where the ratio of police to inhabitants was not maintained as cities increased in size, it was quite clear that undesirable results followed from the lag of the numbers of policemen behind the numbers of criminals. But even in this case there are many other factors concerned in the prevention of crime.

The best way to make clear our hypothesis of the interaction of techniques and values is to give an illustration as we go along from among the recent changes which have in fact taken place as a result of a new invention. Choosing an invention as the starting point is an admission of the powerful social effect of inventions, but does not commit us to any technological determinism since it will be shown that no social change results without the accompanying influence of human interests and attitudes. Let us consider, for our example, the coming of radio broadcasting. Although this appeared to come upon the world quite suddenly it was, like all scientific inventions, a cumulative process depending directly on previous inventions, and resulting from discoveries of scientists from well back into the nineteenth century. It began, if one event has to be chosen, with the prediction of the behaviour of electromagnetic waves by Clerk Maxwell, or even further back with the first electric telegraph. No invention is entirely new, but is a combination of known elements into a new form. The greater the accumulation of scientific knowledge the greater has been the possibility of invention, and this has been expressed by what is sometimes called the law of acceleration in the growth of material culture. A graph of the number of important inventions plotted against time roughly corresponds to a curve showing the growth of compound interest. Such a curve could be drawn for the inventions relating to tele-communication alone, and while there would be few significant points before 1920, when broadcasting began, there has been since that date an increasingly rapid growth of new techniques and subsidiary inventions, including all those associated with the major developments of television and radar.

The coming of broadcasting soon had an effect on industry, politics, religion, education, entertainment, home life, the class structure, and on the whole balance of social forces within our culture. The response of values on a national scale can be seen by the form of control to which broadcasting was submitted. What could reflect the English way of life more than the constitution of the British Broadcasting Corporation, with its independent Governors, its charter, its responsibility to Parliament, and its high record for good standards, and the protection, indeed the education, of the listener? How different from the United States, where their greater attachment to the *laissez-faire* values of free capitalism allowed a freer development of radio, leaving it to be controlled (except for some Federal laws) by private interests, and sponsored by big business and the advertisers. Again, the use of the radio for widespread propaganda for a single party could never happen while we remain a democracy, but has been and is, easily possible in a totalitarian state. This is a clear example of the different uses to which the same invention can be put, and these uses are dependent on the aims, interests and needs of groups of human beings, and determined by what the people who use it consider worth while.

Let us see how the influence of the radio, by interacting with existing techniques and values, affected the whole culture, leading gradually to adaptation and change. It is only necessary to quote a few examples to illustrate our thesis, but in each example a cycle of interaction involving both techniques and values can be observed.

(a) *Economic change*. A new industry was set up. Technicians and designers had to be switched at once to the manufacture of radio sets. This led to improved techniques, further demand, and a larger radio industry. A sub-cycle was here set up within the whole economic setting. Other industries were affected—for example gramophone business at first declined, but later improved its own techniques of recording and reproduction. A new group of occupations appeared in connection with broadcasting; not only engineers, administrators, announcers, and programme producers, etc. but also professional broadcasters and script writers for a new form of entertainment and a new form of cultural diffusion. Techniques were changed and developed in the methods of using the new medium, which affected all broadcasters from comedians to public speakers. The relation to values has already been mentioned, and took the form of control over the subject matter to be broadcast and the refusal to allow advertising or propaganda over the air.

(b) *Political change*. The political possibilities of broadcasting are obviously far-reaching. It extends the direct contact between the leader and the group from small meetings to the ears of the whole nation. Since in Great Britain a strict system of 'fair play' has been observed between party political speakers this has made for the strengthening of democracy. But even more important for the spread of democratic values was the spread of news and information, and the participation in current events which broadcasting made possible. The technique of political campaigning has been changed by the radio, and the strange way a personality gets through the microphone has made the quiet and more rational speakers sometimes succeed where the oratorical tricks of the old style political speakers have failed. These are but a few examples; the reader may add his own.

(c) *Effects on Religion.* As with politics the potential effects are great, and a policy of 'fair play' has been observed between the denominations. There has been a noticeable increase in the open discussion of religious topics, which, whatever its effects, is in line with our tradition of religious toleration and freedom of speech.

(d) *Effects on Social Status and Public Opinion.* The common experiences sustained through the radio make for social cohesion, and have tended to reduce the distance between the social classes. The sound of standard English speech has been more widely diffused, and this tends to reduce the differences between local accents. At the same time the provision of three different programmes has not only shown an acceptance of diversity of interest but has served the variety of cultural levels within the population. The Third Programme is a definite recognition of the needs of a minority of listeners, and also provides an opportunity for anybody to widen his knowledge of artistic and intellectual culture.

Public opinion has been affected through the B.B.C. and the B.B.C. has in turn been affected by public opinion. Here again is a cycle of interaction. Public opinion has affected techniques whether by a demand for better sets and reception, or by a demand for better programmes. Another channel of criticism is through Parliament, which is linked with public opinion by other cycles of interaction. The public have also, in the widest sense, been educated by the radio, and we shall return to this aspect when we consider in general the processes of cultural adaptation in relation to educational change.

Enough should have been said to indicate the multiplicity of factors which must be considered in any analysis of social change. That is why the concept of causation is so dangerous in social science; because we are dealing with multi-variant phenomena. These are events caused by variables which have a tendency to change together, but the measure of their association is only a probability. This probability can be changed by the operation of another variable, perhaps at first unforeseen. For example, it might be said that the introduction of light electric motors enabled more women to work in factories. But more women might have been going out to work because they desired independence or more money or for some other reason. However, if the electric motors make the work easier it is still more probable that more women will work in those factories than if there were no electric motors. If, however, the rates of pay for women are suddenly reduced, the probability of women going to the factories is liable to get less, while the other reasons for going remain unchanged. Again, in an area where it is the established tradition for women to go out to work, there will still be a higher proportion doing so than where this tradition is absent, in spite of the adverse effect of reduced pay. And so on. In brief, it is very risky to say what causes what in human affairs, but very valuable to observe things which tend to change together, and whenever possible to make some kind of measure of the degree of their association with each other. The difficulty is that the variables often cannot be isolated and this is an obstacle to the interpretation of statistics, since the figures may not say how much *each* factor contributed.

The matter is further complicated by factors which appear to be in different orders of reality. How do you relate, or add up, the effects of mechanical machines and beliefs? Yet both change society. Our way of overcoming these difficulties is to maintain that in the end all social changes require the *actions of people*. This at least they have in common. It was in response to human needs that techniques were developed at all, and the whole process of civilization undertaken. People have needs, ideas, attitudes and interests, and call upon techniques to help solve their problems. The forces which integrate, or disintegrate, culture are the forces exercised by groups of people.

THE NATURE OF SOCIAL FORCES

We have been trying to show, by our illustration of the social effects related to radio broadcasting, how the classes of factors we have called techniques and values operate in action within society. We have decided that techniques are operated by people, and values are held in the mind, and spoken or written, by people. In society people associate together in groups for some common purpose and with some common interest. When such a group of people, by its collective action or opinion, is able to influence the action or opinion of other groups or sections of the public, or influence the actions of the government, it can be called a *social force*. It is helpful to think concretely of social forces as groups of people, which in fact they are. Otherwise one connects the use of the word 'force' with the thought of some external power, like a force of nature, which has an existence outside of society. Social forces are human forces which work upon each other within society. As a definition: *a social force is an attempt by a number of the members of a society to bring about social action or social change.*[1]

The social forces at work in a society, at a given time, are the determinants of culture, and are both the media for the diffusion of techniques and values, and change as a result of their interaction. We must not think of culture or society as something apart from the people who live it and change it. A culture is made up of the thoughts and actions of individuals and groups of people and has not any other existence, except as the recorded evidence of people's thoughts and actions.[2]

Social forces will themselves overlap and interact, and they can be

[1] This is derived from the following definition in *The Dictionary of Sociology*: 'Social Force: Any effective urge or impulse that leads to social action. Specifically a social force is a consensus on the part of a sufficient number of the members of society to bring about social action or social change of some sort.'

It differs from an earlier definition which reads: 'Social Forces: The motives which drive men to exert effort, and to associate with others, e.g. hunger, love, security etc.', which was agreed by the American Sociological Society in 1933. These forces are for our purpose called basic human needs.

[2] Robert Lynd: *Knowledge for What*? 1939, stresses this point in his Chap. II on The Concept of Culture, as the following quotations illustrate: 'When culture changes —a new law is passed, a custom falls into disuse, women wear shorts, anti-Semitism becomes a problem, or automatic machinery replaces human labour—it is the behaviour of the people which provides the dynamics of change. Neither a "society" nor a "culture" learns, but people do.' (p. 46.) 'The culture does not enamel its finger nails, or vote, or believe in capitalism, but people do, and some do and some do not. When I give away a still warm and comfortable overcoat because it is beginning to look worn, I *feel* myself responding to people—my wife, my business associates, people at the club—and what they will think of me. . . .' (p. 39.)

classified into such categories as economic forces, occupational groups, political forces, religious forces, social status groups, educational forces, etc. for the sake of further analysis. All such social groups are engaged in a constant conflict of interests, and a struggle for control over change. This dynamic relationship can be diagrammatically illustrated as in Fig. II.

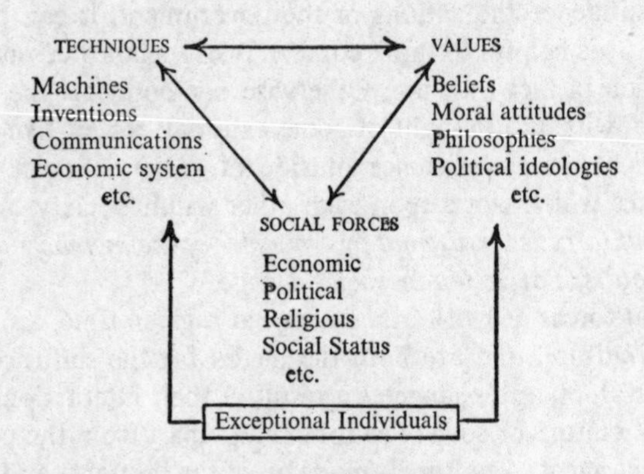

FIGURE II

Diagram representing the dynamic interaction of factors within a society which determines cultural change. Exceptional individuals are shown as having a direct effect on techniques and values, but resulting changes in the culture will only follow through the influence of the social forces.

Social forces are made up of groups of people, but they are not all organized groups. An association of business men, a trade union, a political party, a religious body, will all be to a varying degree organized and able to take collective action as an organization. But a social class is what one might call a quasi-group, and consists of people with sufficient interests in common to make it sensible to talk of 'middle-class opinion' or the 'aims of the working class' if used in the suitable historic context. Even such a vague notion as 'public opinion' can be said to exert a social force, but only because it is made up of many different 'publics' which each exercise their own set of opinions. Such 'publics' are quasi-groups of people, having certain points of view in common.[1]

[1] Thus married women, sports lovers, animal lovers, car owners, listeners to the Third Programme, can on occasion act as social forces when their interests are threatened.

They will usually exert any influence on social action through the particular organized groups to which they belong.

Certain individuals can indeed be considered social forces on their own, because of the influence they have on the ideas and actions of others. Exceptional individuals have a very special place within a society because of the direct influence they can exert in changing the existing techniques and values. Scientists and inventors can cause a sudden change in the techniques of a society, while thinkers and reformers may change its values. The new inventions and ideas have to become accepted by sufficient numbers in the society before they become part of its culture. Creative geniuses and moral leaders may be at first in advance of the changing culture, and their influence must work through the operation of social forces. Thus it may be said that the individual only becomes a social force when his ideas are followed and acted upon by a group. There may sometimes be a considerable time lag before this happens. The influence of great men and women may be fast or slow according to the rate of acceptance and spread of their ideas. We must be careful not to omit the influence of individuals while stressing the social determinants of change. In the end it is the few individuals who make the necessary inventions, state the new philosophies, or make the critical decisions in the policy of a nation. Yet such individuals do not work in isolation from their society, and the extent to which their work is in response to social needs is another interesting study.

SOCIAL NEEDS AND CULTURAL CHANGE

We have introduced the conception that social forces are the active determinants of culture, and must now ask what is the nature of the drive which gives them their force. All human beings are primarily driven to action by the desire to satisfy their needs, and this is the power behind social as well as individual action. Needs may be selfish, altruistic, material, physical, mental, emotional or spiritual, but all the groups which make up the social forces in a society, demand the satisfaction of their needs in some form or other. It is in the process of satisfying social needs that cultural adaptation takes place. As the culture changes new needs are met, new techniques arise, values may change, and so a continuously interacting cycle is at work. It is only for the convenience of analysis that we can take a look at a society at a given time; and purely arbitrary what time we allow before we study the cultural adaptation that has taken place since the first analysis. Along with cultural adaptation goes educational change. We take the view that educational change tends to follow social change, and that education is one of the last functions of society to adapt to new social needs. The elaboration of this point of view is dealt with in the next chapter. Let us now apply our illustration of the development of broadcasting to the new theoretical considerations that we have introduced.

(a) *Cultural adaptation to broadcasting*. Gradually the radio became a widespread necessity, and a part of people's lives. (This process has now taken place with television.) 'Listening in' entered into the pattern of living and family life had to adapt. The radio became the servant of democracy but also increased democratic participation, and increased people's knowledge of each other, of home affairs, and of international relations. Political and social questions are now freely discussed. Public meetings on almost any topic are broadcast, and audience participation through the microphone is encouraged. People's level of appreciation of the arts, and of intellectual culture and thought has tended to improve. This gradually makes an improvement in the standard of values among ordinary people. This has happened at all levels; note the increased popularity of good music and drama. Note also the increased consciousness of citizenship. There are conflicts between the broadcasting authorities and other social forces, such as the press, the entertainment industries, the professional sporting interests, which are gradually settled. (These break out again with the coming of a new medium—television.) Broadcasting has become so much a part of our culture that people consider it a denial of their rights, and get very angry, if any obstacle is placed in the way of broadcasting any public or sporting event, or if there is any threat to discontinue a popular series of programmes.

(b) *Educational change due to broadcasting*. Along with adaptation in the culture the nation profited by a new educational agency for adults as well as for children. New knowledge was spread, for example, on health, child care, travel, agriculture and gardening, by talks, feature programmes, book reviews and criticism. The value of discussion came to be more widely appreciated, and there was a craze for factual 'Quiz' programmes of many kinds. School broadcasting took some time to be fully accepted, but proved a most valuable aid when sets began to come into the schools in any numbers. Some broadcast lesson series were very successful, and tended to spread new techniques of teaching in the schools. The curricula of schools were influenced, for example, by broadcasts on new subjects such as current affairs, citizenship, and international affairs, and new subject matter about radio itself entered the science course. There was an increased need for more technicians for the radio industry, and schools and colleges ultimately increased their technical education. There was a marked lagging behind of education

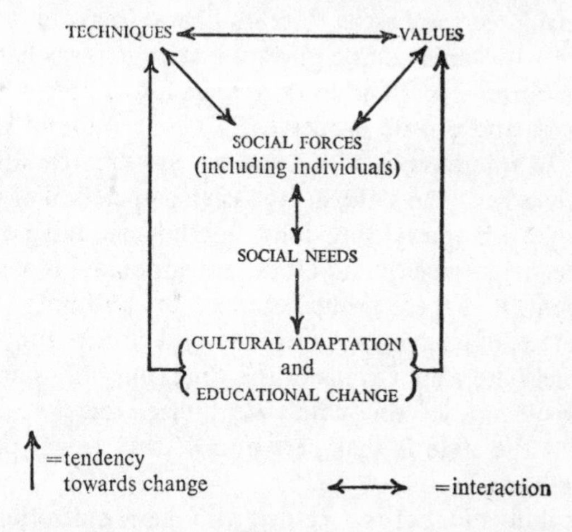

FIGURE III

in this last respect, which is equally true with regard to preparation for all technical occupations.[1]

This completes the general outline of our theory of social and cultural change. The cycles of change may be small or large, but the general direction of movement and the dynamic interaction of the factors which have been mentioned is shown in Fig. III. Detailed illustrations of the

[1] An interesting quotation from W. F. Ogburn: *Social Change*, p. 201, is of relevance here. He writes: 'Industry and education are two variables, and if the change in industry occurs first and the adjustment through education follows, industry may be referred to as the independent variable and education as the dependent variable. Where one part of culture changes first, through some discovery or invention, and occasions changes in some part of culture dependent upon it, there is frequently a delay in the changes occasioned in the dependent part of culture.'

application of the factors of this diagram to recent historical periods are given in the next chapter.

POWER AND THE BODY POLITIC

The place of the state in this interaction of social forces will next be considered. What is the state? It has sometimes been thought of as a mysterious and superhuman entity, over and above the people, which the people must serve with slavish obedience. This idea led to the political doctrine of the Fascist state. In liberal England the state used to be equated with bureaucratic government which was liable to interfere with free citizens, and had to be kept as far as possible away from private business and private property. This conception of state control as unwarranted interference with freedom, or some variation of it, is still frequently heard. The state, in fact, is an association of people: it is a social group with special functions, instruments and powers. Some people are elected to govern and others are appointed to be servants of the government, and these groups exercise the authority of the state. (A despotic state, of course, may dispense with elections.) All full members of a society are also citizens of the state, but only some are given authority as officials of the state. We prefer, therefore, the simple definition that the state is that part of a society which performs the political functions.

The political functions are concerned with the organization of society, with social control, and with the distribution of power within the society. The government is the highest agency of the state, charged with directing its whole organization, and part of its function is the making of laws. The state, through its officials and paid servants, which include the police and the armed forces, has the monopoly of the lawful use of physical power within the society. It has the final power of coercion. The power of the state is, however, limited, except in an absolute dictatorship, and it is limited by a constitution made and accepted by the people. One of the best indications of the type of state is shown by the way in which it uses its power. In a democratic state the power is shared and distributed as widely as possible among different members and agents of society.

Because of confusions over the meaning of the word 'state', and the possible assumption that there is an antagonism between the state and the rest of society, we prefer to follow Karl Mannheim in his use of the term 'body politic' as an alternative, or in addition, to the idea of the state. His definition is as follows:[1] 'By body politic we shall understand all groups and leaders who play an active role in the organization of society. . . . Our concept comprises those political elements *par excellence* that concentrate in their hands administrative functions, military power, and social leadership.' He adds in favour of his definition that, 'It allows political sociology to pay due attention to those social forces which are not state regulated in the traditional sense and not bureaucratically controlled, yet may integrate the political processes of governing, organizing, leading, co-ordinating, and so on.'

This concept relates to our definition of social forces as groups of people attempting to bring about social action. The influence of such groups upon the public may be called a political function when it concerns the public interest, and the more so when a social force is able to bring pressure upon the government. Mannheim continues[2] by pointing out how in the modern state the boundary between private enterprise and state enterprise is tending to disappear. There are private bureaucracies, in the form of large corporations concentrating economic power, which rival state bureaucracies in power. The civil service itself invites the help of advisory bodies from outside its own members. And finally there is a new conception of management which gives more control to the executive function, with or without state authority. This gives a picture of the body politic as groups and leaders who are at the centre of the conflict of interests and values in a society, influencing and being influenced by all the other social forces and needs of the culture. These points may be further illustrated by reference to the place of education.

EDUCATION AND SOCIAL CHANGE

It may be asked: 'What decides the kind of educational system a society provides?' We have answered so far that it depends upon the total culture. Let us begin a closer analysis of how the culture operates. This will be worked out in detail in the next two chapters. 'The fundamental question with regard to any system of education is: By what social group is it given; what are the purposes of that group; why does

[1] Karl Mannheim: *Freedom, Power, and Democratic Planning*, 1951, p. 42.
[2] Op. cit., pp. 43–5.

it will that its members be educated?' The writer of these words[1] points out that education is always the expression of the authority of some social group, and that in our civilization this group is the state. It is true that the largest part of our education is called the state system, and is provided by the state. Is it not then the government which decides on the policy for education? Yes, but who influences the government? The government, as we have seen from our discussion, is the focus of attention from social forces, status groups and associations of all kinds, and must, sooner or later, respond to social needs. Let us take some practical examples of forces which have acted on the government in England in recent years, with regard to the provision of education.

(a) *Comprehensive Schools.* These have been advocated in the programme of a political party, and have been debated in local government on party lines. Comprehensive Schools have been opposed by organized groups of parents and teachers and pressure has been brought to bear on local education authorities to change their plans. There are many conflicting views over this issue, and some of them relate to the defences or ambitions of social status groups. The prestige of the Grammar School, coming from a long way back in history, exercises a marked influence in the controversy. There are some who would preserve the independence and even the exclusiveness of the Grammar School, while others feel that it perpetuates undesirable social distinctions. It is difficult to find arguments on purely educational grounds which are not mixed with feelings derived from the wish to preserve or gain social status. The demand for Comprehensive Schools has come as a response both to changing economic needs and to the growth of political ideas concerning democracy. The development of this type of school is an educational change which will spread only when there is a clear demand for it, resulting from further changes in the social structure of the country. To the extent that the educational system reflects the social system we still need a more comprehensive society before we have more comprehensive schools. Yet the two changes are going on together and the development of new forms of education both reflects and influences the conflict of social forces.

(b) *Technical education.* Because of the growth of industry there was a need for more technical and technological education throughout the 1950's. The Committee on Scientific Man-Power recommended as long

[1] Alexander Meiklejohn: *Education Between Two Worlds*, 1942, p. 279.

ago as 1946, that the university output of scientists and technologists should be doubled. By 1956 the White Paper on *Technical Education* pointed out that we were doing nothing like enough in this field, and that we were in danger of being left behind by the U.S.A., Russia, and Western Europe. The conversion of Technical Colleges into Colleges of Advanced Technology began. In 1959 the *Crowther Report* pointed out the inefficiency of part-time courses in Technical Colleges. The growth of technical education at all levels has come as a result of obvious social needs, but yet it was strangely delayed. There was a certain slowness of adaptation by educational institutions, in spite of leads from the government. There were no clear-cut pressure groups supporting it, and there was some resistance, even when only passive, from well-established interests in the liberal or non-vocational tradition of education. Progressive industrialists finally played a large part by setting up their own training schemes, supporting 'sandwich' courses, and attracting able recruits to them. Again a conflict of social forces influencing educational provision.

(c) *Religion.* There has been pressure from the Church of England and other religious interests for a more Christian education, and for more efficient religious instruction. This had its effect on the 1944 Act, which requires by law an act of religious worship in every school provided by the state. The Roman Catholic Church continues to plead its case for more state aid. To see this latter controversy at its height a glance at recent French politics will show that there was, in 1951, the greatest difficulty in forming a government in France because of conflicting views of political and social groups on questions of education and religion.

These examples indicate the attempts of social groups to change the educational system by direct or indirect influence on the government. In general it may be said that the education a society provides, at a given time, is determined by the dominant social forces at work in that society. Social forces are defined as groups of people trying to bring about social action or social change. As the nature of society changes, through the interplay of social needs, techniques and values, so education tends to follow. The question will be asked; is not education itself a social force and determinant of change? In one sense, yes. It is a force which supports and develops the changes already decided by those in power. The educators, and sometimes the educational administrators (though these are often more tied to public opinion), can play their part in initiating changes because as full citizens they can be critical of their society, and should make every effort to improve it. Teachers in the schools can have a most powerful influence in the community if they choose. The social force of education is exerted by all the adults engaged in its practice. Teachers' professional organizations and unions are among the orthodox pressure groups, and can bring their views before public opinion and the government. Their views will not prevail without sufficient support from the other social forces at work, but this should not lead them to underestimate their powers. Indeed a critical spirit, while remaining constructive, should permeate the schools in a democracy and can prepare a new generation ready for change. But do not let us deceive ourselves. We should put before our children the vision of a better society, we should show them our confidence and faith in the future, we should encourage their power of choice and respect their freedom: all this we can do, but until they grow up, the responsibility for changing society rests on us.

It is true that changes in the nature of education can give rise to social changes which were partly unexpected or unintended. In this country we have seen the development of education against the background of a growing industrialism and in a class-stratified society. The more advanced the technology the greater the need for highly specialized man-power and hence for a longer school life and a greater provision of higher education. Thus an educational change was set in motion in response to new forms of technology, but once started it has had its impact on the whole class structure. It has caused education to become a major agent of social mobility, and given rise to cultural problems through the changed character of the lives of those who have risen in the social scale. The problem of the literacy of the scientist and the scientific ignorance of all the rest has been brought forward in a new form, and caused widespread interest in general education. Secondly, rather than increase social cohesion and solidarity, which would be the obvious intention of the sponsors of equality of opportunity, we can see a danger of education promoting new social differences, this time based on merit instead of birth. Thus the earlier concept of educational opportunity, as a means of moving an able minority up a ladder to places at the top, is challenged by the ideal of making the fullest use of the potential talents of the whole population, along with attempts at developing a new consciousness of community and a common sense of citizenship. Thus we see that the influence of social needs on cultural adaptation and educational change is in a constant cycle of interaction, as illustrated in Fig. III, p. 53. The effects of education can certainly change the balance of social forces, and it then becomes the turn of the new social groups to exert pressure on the educational system to adapt itself to their needs.

However, in the special conditions under which society has developed in England during the past century major changes in the quantity and kind of education provided are most clearly seen as the results of definite social pressures. An analysis of these social and ideological determinants of education is the concern of the next chapter.

CHAPTER IV

The Social Determinants of Education in England

England in the Mid-Nineteenth Century—Social Forces and Elementary Education—The Public Schools and the Grammar Schools—England in the First Half of the Twentieth Century—Social Forces and Secondary Education

An attempt will be made in this chapter to give some illustrations of the thesis that the education a society provides is determined by the dominant social forces at work in that society. The illustrations are chosen from some of the relations between social change and the educational system of England during the nineteenth century and the first half of the twentieth century. In the next chapter our present situation at the beginning of the second half of the twentieth century will be discussed with regard to possible changes in the future.

Let it be said at once that we are not trying to make any new contribution to the history of education. We are trying to outline a way of thinking about the relations between a society and its educational system. A framework or a hypothesis is offered into which some general trends of change can be fitted, and their direction to some extent explained. It is put forward as a sociological method of interpreting the facts. Many of the historical facts themselves should be well known to the student of education. Since our society is, and has been, changing rapidly we cannot understand its present condition without some exploration of its past. This is one of the best reasons for reading history. The attitude of mind we wish to convey is that of thinking sociologically about history. It is equally important to think historically about sociology.

SOCIAL DETERMINANTS OF EDUCATION IN ENGLAND

ENGLAND IN THE MID-NINETEENTH CENTURY

There is no better example of the influence of technical change on the social and cultural life of a country than the results of the Industrial Revolution in England. The dominant techniques and values of the nineteenth century, and some of the related social forces will now be considered. The factors selected could be considered as operative, in changing forms, during the period 1830–80. This period has been chosen as a time of much development in the main types of school the century produced, and during which the influence of social forces on education can be clearly seen. A more detailed picture could be drawn, and other factors might be selected. The intention is only to give an outline of the dominant trends.

The key techniques are the use of steam and steel, and from these follow the machinery, the manufactures, the trains and the steamships which led to Victorian contrasts of wealth and squalor, and to England's position as 'the workshop of the world'. Such techniques represent what Lewis Mumford (following Patrick Geddes) has called the Paleotechnic Phase in machine civilization.[1] By the end of the century the petrol engine and the electric motor were in use, but not widespread, and they belong to the period of the Second Industrial Revolution or the Neotechnic Phase. The electric telegraph, however, was developed by the mid-century, and along with the newspaper began the quicker communication of ideas which grew alongside the more rapid transport of materials and people. The factories and towns changed the face of England, as an agricultural changed to an industrial community, and the handcraftsman was replaced by the factory hand. Fixed hours of leisure as well as fixed hours of work came as a result of the factory system, and this was the beginning of leisure for the masses, which was to grow and become an educational problem.

The dominant technique for doing business was private capitalism, which began to be extended into larger units by the social invention of the joint stock company. Capitalism also comes into the sphere of values since it had its ideology known as *laissez-faire*. This was thought to be not only the best way of doing trade but of securing 'the greatest happiness of the greatest number'. Enlightened self-interest was much talked of and the profit motive accepted as a value.

[1] Lewis Mumford: *Technics and Civilisation*, p. 109, and Chap. IV.

Of the other values Christianity, in its various forms, must be considered the dominant religion, and for the philosophy of the majority of educated people it is probable that idealism was dominant, but in conflict with growing types of realism or empiricism which later tended to overcome it. The growth of science provided new material for philosophic thought, but it was not until the next century that the power of the scientific method was to make a widespread appeal. The most powerful political faith was in what is known as liberal democracy, because it was based on liberal ideas which might be held by members of either the Tory or Whig or Conservative or Liberal parties, and often related in their minds to the Athens of Pericles. It was in any case rule by a privileged class, and must be distinguished from the fuller democracy in which many reformers believed and which developed with the extension of the franchise. The country became prosperous, and the Victorians certainly believed in progress.

SOCIAL FORCES AND ELEMENTARY EDUCATION

One of the most general needs of all groups of the population during the nineteenth century was for more education. Yet a national elementary system did not come until after 1870, there was no organized system of secondary education at all, and little technical education. The increasing numbers of Public Schools for the better-off gave social prestige but a curriculum quite out of touch with the needs of many of their supporters. This was all due to conflicting social forces.

Let us first consider the growth of elementary education in the light of the dominant social forces at work. The strongest forces at the start were religious, and they came to be linked closely with the political parties as we shall see. At the beginning of the century almost all forms of education were under the control, direct or indirect, of the Church of England. Soon an old conflict was to flare up again between the Established Church and the Nonconformists, which has become known as the famous 'religious difficulty'.[1] By 1830 when the period of our survey begins there were the British and Foreign Schools Society, supported by the Nonconformists and the progressive Whigs, and the National

[1] Actually this conflict already had 200 years of history since the Church had tried to exclude the Dissenters by the Act of Uniformity, 1662, and by the Schism Act, 1714. Nevertheless the Nonconformists had succeeded in running their schools and academies in both the seventeenth and eighteenth centuries.

Society for Promoting the Education of the Poor in the Principles of the Established Church, supported in the main by the Tories. This is not to say there were no progressive and reforming Tories. There were; but the section linked with the strongly conservative Church of England group could not be classed with them. This is how politics got linked with religion, and numbers of Bills failed in Parliament over the 'religious difficulty'. The troubles were always the same. The Church of England thought education should be their concern and did not want state interference. The Nonconformists thought they should have the right to do things their way, but would let no money from the rates go to the Church of England, and schemes for a national system with local control involved rate aid. There was also a group which favoured secular schools with no religious instruction at all.

The traditional wealthy upper class, or the 'gentry', allied themselves with the conservatives over education, and remembering the French Revolution were frightened of the labouring classes. A good example of the extreme Tory point of view is given by the following extract from the debate on Samuel Whitbread's Bill in 1807.

'However specious in theory the project might be of giving education to the labouring classes of the poor, it would be prejudicial to their morals and happiness; it would teach them to despise their lot in life, instead of making them good servants in agriculture and other laborious employments. Instead of teaching them subordination, it would render them fractious and refractory . . . it would enable them to read seditious pamphlets, vicious books, and publications against Christianity; it would render them insolent to their superiors; and in a few years the legislature would find it necessary to direct the strong arm of power towards them.'[1]

This brief passage summarizes almost all the attitudes of the ruling class towards the lower orders throughout most of the century. The same attitude of distrust of the working class can be seen at the time of the 1867 Reform Bill when Robert Lowe, then the Vice-President of the Education Department, in speaking against the Bill said: '. . . working men as such ought to be excluded from the franchise on account of their moral and intellectual unfitness.'

Thus the education of the 'lower orders' was for a long time decided

[1] Davies Giddy, M.P.

by what the people in power thought they ought to need, namely hard work, strict discipline, subordination to their betters, and Christian humility. Needs can be of two kinds; those you feel and those which other people think you ought to feel. It is true that the new rich middle class, who were largely manufacturers and industrialists, were in favour of the spread of education, and knew that the growth of industry required real literacy and technical instruction. The workers themselves were at this time not an organized social force, and were singularly dumb on the subject of their own education. Little demand for education came from below. Robert Owen spoke for the workers, as Cobbett had done, and as Cobden and Bright were to do later. There was the gradual growth of Trade Unions. The workers were more interested in Parliamentary Reform, and it is a strange feature of the growth of our democracy that the vote has always been given to the people *first* and their education improved afterwards.[1]

Robert Owen is a good example of an exceptional individual who was ahead of his time. All his main ideas ultimately became a part of our culture, but often many years later. He ran a model factory, he ran an infant school, he tried to start Trade Unions, he had ideas for a co-operative society, and he can be called the first British socialist.

It became clear as the century went on that economic forces alone would demand an improved educational system. At the great 1851 Exhibition, while British goods had beaten the world, it was seen that we were losing our lead and that other countries had better systems of education for their workers. By the 1867 Exhibition in Paris the situation was much worse. There was even a danger that the advancement of our excellent techniques would be handicapped by the lack of skilled workers to operate them. The great increase of population also showed up the ignorance of a rapidly growing working class. By this time we were becoming a great industrial nation with an illiterate population, and this was not safe for our power nor our democracy. So it was no wonder that in presenting the Education Bill in 1870 W. E. Forster had said: 'Our industrial prosperity; the safe working of our constitutional system; and our national power, depended upon it.'

This example shows how changes in education tend to follow social

[1] So it was that Robert Lowe did *not* say in the 1867 debate: 'We must educate our masters', but he *did* say: 'I believe it will be absolutely necessary that you should prevail on our future masters to learn their letters.'

change, and are dependent upon the struggle between rival social forces. The same point could be illustrated by the delay over a state system of secondary education which did not come until 1902, in spite of over a quarter of a century's agitation for it, and the recommendation of three Royal Commissions.[1] But while dealing with the nineteenth century, let us turn to its typical form of secondary education, namely the Public Schools and endowed Grammar Schools.

SOCIAL FORCES AND THE PUBLIC SCHOOLS AND GRAMMAR SCHOOLS

At the beginning of the nineteenth century the old Public Schools had fallen into disrepute, conditions in the boarding-houses were very bad, and there was no social necessity or advantage in attending a Public School, except for Eton and a few others for the aristocracy. The Grammar Schools were also bad, often derelict, and in quite large day schools a few pupils might attend while an absentee master took the endowment. After 1830 reform and development made all those schools known as Public Schools[2] to be the dominant form of education for the upper class and the new wealthy middle class. Dr. Arnold went to Rugby in 1828, and it is well known that he initiated the modern conception of the Public School. But what accounted for the astonishing expansion and development of such schools, the acceptance of many old endowed Grammar Schools into the category of Public Schools and the foundation of new proprietary schools with the same aims and purposes and prestige?[3] The principal factor was that the new rich middle class of the

[1] Royal Commission on Technical Education, 1884; Cross Commission 1888; and Bryce Commission, 1895.

[2] For the history of the term 'Public School' see Fleming Report on Public Schools, H.M.S.O., 1944, Appendix A. This Report also gives a full account of the changes during the nineteenth century.

[3] In 1861 the Clarendon Commission charged with looking into 'certain schools and colleges', chose the nine schools accepted as being in the first rank: Eton, Winchester, Westminster, Charterhouse, St. Paul's, Merchant Taylors', Harrow, Rugby and Shrewsbury. In 1868 The Schools Enquiry Commission (Taunton Commission) considered (a) 800 Endowed Schools, including such schools as Tonbridge, Repton, Uppingham, etc. which were Grammar Schools becoming 'Public Schools', and (b) 122 Proprietary Schools, for example University College School and King's College School and including new foundations of the mid-nineteenth century now known as 'Public Schools', e.g. Cheltenham, Marlborough, Radley, Rossall, Wellington, Bradfield, Epsom, Malvern, Clifton and Haileybury, etc.

industrial revolution supported the boarding schools of England. By the beginning of Victoria's reign the new business men were already a growing class, and as the factories were built, and large new towns appeared, this vigorous commercial class sacrificed everything to the making of wealth. Not only the business men grew rich but the leading members of all the professions, the number of which was increasing rapidly. After the Companies' Act of 1862 which legalized the Limited Liability Company men found they could live by making financial transactions only, and large numbers grew rich with no direct contact with the work or the worker that brought in the money. By the 1870's all the world wondered at the prosperity of England and the men of property, the Forsytes of John Galsworthy's novels, were established in the security of their possessions. Needless to say they accepted the values of *laissez-faire* capitalism and free trade, and believed that the greatest good came by the free exercise on the part of every individual of enlightened self-interest. Of course they believed in progress, which they usually interpreted as money-making and social advancement.

The early members of the new rich class were for the most part uneducated, but they needed schools for their sons, and once they backed the Public Schools development came quickly. Association with the upper class gave social prestige, and by the mid-century it was considered the correct thing for anybody who could afford it to send his sons to a Public School. They served the traditional social needs of Christians and gentlemen, rulers and civil servants; and now they were called upon to serve the needs of leaders of industry and business. The education they gave was, to begin with, very little suited to the sons of business men. When Arnold started his reforms the culture of a gentleman rested on knowledge of the classics. So strong was tradition that the reform of the curriculum proceeded very slowly, but new modern subjects were added. The interesting fact emerges that the subjects which were learnt became not so important as the training in character which the schools gave. The school was to train rulers and money-makers, and for this it must harden the pupils by discipline, and breed the virtues of the stiff upper lip, self-reliance and correct behaviour. Sport became valued partly as a means of physical toughening, and partly because it encouraged the team spirit and loyalty to the group. The important thing about the curriculum was that, although it was largely classical and nonscientific, it was the best that could be got. The demand grew for a curriculum of a more useful kind, criticism was common in journals and reviews, and slowly the Public Schools adapted themselves to the needs of the class which they served. The need for social exclusiveness was one of the needs, not based on educational grounds, but reflecting the class structure of the society.

The English Public School, with its aims and values taken from the society in which it grew strong, has been a model for secondary education ever since. This is important because what the better classes had the classes just below wanted also. It makes sense to talk in terms of social class because this was a much clearer concept in the period being considered, and the consequences and remains of this same class structure can be seen to-day. It has been sometimes suggested that the Public Schools created the social distinctions of the nineteenth century. The *Fleming Report*[1] says: 'They were, in fact, called into being to meet the demands of a society already deeply divided', but goes on to add that 'nothing could have been better devised to perpetuate these class distinctions than this educational development'. Once the standard was set all the middle class, which was expanding in numbers throughout the century, aimed at money-making and social advancement, and needed for their sons some technical competence and professional opportunity for the world of enterprise and industry, in which other countries were becoming our rivals. A growing industrial system required not only skilled manual workers, but clerical workers, technicians, and routine brain workers. These 'white-collared' workers were in demand and were drawn from the poorer middle classes. They had to get what education they could from the lesser Grammar Schools, and the large number of small private proprietary schools which sprang up and were usually of poor quality, and sometimes scandalously bad. By the turn of the century the situation was so bad that thousands of well-educated German clerks had to be employed in London offices to carry on the work of commerce.

Entering into the twentieth century to complete this stage of the story, we find that a system of secondary education came with the Act of 1902. It still did not provide for adequate scientific or technical education. That struggle is still being fought sixty years later, Germany having been ahead of us in 1914 and again in 1939; the United States and

[1] Op. cit., p. 23.

the U.S.S.R. being ahead of us to-day. The secondary school copied the Public School with its academic, classical, and linguistic bias; its sports, its prefects, its colours and old school ties; and all the concern with social distinctions and gentility. Thousands flocked to the secondary school searching for a means of making money, and a means of social advancement. These same dominant aims still operated, and the educational values that were accepted by the new members of the professions, and the new suburban-dwelling clerks, were those of their better class leaders. What did it matter if the education were relevant or not to the actual needs of their future careers? So long as getting to the secondary school meant getting a better job, parents would let their children learn anything, if they could pass the examinations and win the scholarships.

THE FIRST HALF OF THE TWENTIETH CENTURY

The Second Industrial Revolution can be considered to date from about 1900 when the new power techniques of electricity and the petrol engine began to come into general use. The effects of a light movable engine began to be felt quickly. Road transport by motor began, and flying by a heavier-than-air machine became possible for the first time. Factories could now be built anywhere, and did not need to be near sources of coal, nor to be operated by heavy steam engines. Light industry developed with the use of new light metals. Mass production soon became a term in common use. Increased transport, and the growth of industry, led to the growth of still larger towns and suburbs. Ultimately towns merged together and the vast conurbations of London, the Midlands and the industrial North, changed the landscape and the lives of the people.

The first fifty years of this century, throughout its wars and its slumps, showed a steady mechanization, industrialization, and urbanization, with the growth of the mass society as we know it to-day. Telecommunications linked together and speeded up the business, the politics, and the news services, within the country and with the rest of the world. Transport from place to place became more rapid and more frequent. People became more mobile than ever before. The two major inventions of the cinema and radio broadcasting served the multiple purposes of entertainment, education, and cultural diffusion.

The growth of the physical sciences and their application to the technology of war and of peace is obvious enough. They have led us to the turbo-jet engine and the release of atomic energy, which have already started a new revolution in the use of power.

The social sciences made a beginning, and the study of economics helped to make the control of capitalism more possible, and to make the predictions necessary for economic planning. Capitalism reached its height with the development of extremely 'big' business, the large-scale corporations, the monopolies, and cartels, which placed great economic power in the hands of relatively few people. Left to free enterprise alone the system proved unable to manage its own complexity, and there was not only mass unemployment, but the problem of too much production while people were in poverty and need.

The ideal of full democracy became a leading value in the minds of the mass of the people. Was that not what they fought wars for? Political democracy reached its height, but not until the Reform Bill in 1928 extended the vote to all adults, men and women, over twenty-one—except criminals in prison, lunatics, and peers. But democracy was also associated with the values of freedom and equality. So inevitably a struggle was intensified among the social forces connected with economics and politics. The conflict of capital and labour meant in terms of people (for social forces are groups of people), the employers against the employees, or organized management against the Trade Unions. In terms of politics it meant the rise of the Labour Party to challenge the Conservatives, and towards the mid-century the decline of the Liberals as a separate political force. Names of parties may change, and extreme points of view can be found within the same party, but clearly the main struggle has been between the 'two nations' in Disraeli's words of a century ago.

With regard to social status there was a tendency to break down class distinctions, which is a tendency towards the greater integration of society. The members of the upper class have during this period lost their dominance, though they still have power out of proportion to their numbers. The outstanding feature of this fifty years with regard to class structure was the great expansion of the middle classes, and the coming to real power of the working classes. In talking of status in society this is perhaps the best place to mention the changes in the place of women in our society, which is sometimes called their 'emancipation'.[1] This has meant that women have taken more part in the productive and intellectual work of the community; they have gained full citizenship; and they have been able to alter the balance of social forces through any of the organized groups to which they have tended more and more to belong.

Of the aims and values stemming from religion and philosophy we have to estimate the major trends among the more educated sections of the community. There are many more 'educated' people to consider during this century owing to the increase of secondary and university education, the greater circulation of serious journals, and the widespread interest in discussion, no doubt partly stimulated by 'spoken word' broadcasting. We must say nevertheless that while interest in fundamental values has remained strong there has been a decline in adherence to traditional religion. Part of the reason has been the growing influence of the scientific attitude on all departments of thought. Hence it could be said that some form of empirical realism had been gaining in influence over idealist philosophies among those who thought hard about such matters as well as among ordinary people.

Finally the belief in automatic progress which the Victorians had in the Century of Hope gave way to a desire for security. This showed itself in fear of war or slump, and by the development of what began as a scheme of national insurance into a demand for total social security from a 'Welfare State'. Some have even seen a danger of our valuing security so much that we might give up too much of our freedom for it.

SOCIAL FORCES AND SECONDARY EDUCATION

The two major traditions of education which were established by the end of the nineteenth century were the elementary schools for the mass of the people, and the Grammar and Public Schools for the privileged few. The twentieth century began with a first-class muddle in education, and still no state system of secondary education. In spite of Matthew Arnold's cry of 'organize your secondary education' of over thirty years before, the progress of secondary as well as scientific and technical

[1] This of course was begun by the feminists of the latter half of the nineteenth century, e.g. the pioneers of girls' education, Miss Buss and Miss Beale in the 1850's, *The Subjection of Women* by J. S. Mill, 1869, the foundation of Girton, 1869 and Newnham, 1871, but did not become a dominant force until this century.

education had not made much headway against upper-class government and conservative church interests. The coming at last of the 1902 Act has already been referred to. (See p. 65.)[1] The most influential and the most needed type of formal education in the first half of this century was provided by the new secondary schools. It is now proposed to touch on their development in relation to the social forces involved.

(i) First there was a great public demand for secondary education. This demand remained and increased, there being at no time sufficient places in the state system to satisfy it, in spite of the tremendous expansion since 1902. This is not surprising since parents at the lower end of the social scale realized that education had become one of the main agents of occupational and also social mobility.[2] In plain words if you wanted to get a better job you needed to obtain a place in a secondary school, and before 1944 this meant of the 'grammar' type, which only held 500,000 of the population between eleven and eighteen. And such education also had status value, since social position depends to a great degree on a person's occupation. It should also be noted that the pressure of the middle classes to hold their position against competition from below has not only kept the private and independent schools (including Public Schools) full in spite of their relatively greater cost, and increased fees, but has been a factor in the reduction of the size of families in these otherwise vigorous and intelligent classes of society.[3]

(ii) The social needs of our growing and complex industrial society required a better educated population. Making and selling goods abroad became essential to our lives as soon as the population became too great to be fed by the produce of our own land. The lesson had to be learnt that we live by exports. Still greater diversity of occupations kept arising among salaried professional workers, the civil service, office workers and business men. The demand for technical education has still not been met.

(iii) The Great War of 1914–18, as all wars do, made us examine the quality of our people, and was followed by an Education Act.

[1] The struggle of the different pressure groups at work behind the passing of the 1902 Act makes fascinating reading as it is described by Lester Smith, *To Whom do the Schools Belong?* pp. 137–44.

[2] See *Year Book of Education*, 1950, Chapt. 5, 'Educational Opportunity and Social Mobility' by Jean Floud, and also D. V. Glass (Ed.), *Social Mobility in Britain*, 1954.

[3] G. Leybourne and K. White: *Education and the Birth Rate*, 1940.

(iv) The general trend of democracy and the belief in equality led to a demand for equal educational opportunity. The rise of the Labour Party brought with it as one of its cries 'Secondary Education for All'. The Committee which produced the *Hadow Report* on *The Education of the Adolescent* was set up by the Labour Government of 1924 and reported in 1926. This pointed the way and made quite clear what was needed, namely, (a) two different stages of primary and secondary education as part of one continuous process, (b) different kinds of secondary schools to suit different abilities, aptitudes, and needs of the pupils. Yet these reforms, and others then suggested, were not to come until twenty years later, after another Great War.

(v) The cry for equal opportunity included, of course, the education of girls, which was far behind that of boys before the 1914 war. The opportunities for women to take salaried occupations and skilled work increased at a great rate from that time onwards.

Now let us see what actually happened to secondary education, because compared with the obvious needs progress was slow, and obstacles were encountered which did not arise from educational considerations but from social prejudice and political expediency. Society had in fact changed, but educational change to meet the new needs was far behind.

(1) First a general note on economic forces. The unfortunate facts to be recorded cannot easily be put down to the operation of any particular social pressure groups, as they are a reflection of the economic condition of the country as a whole, and the alternation of wars and slumps which has characterized the century so far. However, it is worth noting that when there is a question of priority of expenditure education does not always come high on the list, and this must be related to the value it is thought to have by those in power at the time, and also related to public opinion.

The bare facts are as follows. Hopes for day continuation schools and raising the school-leaving age to fifteen, as proposed by the Fisher Act of 1918 were dashed by the economies of the 'Geddes Axe' in the slump of 1921. Hopes for the Hadow 'reorganization',[1] spurred on by the Board of Education's pamphlet *The New Prospect in Education*, 1928,

[1] The separation of children at 11 plus into Senior Schools or Central Schools, the forerunners of the Secondary Modern Schools, but still at that time under the Elementary Code.

and by a 50 per cent grant for new buildings, were high in 1930 and then were dashed by the economic crisis which then occurred. Recovery from 1935 onwards led to further building and development preparatory to raising the school-leaving age on 1st September 1939! During the war a genuine and widespread interest in educational reform led to the Act of 1944 which appeared to give a real chance for progress. By 1949 the country could hardly produce enough goods to prevent itself from going bankrupt. By 1950 another new factor: rearmament. People began to ask: 'What about the county colleges, or raising the school-leaving age to sixteen, or smaller classes, or new schools?'[1]

It is said that we now understand the economic techniques for avoiding slumps—at least in part—and that in fact we did quite the wrong thing before in cutting expenditure which only made things worse. This view will please those who say there is always money to spend for the things you really want. But it must be added that the spending of *money* is not in these days the critical factor. It is man-power and materials. While the society uses such an enormous amount of man-power and materials, such a high proportion of the national product in real things, on large-scale war, or recovering from war, or preparing for defence, it has not the men or the bricks to build schools. We have not yet understood the technique for avoiding wars.

(2) It has been pointed out how the new secondary schools tended to imitate the old grammar schools. This is confirmed by the *Spens Report* published in 1938 which says: '. . . The force of tradition was so great that, when, under the Education Act, 1902, the state undertook for the first time the general organization of secondary schools, the ancient Grammar School, local or non-local, was taken as almost the exclusive model for secondary schools.'[2] The *Report* points out that this policy was supported by the 'Regulations for Secondary Schools' issued by the Board of Education in 1904–5, and that from that date was introduced 'an unnecessary and unreal cleavage between secondary and technical education'. It states further that also from 1904 a confusion began whereby the traditional academic course directed towards the universi-

[1] Perhaps the Report, *School and Life*, 1947 (First Report of the new Advisory Council for Education in England), is right in saying: '. . . half a century's unremitting efforts will be required before we can hope to have good primary schools for all.' (p. 12.)

[2] *Spens Report*, op. cit., p. 351.

ties was the type of education preferred even when it was not appropriate to the needs of the boys and girls. What happened is clearly set out in this *Report*[1] and one of its conclusions gives support for the view we are holding, that the 'existing arrangements . . . have ceased to correspond with the actual structure of modern society, and with the economic facts of the situation' (p. 353).

Many obstacles to change can thus be traced back to the social prestige of the Grammar School, and the traditional belief that the man who works with the tongue and the pen is superior to the man who works with his hands.

(3) When we look at the types of school the *Spens Report* proposed it is interesting to make a comparison with the proposals of the Taunton Commission reporting in 1868, seventy years before.

Taunton First Grade School. To age 18 plus. No attempt to displace the classics, but curriculum to include mathematics, modern languages and science. In general like a Public School but with lower fees.

Spens Grammar School. To age 18 plus. 'No reason to recommend any revolutionary change in the subjects and activities' of the Grammar School, except that the curriculum can be lightened after 13 plus so long as the subjects include English, a language, or science or mathematics. (pp. xxiii–xxiv.)

Taunton Second Grade School. To age 16. Latin and 'those subjects which can be turned to a practical use in business'. For boys wishing to enter the professions, for example, engineering.

Spens Technical High School. To age 16 plus.[2] Intellectual discipline along with technical value in relation to a group of occupations—notably engineering and building. (See p. 373.)

Taunton Third Grade School. To age 14. General education, and not

[1] A good account of the development of the tradition and social prestige of the Grammar Schools is given in Chaps. I and II of the *Spens Report*, with a summary of the conclusions on pp. 349–53.

[2] Note the leaving age of 16 plus. This was changed by the *Norwood Report* of 1941, but Spens recommended it as 16 and note the reasons on p. xxix. They say that the boys will be matured sooner by contact with men who normally teach adults, i.e. in the Technical Colleges. Also, while it is not directly stated, one gets the impression that the Committee did not really want Technical Schools to have a Sixth Form, which is the glory of the Grammar School, and whose 'tradition depends on its existence'. (See p. xx.)

vocational. 'The most urgent educational need of the country.' For farmers, tradesmen, and superior artisans.

Spens Modern School. To age 14 (then the school-leaving age). General education with a practical and concrete approach, but not vocational. For the majority of boys and girls in the country.

Can we not detect here the continuance of a social class distinction? It should be added at once that the *Spens Report* called for equality of status in every respect between the Grammar and the Technical School, and made it essential that there should be parity between all types of secondary school, with methods of transfer between them, and so on. The Taunton Commissioners openly stated that the distinctions between the schools corresponded 'roughly, but by no means exactly, to the gradations of society'. The demand for parity may not in every sense be a possible one, its meaning needs analysis, but that our present 'gradations of society' have strong views on it can be seen from any current controversy on the Comprehensive School. That parity of status has not been achieved, economic considerations apart, is because the educational system reflects the structure of the social system.

(4) Continuing the story of what happened in secondary education the *Norwood Report* published in 1943[1] supported the idea that all the children of the country could be separated into three groups, and they described three types of mind to which corresponded three types of curricula. These types of mind also conveniently fitted the three types of school which already existed or were proposed. The unscientific basis of this division of abilities has been widely criticized by psychologists, but we are here concerned with its sociology. The interest in the present context lies in the social overtones and undertones of this *Report*. It might be cited as an example of a tendency to find in human nature what you want to find, in order to fit your social theory. Further, as an exercise in clear thinking, the ambiguities and lack of logic should be studied in pp. 2–4. Of these types of children, Type 1 is the Grammar School boy (or girl), and a good description is given of a pupil with high intelligence and powers of abstraction. Type 2 is the Technical School boy, and his interests lie in the 'field of applied science or applied art'. 'He often has an uncanny insight into the intricacies of mechanism, whereas the subtleties of language construction are too delicate for him.' It may be asked could not a boy of high intelligence be found in a tech-

[1] *Curriculum and Examinations in Secondary Schools*, H.M.S.O.

nical school? Why, yes, the *Report* admits that he may. And do not some Grammar School boys have interests in applied science or art, e.g. become doctors, engineers, architects, etc.? And may they not sometimes be unsubtle in language? Why, yes, but ought they to have gone to a Technical School?

Type 2 'may or may not be good at games or other activities'. This kind of statement, which gives no information of what is or is not the case, like 'either it is raining or it is not', finds a frequent place in these pages. Of Type 1 it is said: 'He may be good with his hands or he may not; he may be a good "mixer" or a leader, etc.' Quite so, but how does this distinguish him from Types 2 or 3? We read on to Type 3 and find that 'He may or may not be good with his hands, or sensitive to Music or Art'. Now why only this type may or may not be that? And may not any of them be good at games or only Type 2?

It appears that Types 2 and 3 have a lot in common. In the Technical School boy 'knowledge must be capable of immediate application, and concerned with the control of material things'. But Type 3, the Modern School boy, his mind also 'must turn its knowledge or its curiosity to immediate test; and his test is essentially practical'. Grammar School boys do not, of course touch material things, nor are they practical!

Type 3 is a queer boy. He can't deal much with 'ideas' but his ability is 'in the realm of facts'. This distinction is clearly one of the subtleties of language construction, but the boy has *some* ideas for 'his career is often in his mind', which marks him off at once as having a very limited horizon. One finds a page later that the curriculum for this Type 3 should 'enable pupils to take up the work of life', while the second type of curriculum provides, 'special data and skills associated with a particular kind of occupation'. But in the Grammar School they must pursue study for its own sake: did they not inherit the tradition of the gentlemen who need not soil their hands nor worry about earning a living?

(5) When the 1944 Education Bill came before Parliament it had been well prepared and well discussed in advance. It is a good example of the working of modern democracy, by the consultation of all interests likely to be concerned, and by the publication of pamphlets, programmes of

[1] This story is well told by H. C. Dent in *Education in Transition*, 1944, especially Chap. IV in which he describes the prevailing aims of educational thinkers and theorists, and the direct influence of religious, professional, political and industrial forces and of public opinion.

reform, and memoranda by organizations of all kinds.[1] Any teacher or educationist at that time had a chance to influence the Government, not only through existing professional bodies, but through quite new organizations which were set up for the specific purpose of advocating educational reform. The Government played its part well in dealing with the diverse pressures brought to bear on it, and the result was an Education Act welcomed by all parties, and to which even the most ardent reformer could raise little objection, except perhaps that it leaves untouched the Public Schools and independent schools which still constitute a system of their own separate from the state system. It cannot be said that there is yet a fully unified educational structure.

How far, and how quickly, the provisions of the Act could be carried out remained to be doubted as the years went by, and obstacles arose. With regard to secondary education, which is our present theme, the 1944 Act opens the way to all the developments desired since the *Hadow Report* of 1926. The Act says nothing, however, about *types of school*, it only lays it down as a duty of the local authority to provide (in accordance with the oft-quoted clause 8 (b)), education to suit the 'different ages, abilities and aptitudes' of the pupils. It is not therefore stated by the Act that the Grammar–Technical–Modern division of schools is the one that should continue, or is expected to continue. This problem, along with many others, must be worked out in the course of the next half-century, and under the influence of the social forces of the future.

[1] The Board of Education issued a confidential memorandum in 1941, known as the Green Book, as a basis for discussion with L.E.A.'s, teachers' organizations and other bodies. A summary was made public, and there followed the prolonged interaction of social forces so well described by Dent, op. cit. The White Paper of 1943, *Educational Reconstruction*, summarized the Government's position, and by then the main decisions were made, and many compromises already effected. Mr. R. A. Butler well deserved the praise he received for steering the 1944 Bill through Parliament.

CHAPTER V

The Educational Needs of our Future Society

England in the Second Half of the Twentieth Century—A Mass Society
The Changing Nature of Our Democracy—The Role of Education

THE SECOND HALF OF THE TWENTIETH CENTURY

WE are now entering a new phase of scientific and technological development. Man has acquired the possibility of unlimited physical power, and the complete conquest of materials. Even before the discovery of the use of nuclear power, new engines, resulting in the turbo-jet, were developed which made the piston engine out of date for aircraft. The use of nuclear energy is completely revolutionary, and the reaction of the hydrogen bomb, when controlled for peaceful uses, taps the source of power which heats the sun. Nuclear power stations for generating electricity are making the use of coal for this purpose unnecessary. Atomic engines are in use in submarines and liners. To-day our planet has man-made satellites, live men have circumnavigated the earth in space, and will soon be landed on the moon. Space travel is leaving the realm of science fiction as sufficient power, through nuclear fuel, is being harnessed to the rocket ship. There is an International Conference on Astronautics which meets annually, and the British Inter-Planetary Society is supported by serious scientists.

The conquest of materials means that the chemist can say 'What have you got? And what do you want?' and turn the one into the other. During the first World War the Germans literally made explosives from the air, by the fixation of nitrogen and subsequent manufacture of nitrates. During the last war the Germans were short of oil so they made it from coal; the Americans were short of rubber so they made it from oil; and the Japanese were short of oil so they made it from rubber, of which they had plenty after seizing Malaya. For some time the world has used synthetic materials, which do not occur at all in nature, and which are often better for their purpose than natural materials. The plastics and the artificial textile industries are both examples of this. The development of plastics is such that metal and wood are being replaced for many purposes. Car bodies have been made of plastic, with seats from a derivative of soya bean. Everyone knows about nylon, orlon, terylene, courtelle and the other synthetic fibres. The fantasy of *The Man in the White Suit*,[1] which it was hoped would never wear out, may yet become a reality. Any kind of material might be used as a starting-point. An artificial wool has been made from the chemicals of grass without the intervention of the sheep. What, after all, is a cow to the chemist but an apparatus for turning grass into milk! It is only a matter of time when synthetic foods will be made from simpler components. An easy synthesis of starch or sugar, which so far only plants can make, would be a good beginning.

Lewis Mumford foresees the coming of a Biotechnic Phase, when the bio-social sciences such as medicine, agriculture, nutrition, and psychology will take precedence over the mechanical. Certainly the development of chemotherapy by the use of new drugs and medicines is giving us new power over disease. Note only the sulphonamide drugs, and penicillin and the other anti-biotics. Some experts regard the scientific control of food production, by the decrease of plant and animal disease, by plant and animal breeding, and by the better utilization of land, as absolutely necessary for the survival of an increasing world population.

More exciting and far-reaching are the new discoveries being made with regard to the nature of life itself. Research on the nucleus of the living cell can yield results as important as that on the nucleus of the atom. The biological equivalent of nuclear power remains to be discovered. In the future we may yet be able to produce a better race as we learn more about the mechanism and control of the genetic factors in inheritance, and the bio-chemical factors in growth.

The social sciences were certainly well established by the half-century, and look like growing very rapidly, in particular economics, psychology and the composite group of sciences concerned with the control of

[1] A film of 1951.

human behaviour. These sciences provide the necessary theoretical basis for social and economic planning which have become inevitable in the life of a modern industrial nation. We have conquered the material world *on* which we live, can we also conquer the social world *in* which we live? This is largely a matter of social techniques, in particular the methods of mass communication and any form of influencing human behaviour on a large scale. And we have television, which will become one of the dominant techniques in the cultural and political life of the next fifty years.

Another new technique which may lead to astonishing results in the future is Cybernetics or the science of automatic control. This deals with the theory of a large range of mechanisms including electronic calculating machines, self-guiding missiles, and machines for running other machines. This new science can thus save the brains of man, as well as his hands. We see here the beginning of the manufacture of a mechanical brain. The prospect of automatic factories guided by only a few technicians leads one to speculate on the social changes involved.[1] Yet the decrease of drudgery and the increase of leisure is one of the desirable results of the progress of science—if we can find something sensible to do in our spare time.

The power and techniques which are already under human control make a world of plenty a practical possibility for the first time in history. It all depends on the choices made by human beings. Not only our society but the whole world is involved. The greater the power the more acutely the moral problem is focused. It is always a problem of choice, and the outcome depends on the aims and values of those who choose. In our society there is a widespread lack of faith. Relativism and uncertainty tend to dominate the philosophy of the ordinary man. We have not made a new synthesis, or reinterpretation of belief to fit our changed world. The old religious forces are still at work but becoming less and less effective in their present form except on a small scale. Three main trends can be observed, which will probably co-exist until one becomes dominant or a new synthesis develops. First the uncertainty may lead to a renewed dogmatism or absolutism, perhaps of an undesirable kind. Or we can learn to tolerate the unavoidable uncertainty, and a secular humanism may develop into an acceptable faith, without reliance on the traditional beliefs. Thirdly there can be a rebirth

[1] Norbert Wiener: *The Human Use of Human Beings*, 1951.

of spiritual religion, basically Christian but perhaps involving profound changes in the existing Churches.

In what do we firmly believe and put our trust? The strongest faith is in democracy and freedom, however differently or vaguely those words may be interpreted. Democracy and freedom are not ends in themselves, yet they are held as important values by the majority of English people. Yet freedom is relative, and can only be had on conditions. Hence the paradox of planned freedom. We all hope that in a society which is becoming more collective in its organization, and more centrally controlled, we can still retain our essential freedoms. Above all, and in spite of the possibilities for human welfare, we look to the future with anxiety and live in fear of a war which will again destroy our hopes.

A MASS SOCIETY

It is within the socio-cultural framework of our society during the immediate future that the educational system promised by the 1944 Act has to be developed. While we do not claim to predict the future, there are some general trends which can be observed. How the social forces will group themselves is not so clear as the needs which face our people at all levels. In the long run education will adjust itself in response to social needs, but there are several different ways in which the response can be made. Let us first look a little closer at the kind of society in which we are now living, and as it is likely to be in the near future.

Great Britain is a mass industrial society, and to-day that means that our principal material problems are economic. We live close together in towns. Over 50 per cent of the population of England live in dense conurbations and large towns of over 100,000, most of the rest live in smaller towns, and only one-fifth live in what is still called the countryside. We can only produce enough food to feed one-half of our population, and we cannot provide all the raw materials for our industry. From these basic facts follows the familiar economic argument which concludes that our standard of living depends on our exports and our total productive capacity. Through nationalization the state has now entered the spheres of production and distribution, so that industry is divided into the two sectors of private enterprise and state ownership. At the same time organized labour is a social force protecting the workers' interests against the employers, if necessary, whether they work for the state or for private capitalists. The organized professional workers are becoming a more powerful social force because of the greatly increased size of the professions, and the development of new professions, all dealing with the highly specialized scientific, technical and administrative work of industry, commerce and government. These facts create the social need for efficient and productive workers at all levels, and the best possible use of educated man-power.

Politically we will assume that we are likely to retain what is virtually a two-party system for some time to come, and even if the names change there will be 'left' or 'right' attitudes corresponding to what we now call the socialists and the conservatives. If we fall, through whatever kind of crisis, into a one-party government then our present democratic way of life will be in danger. A new political force is growing up which can be called 'managerial' and which will have its influence within the body politic (see p. 55), through the exercise of executive power on a large scale. The 'managers' are those who have charge of the actual processes of production.[1] Planning directors, production managers, operating executives, administrative engineers, supervisory technicians, superintendents, bureau heads, etc., have functions within industry, but also exercise political power since they play an active role in the organization of society. Whatever the politics may become we assume the maintenance of democracy, and this demands of all the people the responsibilities of full membership of society. These responsibilities become greater the more democracy spreads.

With regard to social status, the growth of equality and the increasing social mobility have done much to make the old class distinctions meaningless. This does not mean, however, that there is no hierarchy of prestige groups in the social order, but that they tend to be based more on income level and occupational status. Public opinion is becoming more of an influence on the government, as well as on salesmanship, and the different 'publics' are zealously 'polled' for their preferences, be it in prime ministers or biscuits. The polls in fact specify to what groups in terms of age, sex, income, class or other categories the public belongs. The differences of needs and opinions, and hence the social pressures, of youth as against age are likely to become more acute, because the proportion of old people in the population is increasing and that of young people decreasing. This is already certain to con-

[1] James Burnham: *The Managerial Revolution*, 1941.

tinue, because of the decline of the birth rate earlier in the century, and the increased longevity due to the advance of medicine and improved social conditions. No increase in the birth rate, even if it is maintained, can alter this trend for a long time ahead.

The techniques of our present society have also brought the phenomena of mass production and mass communication. Both can tend towards uniformity; the first of goods, the second of minds. When the same things are produced in large quantities there is an obvious standardization, and often a restriction of choice. The situation has an aesthetic aspect, since it becomes more difficult to show individual taste even in personal things like food, furniture and clothes. The effect upon the worker is also significant since the same sort of repetitive, button-pushing, lever-pulling work is needed to produce almost any kind of goods. Hence a tendency to dehumanize the worker, at least during working hours, and make him or her function like a part of the machine. This state of affairs is not only found in factories, since there are large numbers of 'white-collar' workers in offices, whose work is just as routine and monotonous as that of the factory workers. They have their leisure but this is becoming more and more dependent on the machine, and leisure also tends to become mass produced. It has often been asked, as an educational question, whether leisure can be used to give the satisfactions which the less skilled workers cannot get from their work. It may be that they only seek excitement and pleasure, and are content with stimulants and entertainment. With regard to numerical facts all we can do is to report an all-round increase, over a long period, in the expenditure on entertainment and gambling, and in the consumption of alcohol, tobacco and cosmetics. Many new means of mechanical amusement have been created. We have the telecinema; shall we even yet have the 'Feelies' of *Brave New World* as imagined by Aldous Huxley. 'An all super-singing, synthetic talking, coloured, stereoscopic, Feely, with scent-organ accompaniment', with suitable smells of orange-blossom wafted through the theatre as the audience tactually experience the most touching love scene. It has been reported that a scent-organ has indeed been made by an Italian professor who speaks of the synchronized odours which make the 'Smellies' a reality. One gets the impression more and more that anything is possible—if people really want it.

The moral problem, as always, is concerned with how we choose to use our inventions. The media of mass communication such as the cinema, the radio and the press are continuously spreading ideas, and establishing common interests and tastes. These can either spread a more enlightened culture or stereotype thinking and standardize ideas. Up to a point social solidarity through a set of common beliefs is a good thing, and something our chaotic society badly needs. But we must not accept indoctrination without the free play of criticism, or else something much more valuable will be lost.

The use of television will provide a test for our social morals, and it may become of very great importance. Even more than with the sound radio actuality can come into the home. It possesses all the intimacy and personality of the radio voices, with the apparent reality of vision, and the hypnotism of the cinema screen. There is the maximum possible participation of the population in what is going on in the world. This could be used to encourage active citizenship, and the awareness of the machinery of democratic government. Before long common knowledge of world events will be instantaneous in many countries, and we should note that the commentary can be in any language, which solves the problem of the world film understandable by all. In March 1951 the televising of the Senate Committee Investigating Crime in the United States created an enormous interest, and brought home to the public the reality of the crime problem. Later in the same year the first 'coast-to-coast hook-up' gave the whole nation a view of the Japanese Treaty Conference in San Francisco, thus bringing into people's homes the personalities of world affairs, and enabling them to be critical of the actual proceedings as they took place. The public in England now expect to look in at all important national events, and it is only a matter of time before some of the debates of Parliament will appear on television. It is true that by seeing for themselves people are to some extent protected against the distortion or withholding of news by other forms of reporting, but it puts an increased strain on their capacity for critical judgment. There are no doubt many arguments for and against this kind of increase of public knowledge, or the policy of 'trusting the people', but any conclusions about the television of political events must await more experience of its effects. In any case it is difficult to see how the public demand to see and hear can be refused.

Television has also been claimed as the 'Visual Educationists' Dream' come true, but we must remember that it is already becoming less and less necessary to read. Reading is an essential tool for higher education, as well as preserving the individual's capacity to choose for himself what he likes to study, and when he wants to do so. As time goes on there may arise a new *élite* of those who remain able to read, and thus the only people who can develop an *individual* taste in literature from the use of books.

THE CHANGING NATURE OF OUR DEMOCRACY

The idea of our democracy has taken on a new form during this century. Let us remind ourselves of its basic principles, and see how these are being reinterpreted. There are three general statements which express our democratic theory.

(i) *All people are in some sense equal.* This principle has often caused confusion of thought, since people are obviously *not* 'created equal' in abilities or talents, either physical or mental. What is meant is that each person is unique as a personality, and has an equal right to respect as an end in himself. When we had given men equality before the law, and as citizens with certain political rights, it was found that they could still be subject to economic exploitation, and many lived in extreme poverty. Hence the demand for a more equal distribution of wealth, which is the basis of the Welfare State.

(ii) *All people have certain essential freedoms.* Freedom of worship, freedom of speech and opinion, freedom of assembly for political or economic ends, all these are well known, and only restricted by the necessary laws for our protection. But a new series of freedoms have appeared which can be called social freedoms, and are demanded in the interest of social justice. They are best expressed in the language of the Beveridge Report on Social Security as freedom from want, disease, ignorance, squalor and idleness. Such freedoms can only be achieved by some form of collective action, which means central planning by the authority of the government. All planning involves restrictions of some kind on somebody, and the discussion of its value centres on whether it is in the interest of the people as a whole. The co-existence of freedom and control is the paradox of planning. In giving more equality we have also attacked some of the traditional freedoms; the freedom of management of personal income and property, or the freedom to own the means of production and to employ others.

(iii) *Government by consent* is the third main principle of our democracy. The coming of full political democracy, when *all* are consulted about their government for the first time in history, means that *all* the citizens must accept the responsibilities of full membership of their society. This can still be called a new idea, and the acceptance of such responsibility is one of the social needs for the future.

Let us return to economic planning and the social freedoms, for this is the essentially new factor in our mass industrial democracy. We have said that all planning involves control. This is not a party political matter but is inherent in the economic situation. The political parties will differ over what should be planned, and over the rate of change attempted. The controls necessary are on the whole economic. To achieve freedom from want and freedom from disease a compulsory insurance scheme for everybody was required. Since the benefits are not all paid from contributions but partly from taxation (for instance family allowances are paid entirely from the Exchequer), this involves to some extent a distribution of wealth from the richer to the poorer as well as from those not in need to those who are. Food subsidies also come from the taxpayer, and the benefits of cheaper food are mostly provided by those who pay most taxes. And a National Health Service means less freedom for the doctors, and planned food production less freedom for the farmers. Freedom from ignorance was the objective of the increased educational provision of the Act of 1944. But note that this gave more control to the central authority, and thus less freedom to the local authorities. If all parts of the Act are implemented it will mean that employers will not be free to employ youths under eighteen every day, but that the young people *must* attend county colleges a specified number of days. It means that independent schools have to be inspected and can be closed. Are parents free to choose a school for their children unless they pay for entrance to an independent school?

Freedom from squalor involves town and country planning. The individual cannot build his house or his factory where he wishes. There is control over the ownership of land, and authorities may receive orders for compulsory purchase.

Freedom from idleness is the key problem, but full employment cannot be achieved without central economic control. This means control over the use of capital and the control of investment. Some of these freedoms we are losing may not be important, some may be necessary for the sake of greater gains to society, but it is worth pointing out that the spirit of freedom that was at one time thought essential to the growth of British prosperity under free enterprise, has had to change its nature.

That the situation is not without danger has been shown by Karl Mannheim in his *Diagnosis of Our Time*, 1943.[1] His main theme is expressed on the first page of that book as follows: 'We are living in an age of transition from a *laissez-faire* to a planned society. The planned society which will come may take one of two shapes: it will be ruled either by a minority in terms of a dictatorship, or by a new form of government which, in spite of its increased power, will still be democratically controlled.' He then develops his conception of planning for freedom, which will result neither in Fascism nor Communism but in a Third Way. This may be achieved by using the new social techniques in a suitable way. These social techniques are methods of influencing human behaviour on a large scale both by the modern means of mass communication, and by the economic and psychological inventions for achieving social control. Mannheim sees the danger of these techniques making the centralization of power and minority rule much easier. We have seen this happen in totalitarian states and in the future it will be easier still.[2] Public opinion can be conditioned and education controlled; civil power as well as military power can be concentrated and operated from key positions. This would be planning, but in terms of a dictatorship. The alternative is planning for freedom. How can this be achieved? We give an outline of some of the conditions Mannheim proposes.[3]

(i) You need not plan for conformity, but can plan for variety. Regimentation is not necessary; co-ordination need not be that of the goose-step, but can be that of the orchestra.

(ii) Part of planning is deliberately to refrain from interference. Leave to free enterprise the largest place possible, and do not control for the sake of control.

(iii) To give greater social justice (the new social freedoms) we *must* plan, but the objective is itself a democratic move, and will be freely accepted by the majority. Also it can be done by the existing machinery

[1] His analysis of society in an age of reconstruction is given in greater detail in *Man and Society*, 1940, which is a much more difficult book to read.

[2] See George Orwell: *Nineteen Eighty Four*, 1950, which is a fantasy with a perfectly serious moral.

[3] From *Diagnosis of Our Time*, Chap. I.

of our government, and no revolution or dictatorship is required to improve the living conditions of the people.

(iv) Democracy must no longer be neutral over its aims or tolerant of those who would destroy it. It must become a militant democracy. We have a 'perfect right to exclude those who wish to abuse the methods of freedom for abolishing freedom'. For example we can only allow the government to be changed by peaceful means, and must prevent by force those who would use violent means.

(v) There is no need to dictate everything that people should think. Agreement is possible over a set of basic values, which should be propagated widely, while the more 'complicated' values could be left open to choice and experiment. Mannheim thinks that, 'the democracies have a set of basic values in common, which are inherited from classical antiquity, and even more from Christianity, and that it is not too difficult to state them and agree on them'. This corresponds to Fred Clarke's suggestion that we must 'communicate the type and provide for growth beyond the type'.

(vi) We must realize in England why we don't like thinking, and especially thinking ahead or planning. Things are changing in the world, our secure and insular position has gone, and we must give up our old ideas. We suspect 'intellectuals' too much, we are too attached to tradition, and we neglect the energies of youth and link prestige with the elderly. At the same time Mannheim always insists that the moral force, the sense of balance, the political maturity and genius for peaceful reform of the British, make us the most likely people to carry out the new pattern of democracy.

We have given a picture of how democracy is changing its nature in this century. The chief features of the change are two. First the much greater *participation* of the mass of the people in all the ways of their society. This is primarily a result of the increased communication of ideas and of the mobility of people. Second the improved standard of living of all the poorer and lower middle sections of the community. This is due to a combination of a new understanding of the ideal of equality, with the machinery of economic planning. The potential experiences of most people are therefore greater than ever before. The effectiveness of education depends on the experiences people select and which are selected for them. We thus turn to the role of education in our future society.

THE EDUCATIONAL NEEDS OF OUR FUTURE SOCIETY

THE ROLE OF EDUCATION

We are educating now for twenty years later. That is the time when the population of our schools will be taking on positions of responsibility in our future society. How will our educational system respond to the needs of the socio-cultural situation we have just been describing? If it is true, as our theory has suggested, that education tends to *follow* social change, then by observing the present trends of society we should be in some position to predict the possible responses in the sphere of education. Let us consider some of our present social needs in turn, remembering that they are all part of the same complex situation.

1. *To maintain the scientific and industrial techniques, and the body politic of our society, we need a large number of intelligent men and women for such occupations as those of scientific and professional specialists, administrators, planners, managers, technicians and sub-professionals.*

By glancing at the advertisement columns of our newspapers we see the demand for engineers, physicists, chemists and mathematicians. We see also vacancies for specialists in the fields of electronics, aerodynamics, telecommunications and the sciences concerned with automation and nuclear energy. There is a whole range of occupational specialisms, and new ones continue to arise, which are essential for the running of our technological society. Not only are scientists and technologists required but administrators, executives, directors, planners and all those occupations concerned with management. These advertisements can be taken as an indicator or symptom, of the most important single change in our class structure during the last half century, and one which is still continuing. This change is the growth of the professional and managerial class; in other words an increase in the number of people with middle-class incomes.

Up to the present the school education of those who will enter such occupations has been mainly the task of the Public and Grammar Schools and the Technical Schools or Colleges. The Report of the Central Advisory Council in 1959, known as the *Crowther Report*, gave the fullest review and forecast of the changing pattern of secondary education. It states as a main objective, 'At present only 12 per cent of the 17-year-old age group get full-time education; we think that by 1980 half should.'[1] It is shown in the following chapter (p. 110) how fast this percentage is increasing, and why it is a key figure as a measure of educational progress. In this decade we are witnessing a vast national effort to adapt our educational institutions to the needs of an advanced technological society.[2] The role of education is to become a major agency of selection and training to fill all the ranks of the occupational structure. The first general point to make is that those who will fill the upper ranks, whatever type of school they go to in the future, are ultimately going to undertake work requiring relatively high intelligence. There is no need to discuss here how accurately intelligence can be measured, nor when is the best time to measure it. The fact remains that some people have more units of brain power than others, however it is measured, and it is those among the upper ranges of mental capacity who are required to be trained as the future specialists in their professions. Both the report on *Early Leaving* and the *Crowther Report*[3] have shown that many pupils of high ability have left school early, and there seems little doubt that we have underestimated the capacities of our population. At the same time, in our enthusiasm for the principles of equality we must not, through misinterpreting them, also underestimate the overriding importance of the power of intelligence. It seems likely that we shall have to give more and not less attention to educational methods and curricula most suited to specially gifted children.[4] If we do *not* we shall find that some of the most skilled work of our society is not being done properly, because insufficient intelligence or improperly applied intelligence is being devoted to it. There are strong advocates for reserving the Grammar School, or some Grammar Schools, for the most able children. This would require considerable changes in the nature of the schools. For example, in our type of society, as many people are required with high intelligence to be tech-

[1] 15 *to* 18 (Crowther Report), p. 407.

[2] Among the many documents of the early 1960's estimating future needs the Morris Report of a committee set up by the National Union of Teachers, *Investment for National Survival*, is typical. It estimated that by 1970 about 100,000 more teachers than in 1959 would be needed, and that expenditure on education would need to rise from 4½ per cent of the national income to 6 per cent or more. This is a modest estimate, taking no account of raising the school leaving age, or increasing part-time education over 15.

[3] See next chapter pp. 113–16 for details.

[4] *The Year Book of Education*, 1961, on 'Concepts of Excellence in Education', gives full attention to this problem.

nologists and applied scientists as to be administrators or members of the liberal professions. Most Grammar Schools will need to become better adapted to the future technologist; but we shall return to this matter later.

Now there is still a certain cultural conflict between the idea of a technical education and the idea of a liberal education. Let us remember that the definition given by the Oxford Dictionary is: 'Liberal (of education), fit for a gentleman, of general literary rather than of a technical kind.' For too long technical education was regarded, on the whole, as inferior, and the term 'vocational' is also applied to it in a disapproving manner by the supporter of the pure liberal-cultural tradition. This is 'culture' in its literary, intellectual sense. The failure of the Technical High Schools to develop on an adequate scale was partly due to the feeling that what they would offer would not be *real* education. How the literary prestige of the Grammar School lingers on! In fact there are very few Secondary Technical Schools of equivalent status to Grammar Schools, and the overall proportion of their pupils staying on to the sixth form is much lower. An essential condition for their improvement would be to have sufficient entrants of equal intelligence with the best of the Grammar School. While the next best are sent to the Technical School there will never be parity. Clearly the liberal versus vocational conflict must be solved.

To clarify the issue let it be admitted that the present Grammar School is vocational anyhow. Most of the sixth form on the science side, if they stay on, will be learning their science or mathematics with their future careers in their minds. If a boy takes the first M.B. (premedical examination), at school it is with the intention of becoming a doctor. The large number of future teachers who come from Grammar Schools are learning the subjects they will teach. The boy who is going to write, be it articles, books, or laws, practises writing. The whole distinction between technical and secondary (grammar) education should have been abolished by the famous passages in the Report of the Bryce Commission in 1895.[1] But in our historical setting that could

[1] For instance: 'Secondary education is technical, because it teaches the boy so to apply the principles he is learning, and so to learn the principles by applying them, or so to use the instruments he is being made to know, as to perform or produce something, interpret a literature or a science, make a picture of a book, practise a plastic or manual art, convince a jury or persuade a senate, translate or annotate an

not have happened, because of the social prestige of the classical tradition and the Public School.

As time goes on the matter is getting more serious. One solution is to extend the vocational function of the Grammar School. Let all the future professional specialists go to the same school, but provide sufficient new courses for them to choose from. This would involve a thorough-going and radical curriculum reform. To decide what new subjects would have to be offered it is only necessary to look at the needs of our society. It would be essential to have the preliminary studies for engineering of all kinds, statistics and more varieties of mathematics, more advanced electricity, agricultural science, economics and higher commercial subjects. Practical work would have to be offered in mechanical and technical laboratories and workshops. As the Grammar Schools already carry some sciences to a high degree of specialization there is no reason why they should not take on new ones, once the difficulty of finding teachers is overcome. In any case it looks as though the Grammar Schools will have to adapt or perish. They are losing pupils because they are not satisfying the social needs of the time. Until 1960 there were still over 60 per cent of the pupils leaving before the age of seventeen. There are many reasons for this drift, but among them must be considered the possibility that the schools are not providing what the boys and girls and their parents want.

Another possible solution is the Comprehensive School. It is argued that with their greater range of subjects and classes they can more easily develop to the full the varied abilities of all the pupils, avoid the mistakes of selection, reduce the incidence of early leaving, and provide better educated recruits for industry and other occupations. It is also thought, by those who advocate it, that the mixing together of all social classes at school will prevent snobbery, and promote a desirable feeling of basic equality among those who in later life will have to work together even though at different levels of the occupational structure. The *educational* test will be whether an adequate education can be given to all ranges of intelligence in the same institution, In particular we must

author, dye wool, weave cloth, design or construct a machine, navigate a ship or command an army.' This passage, describing a secondary education as it *should exist*, was quoted by the *Spens Report* (p. 59) which later says: 'These statesmanlike and far-sighted recommendations were passed by. An unreal and unnecessary division was introduced between secondary and technical education.'

watch that the more able children are well catered for. However, we must remember the significant fact that the *Crowther Report*, looking ahead as far as it did, still based its whole argument and recommendations on the assumption that what it called 'the ablest boys and girls' would still, on the whole, be segregated in Grammar Schools or the equivalent, and that selection would still be at 10+ to 11+. But it also predicted that over 11 per cent of pupils of Secondary School age would be in some type of comprehensive education by 1965.

2. *Our society needs productive workers who enjoy their lives. This means the most economical and effective use of man-power, and it also means that happiness is a factor in efficiency.*

We now come to the education of the majority of the population. These are the 65 per cent of all children, who at present attend the Secondary Modern School.[1] They will grow up be become the majority of the population of the country. They include the large mass of manual workers, with all the varieties of craftsmen and skilled labour. They will become the workers in factories, in mills, in mines, in agriculture, in building and construction, and in transport and distribution. Many will become clerks and office workers, tradesmen and shop-assistants, minor technicians and mechanics, and men, women and non-commissioned officers of the armed forces. Whether all of these people are educated in the same school as the other third of the population or not, the *educational problem* remains. When we consider the different varieties of intellectual ability and natural talent, it is quite clear that they do not all require the same education, and it should be even more clear that the curriculum and methods of the Grammar School is entirely the wrong model to follow. This is true whether we consider the economic problem of sorting out the population into the right jobs, or the human problem of helping them to be creative and happy human beings. There is no measure of these things, but it is fairly safe to estimate that for more than half of our present adult population education was on the whole boring, inefficient and unpopular. It has improved, and our children in the schools of the 1960's enjoy it more, but for the majority, the content of the curriculum and the methods of teaching

[1] At age 14 in 1960 there were, in round figures 64 per cent of children in Secondary Modern Schools, 24 per cent in maintained grammar, technical and comprehensive schools, 2½ per cent in direct grant schools and nearly 7 per cent in independent schools.

will have to be greatly changed in order to become more significant *to the child*, and more related to his future. Equal opportunity for education does not mean identical education for all; it means that education at all levels should be of the best possible kind to suit each child, and that the highest education should be *accessible* to *anyone* able to profit by it. It is useless to copy the Grammar School for everyone, because it is not the best for everyone, but of course it will go on being the model while the social prestige of the literary tradition retains its grip. The Ministry of Education may say, as they do, that the purpose of the Secondary Modern School is 'to provide a good all round secondary education, not focused primarily on the traditional subjects of the school curriculum, but developing out of the interests of the children',[1] but most of the schools go on teaching history, and English, and mathematics, and French and the rest, in the *same kind of way* as the Grammar School, and merely to a less efficient level of attainment. There is the same kind of superior sniffing at 'vocational' education, as if there were a special merit in studying subjects which *appear to the child* to be entirely unrelated to his future economic role or to his enjoyment of life.

One cannot see at the moment what social forces are making for change. It is one thing for the progressive educational theorist to say it should be different, but what support has he in society at large? The more influential parents do not object to an academic bias since they often wish their children were in a Grammar School anyway. Their demands will most likely be for their children to take the General Certificate Examination. After all, what parity of status have they with the other forms of *secondary* education if they don't receive some kind of certificate? The less responsible parents don't object because they think the teachers should know best; and the teachers have no other practical model to follow. Change is coming, and mostly through progressive education authorities, but it is likely to be slow. The great change in provision which is certainly coming is the increase in the number of extended courses for pupils of fifteen-sixteen. This will suit the more able who can take examinations even if they dislike the subject-matter, but it will not solve the problems of the less able who form the majority. (See p. 122.)

One might predict a great development in the use of new media of

[1] Ministry of Education Pamphlet No. 9, *The New Secondary Education*, 1947, p. 29.

instruction, if the education authorities could afford the apparatus for audio-visual aids including cinema and television. Every device to further active understanding, and avoid over-emphasis on book work is a gain when dealing with the less intellectual minds. But we are again hampered by our economic situation.

One imagines that ultimately the search for talent will bring about the needed attention to the Primary Schools.[1] The loss of the nation's ability starts at the age of five or below. The real advances will follow further research on the psychology of early concept formation, and the relation of language to the development of thinking. Adverse environmental conditions can handicap the foundations of intelligence as much as they can handicap any other form of growth, and it is probable that an enormous increase of mental capacity could be realized in our population. In the meantime too many Primary Schools cannot even get decent buildings. A report of the N.U.T. states that the last national survey of school buildings was undertaken in 1925–6 and of the schools then included on the 'Black List' there were 549 still in use in January 1958, even though some of those were 'originally condemned as unsuitable for continued recognition and incapable of improvement'.

3. *Our society needs a new concept of general education*

We have so far placed most stress, and we think rightly, on the kind of education needed to satisfy the economic and productive functions of our society. There is no other way, during this next half-century, to maintain our standard of living and our place in the world, than by gaining a position of economic security by our own productive work. But some concept of the general education of the personality is also required at all levels. New values are needs too; not so obvious as new techniques, but at all times really more important. Let us first consider our future professional and technical specialists. It is with them that the problem has become acute with the demand for general 'culture' in the scientist and technologist, and a condemnation of over-specialization both at school and university. The first trouble is that in our society to-day we no longer agree on what is the pattern of the well-educated man. In the past the leading members in almost all professions had a classical education, and the majority of the rest were attached in some way to the Public School tradition. To-day we have highly skilled

[1] *Fair Play for Our Primary Schools*, 1960.

experts, and business or public service administrators who may have been selected from any level of society and perhaps have had no background, at home or at school, of a 'liberal' education in the old sense of the word. What content of knowledge does the well-educated man or woman need to-day?

(a) We will take for granted the need for some elements of the old liberal education, with Latin and Greek left out except for the few. This means a general knowledge of some of the great works of our literature past and present, practice in the proper use of the English language, and some appreciation (and, when possible, practice), of one or more of the arts. This essential background we will not enlarge upon, though the selection of its content and methods of teaching raises many problems. What is interesting, in our context, is to consider the new needs which living in the present day world force upon us.

(b) The old liberal education taught responsibility to society but to a different kind of society, and from the point of view of a ruling class. The present-day citizen needs to know and understand the meaning and implications of modern democracy, and the social philosophy behind it. This should be seen in its historical setting, and against the general world background of other systems of government.

(c) The rapid development of science and its influence on our way of thinking and our beliefs cannot be ignored. The place of the scientific method in civilization concerns us all. Science specialists, just because they are *specialists*, as well as non-scientists would profit by studying the general contributions of physical science to culture, and the problems which it imposes. Of course the problems posed are often value problems, so we are really asking for courses not only in the history and philosophy of science, but also in morals and ethics.

(d) More important still, in some respects, is the study of the contributions of social science, which are leading to an understanding of society itself. It is probably too soon to ask that some knowledge of this kind be expected of the ordinary well-educated man. We should be asking for an education in the things which most of us ourselves do not know, since we are not well-educated in this new sense. But such knowledge will become so important that it is likely to form a background to the minds of many of our future leaders. This means studying the science of human nature and the science of society, and includes the contributions of the newer subjects such as psychology, anthropology, economics and sociology, in addition to the history of ideas and social behaviour.

When we ask who, in our society, is aware of this need for a new general education, we find that there are not many outside academic circles. It is indeed difficult to persuade those who have not got it that it is necessary. A young man who is, let us say, a research chemist, or a radio engineer, doing a socially useful job, taking an interest in current affairs and using his vote might say: 'Why should I know anything about psychology, or economics, or Beethoven or Picasso, or Shakespeare and Shelley and Dickens for that matter, though the last three were rammed down my throat at school?' It is true that some people go voluntarily and study these things at adult education classes, but not very many compared with the size of the population that might go. In fact there is little demand for general culture.

It is some ideal of a better civilization, even in the minds of a few, which is the real justification for a general liberal education. Our technical society, as such, does not demand it. The machines could be worked by conditioned robots or ignoramuses; the cleverer people could mend them, and the cleverer ones still invent them. But this would be a slave society. If men are to be democratically governed they must take a share in responsibility, and understand what is going on in order to make personal judgments. This means we must understand the world we live in outside our own small circle of activities. But this is not all. The knowledge which makes us politically free might still leave us ignorant of the arts, and in this sense vulgar and without taste. A democratic society can be vulgar. The arts are necessary to make us more agreeable, or more interesting, or happier, or whatever else comes from being more expressive, gaining emotional experience and using imagination. All these things come from creation in the arts and humanities, or through the recreation which is called appreciation.

It is interesting to see the struggle for a more general education developing in England in the 1960's. The competition for university places is the basic reason for the growth of sixth form specialization. Pupils simply could not afford not to specialize, since they wanted to gain the highest possible marks in the 'A' and 'S' level papers. In turn this led to a streamlining of the Grammar School syllabus, and the introduction of 'rapid' forms, taking their 'O' levels earlier so as to gain an extra year in the sixth form. Art and music were neglected, the choice of future courses was pushed earlier—there might be a choice between literature and physics in the fourth forms—and general education was sacrificed to gaining the examination passes in the subjects thought most useful. For years the narrow specialization of the Grammar Schools was condemned by educationists, but the situation got worse rather than better. No effective body of opinion was behind a change, and many university teachers were also equally narrow in outlook. The *Crowther Report* supported sixth form specialization, on various theoretical grounds, which avoided mentioning its plain vocational significance, and suggested that any bad effects could be mitigated by the better use of pupils' 'minority' time. This, it was held, could be used to ensure both the literacy of the scientist and the 'numeracy' of the arts student. Other groups of educationists got together and advocated different means of broadening the sixth form curriculum. A simple method of solving the problem was initiated by Professor Oliver,[1] who, working through the Northern Universities Joint Matriculation Board, succeeded in experimenting with and establishing in 1959 two General Studies papers at 'A' level, which could be offered for university entrance as the equivalent of any other subject. If all the universities were to demand, through their examination boards, that some set of General Papers be taken as an essential requirement for entrance then the schools would take the preparation for them seriously. A committee of Vice-Chancellors has discussed a proposal of this kind. At the time of writing it is by no means certain what will happen. The very expansion of all forms of higher education may make some common means of selection more necessary. Again, if our society gets more wealthy it may be possible to contemplate a longer period of higher education, and thus be able to accept less specialized qualifications on entry. If some new concept of general education does *not* spread we shall have a society more and more filled at the top with narrow specialists, and this in itself may be a cause of inefficiency, since they will lack understanding of each other's work and outlook.

A comparison can be made with the U.S.A. where they have sufficient wealth to make general education on a large scale possible. Nearly all the population go to High School. In many States the school-leaving age is eighteen or seventeen, and for the country as a whole an average

[1] R. A. C. Oliver: *General Studies in the G.C.E.* Northern Universities Joint Matriculation Board, 1960.

of over two-thirds of the age-group will stay on at school until the age of eighteen. The proportion of the age-group going on to College of some sort was about 30 per cent at the same time as it was about 4 per cent in this country. It is true that large numbers drop out after one or two years, and already there are doubts whether many more young people will want to go to College. The problem is one of *motivation* and is not economic. Obviously average standards in the universities of the U.S.A. tend to be lower than in this country, but the conception of university education is different, and the better students all proceed to higher degrees so that the first degree does not count for so much as ours. Again there are many different university institutions, and some at the top have as good a reputation for scholarship as any in Europe. While the further expansion of occupations requiring College training is expected to increase in the U.S.A., the contention is that a general education to the bachelor's degree is of value to the holder whatever future place in life he chooses to take. The aim is therefore a better educated society, and is an attempt to increase the common intellectual and social experience of the population. This will make for greater social cohesion, greater mobility, and a reduction of the class stratification of the society. We must realize that as things are at the present the problem of specialization, as we have it, has been solved in America; it is postponed to the university stage. They can afford in their High Schools to spend more time in learning less. The problem of competition for the university, and cramming for scholarships, is also solved. Almost any young American can be certain of receiving, if he wants it, all the education of which he is capable up to any level. The task of the general education of the people is being undertaken on the largest possible scale. This is a measure of the wealth of their country.

The culture and traditions of our society are not the same as those of the United States, in spite of many things in common as English-speaking people, and what suits them may not suit us. At the same time we can perhaps learn from their experience when dealing with similar problems. We are in Britain faced with the same two tendencies of an increasing technology and an increasing democratization of society, which will lead us, as it has led the Americans, to the need for still further expansion of our education, both in universities and schools. When we can afford it, what shall we do? That is the question we must ask ourselves. There will come a point when we cannot both expand the provision and maintain the same standards in our universities. In good time we shall have to decide whether to open colleges of a different kind for the lower ranges of studies, or provide for a different range of standards, and perhaps new types of degree, within our existing system.

4. *The need for humanization, or the preservation of whole human beings in a machine-dominated society*

In the meantime another problem is pressing upon us. To talk of a liberal education for the mass of the workers is more difficult still. They need to be preserved as whole human beings. As we have seen the tendency of mechanization is for the automatic machine to replace the hands. The work becomes repetitive and monotonous and attention rather than adaptive effort is required. The worker tends to become a part of the machine. The break-down or 'atomization' of the process into one operation per worker leads to a lack of interest, and gives no chance for the creative development of the personality through the work. The worker, unless of very low mentality, tends to feel frustrated, and to lack significance as a person except outside his work. It is difficult to be happy while doing much of the work that people have to do; hence the low industrial morale and the need for new incentives. More leisure is often chosen rather than more pay, and even the powerful money motive is not enough after a certain point of disinterest or strain is reached. Let us remember also that many 'black-coated' workers suffer from similar occupational diseases. They are becoming paper-minders in offices and just as bored as the machine-minders.

It is difficult to see what solution can be found. The problem is not necessarily so great as it appears. We have probably exaggerated the monotony and boredom of industrial work. About one-third of the industrial workers are engaged in this type of work, but this is a large number. Many of these do not complain, which in itself might be regarded as a bad symptom. But if the work is not in itself monotonous, or can be relieved by human contacts, and by the variety which comes from agricultural, building, transport, and all outdoor jobs, there may still be the lack of personal satisfaction from the work, which the better-educated worker of to-day requires. Of course we do not know how far lack of satisfaction in family life, or discontent and lack of purpose brought on by other troubles of our time, are transferred to the work situation. A man is a whole personality, and the happy man in his leisure is usually happy in his work.

It looks as though for many the full development of personality will have to be realized outside the hours of paid employment. Education for leisure is an old cry but it still seems to be the best solution since in most cases the nature of the work cannot be changed. There are of course attempts at better human relations in industry, joint consultation of managers and workers, and the greater participation of the worker in the enterprise. All these are a help in giving a feeling of greater significance to the worker, who undoubtedly has to some extent been 'depersonalized' by the growth of large firms and large-scale processes, and the lack of that personal contact with the management which is a feature of the small family business. But one cannot disguise the fact when the work itself is dehumanizing. For such jobs we can only look forward to the progress of cybernetics and the coming of the automatic factory, with more and more repetitive work eliminated.

Perhaps we shall have to take a different view of leisure. The invention of leisure was a great sign of progress, and one might suggest that the more we get the better. Yet we already fear that the nuclear age and automation will reduce the need for large numbers of the less skilled workers. Even for the skilled the four hour work-day is beginning in the U.S.A. The moralist is apt to blame others for the misuse of their leisure, but we presume he knows well enough how to use his own spare time. Education *does* help people to enrich their leisure. Above all it could give more help in developing powers of criticism, so that even in entertainment people could choose the better *for them* and reject the worse. It is very curious that people often don't know that they could enjoy themselves better, and have even forgotten the enjoyment of making something for themselves. It is no use the 'highbrows' turning up their noses; the mass of people must begin at the beginning in learning to appreciate the good things of life. There are schools which give lessons on how to dress, and use make-up, and behave appropriately in social situations. Such attempts are often made in the teeth of opposition from the educational purists. Why not courses in eating and drinking? We in England have a lot to learn about these enjoyments and refinements of civilized life. Television will help, and the spread of culture through the mass media is one of the hopeful signs of our times. An appreciation of the visual arts is growing, as an interest in music grew through sound broadcasting. Perhaps better models for happiness in family life, and in the bringing up of children may imperceptibly be disseminated through the televised lives of the Dales or the Archers.

These suggestions are made in all seriousness, but above all the renewal of the creative spirit in all human beings is the best solution to aim at. A person is happy when creating something which expresses himself, and his own reaction to his world. This is the reason for the encouragement of individuality in a world which makes for more and more conformity. At the root of all our social needs is the individual's need to be himself, and by his own creative act, however small, to contribute to the general welfare. A respect for the uniqueness of each child is always deeply felt in the heart of every real educator.

CHAPTER VI

Education and the Social Structure

Social Mobility—Education for the Professions—The Wastage of Ability—The Social Demand for Education

With the growth of our industrial and technological society the educational system has taken on a new and closer relationship to the productive and economic life of the community. This chapter and the one that follows are concerned with the relations of education to the occupational and social hierarchy of England and Wales.

To say a person belongs to a certain social class is to refer to a very vague type of group. Social class in its everyday usage is spoken of in terms of social habits, attitudes and values. It is largely determined by cultural criteria, by the degree of social mixing, including intermarriage, and refers back to its older connections with rank, family tradition and the ownership of property. Type of education and occupation have always been factors in the determination of class, but to-day, in advanced industrial societies, they have become the dominant criteria as well as the most easily classified. Nevertheless in the older sense of the word we still live, in this country, in a highly class-stratified and class-conscious society. Until recently this had become almost an embarrassing subject, since it conflicted with the democratic ideals of social equality which are widely held. The concept of 'class' implies that some people are superior or inferior to others in some respect. This is what we do not like to say, and we feel we must avoid or deny this implication. The 'taboo' has been released, the facts are emerging, and hence the excitement which revelations on social class sometimes cause, and its popularity as a topic in even the best Sunday newspapers.

On the occasion of great national events such as a Coronation or a Royal Wedding the class structure of Great Britain is laid before the observant spectator. At the Coronation of Queen Elizabeth II we saw in the Abbey the peers and peeresses, wearing their coronets. The clubs of the Mall and St. James's were resplendent with the top hats and morning coats of the Public School boys and the upper middle-class. The stands erected by the Ministry of Works along Piccadilly and Hyde Park were thick with members of the Civil Service and the major professions. Lining the streets were the lower-middle and working-classes, with, in addition, the classless university students and impoverished intellectuals, and a certain number of high class girls who camped all night for the fun of it. But the modern sociologist is not content with such a rough and ready classification.

Scales of occupational status used for investigations in the sociological aspects of education are usually based on some modifications of the Registrar-General's Census classification. A bare outline of this is given in Table 1. It will be seen that there are five main social class groups, numbered I to V. The working population is divided into fifteen socio-economic groups, which in turn are made up of a number of occupational unit groups.[1] Each occupation is classified on the basis of the kind of work done, and each occupation is given a basic social class. However, in assigning any individual to a social class, account must be taken of his employment status as well as his occupation. Thus all at the level of foremen or supervisors are in Class III regardless of the occupation. The position of employers and managers varies with the size of the establishment, and with the nature of the work, for example manual or non-manual, so that they can be assigned to any of the classes except Class I which is reserved for professional workers, who normally require qualifications of university degree standard. It is significant that an *educational* qualification is the one demanded for membership of the top class. Teachers, except university teachers, are in Class II whether they have a university degree or not. Upper clerical workers are also in Class II. The largest group of all, that of the skilled occupations, consists mostly of manual workers, but contains a non-manual section composed of clerical and intermediate non-manual workers with less responsibility than those in Class II. Farmers and agricultural workers are allocated according to their employment status. There are many difficulties in making any such classification quite satisfactory in all its details, and objections can always be raised

[1] See *The Classification of Occupations* 1960, H.M.S.O. Bluebook.

about the position of particular occupations. In the social surveys to be described later in this chapter the subjects, whether school pupils or young adults, are classified in accordance with the occupation of their fathers. The usual classification into occupational groups is the modification of the census classes as given in Table 2.

TABLE 1

Social Classes according to the Registrar General's classification. (Occupied and retired males.)

Class	*Description*	*% of total 1951*
I	Professional	3·3
II	Intermediate	14·5
III	Skilled	53·0
IV	Semi-skilled	16·1
V	Unskilled	13·1

TABLE 2

Occupational Status Groups as commonly used in Social Surveys

Occupational Group	*Census Classification*
Professional and Managerial	Class I and most of Class II (e.g. Professional, administrative, large employers and managers, civil service, teachers, higher clerical, etc.). About 14% of total.
Clerical and other non-manual	Rest of Class II (e.g. shopkeepers, small employers), and non-manual in Class III (e.g. ordinary clerical workers, shop assistants). About 12 % of total.
Skilled Manual	Class III manual, including foremen and supervisors.
Semi-skilled Manual	Class IV
Unskilled Manual	Class V.

SOCIAL MOBILITY

Whatever views are held over the reality of the social stratification nobody would deny the intense competition in much of our society to move upwards in the social scale. In the nineteenth century, as was pointed out in Chapter IV the dominant aims of the new rich class were money making and social advancement, and those who could afford it sent their sons to the rapidly increasing number of Public Schools. This was the ladder of wealth. In the twentieth century some children from lowly homes have been able to get a good education, relatively high occupational status, and sometimes wealth. This is the ladder of ability, or merit, and it was the increasing educational opportunity and the new concept of democracy which broadened and strengthened this ladder. It is now well recognized that gaining a better education has been, and is, one of the chief means of achieving upward social mobility. The evidence for this can be seen in *Social Mobility in Britain*, published in 1954. The responses of a sample of 10,000 adults were analysed with regard to the social origins, education and occupation of the subjects, their parents and their grandparents. For the first time some fairly clear indication was obtained of the movements between the social classes of this country. The measure of social class used was the occupation of the father or male subject. To relate social status to occupation the Hall-Jones scale[1] was used in these investigations. It was found by Hall and Glass[2] that the type of education undergone was a most important factor in the movement of children to a higher or lower position in the social scale than their parents.

Thus the last sixty years have seen the forward march of that great middle-class movement, the Secondary Grammar School. Achieving entrance to the Grammar School (or its equivalent) was the critical step for upward social mobility, since this was the means of facilitating entry into middle-class and professional occupations. Further education after leaving school, especially university education, reinforced the upward

[1] D. V. Glass (Ed.): *Social Mobility in Britain*, 1954, Chap. 2, 'The Social Grading of Occupations', by C. A. Moser and J. R. Hall. The standard categories used are: (1) Professional and High Administrative, 3 per cent; (2) Managerial and Executive, 4·5 per cent; (3) Inspectional, Supervisory and Clerical, higher grade, 10 per cent; (4) Supervisory, etc., lower grade, 13 per cent; (5) Skilled manual, and routine non-manual, 41 per cent; (6) Semi-skilled manual, 16·5 per cent; (7) Unskilled manual, 12 per cent.

[2] Ibid. Chap. 10.

movement. Parents became well aware of this. Hence the continuous demand for Grammar School education, and the willingness of parents to pay fees, when fee-payers were permitted, if a free-place was not gained, or to make considerable sacrifices to send their sons to a Public School if they aimed higher still. The prestige of a school came to be judged by the prestige of the occupations which its old pupils succeeding in entering.[1] Education, in this context, can be defined as a process used by parents to get their children better jobs.

This process continues and has been accelerated by the demands of our society for highly trained specialists. It is accompanied by corresponding demands for middle grade technicians supervisory and clerical workers. Our society is thus faced with making an educational response to a rapidly changing occupational structure, and education is likely to play an even greater part in the process of occupational and social mobility than it has done in the past.

EDUCATION FOR THE PROFESSIONS

A key figure which indicates the main source of recruitment to the professional and managerial class is the number of pupils still in full-time education, of any kind, at seventeen years of age, i.e. in the age group 17·0 to 17·11. Whether in the sixth form at school, or in a Technical College or other establishment of further education, these are the pupils who have the best chance of gaining a university qualification or a technological or other professional qualification if they choose to continue with a higher education. The new type of 'sandwich' course, which involves a continuous period in a college alternating with work in industry, is considered, as it is in the Ministry of Education's statistics, as a form of full-time education. There are, of course, some part-time routes to technological[2] qualifications but these are difficult and in-

[1] See Olive Banks: *Parity and Prestige in English Secondary Education*, 1955, specially Chap. 16.

[2] The distinction as made in the White Paper *Technical Education*, 1955 is: A *technologist* has the qualifications and experience required for membership of a professional institution. Most university graduates in engineering and other applied sciences, and a good proportion of holders of Higher National Diplomas or Certificates or similar qualifications become technologists. A *technician* is qualified by specialist technical education and practical training to work under the general direction of a technologist. Consequently he will require a good knowledge of mathematics and science related to his own speciality.

efficient means of reaching full professional status. The tendency is to increase the number of full-time and sandwich courses as the best means of providing specialist technologists.

The figures here discussed refer to England and Wales in 1964 and are given in Table 3, columns one and two. At the beginning of that year the total age group of boys and girls aged seventeen last birthday was 776,000. The number of these who were in fully maintained schools of any kind (i.e. Grammar, Technical High, Comprehensive, bilateral, etc.) was, in round figures, 75,500, which was 9·8 per cent of the whole age group. To this should be added another 9,300 or 1·2 per cent in Direct Grant Schools, and 2·0 per cent in the recognized independent schools, which includes all the Public Schools, day and boarding. There were only a small number still remaining at age seventeen in the unrecognized independent schools, which mostly cater for the younger age-groups. To the above pupils, who were sixth formers in all our schools, must be added the numbers in full-time further education, including sandwich courses, which came to 26,600 representing another 3·4 per cent of the seventeen year age-group. Thus there were in all 16·6 per cent of the age-group in full-time education of any kind, and this amounted in 1964 to 101,000 boys and girls. This number is an indication of the total pool, apart from part-time students, provided in that year as potential entrants for all the major professional and managerial occupations. Many of them left school that year or the next and went direct into various forms of clerical and business employment. These were lost to higher education, although some will no doubt ultimately obtain important positions in their chosen occupations. It must also be remembered that the number of girls entering the professions of a technological, scientific and managerial nature is still very small, and there were only about 70,000 boys in the above total. Nevertheless we think it best to base our educational plans on the total of boys and girls, since there is an increasing demand for the services of women in occupations requiring specialist training. In any case it is desirable that girls should have equal opportunities with boys to carry their education as far as possible. A higher education for girls should never be said to be wasted even though the duties of family life subsequently take many of them away, temporarily or permanently, from their careers. It should also be noted that a large proportion of the girls in further education at seventeen will drop out within a year, and these are usually doing some form of commercial course. In addition it should be mentioned that a certain number of boys not in full-time further education at seventeen will come back into it later through various schemes of education within industry.

TABLE 3

Numbers of boys and girls aged 17 and the percentages of the age-group still in full-time education of various kinds in 1964 (*England and Wales*).

Type of school	*Numbers Boys and girls age 17 in 1961*	*% of age-group*
Maintained Schools (i.e. Grammar, Technical, Comprehensive, etc.)	75,500	9·8
Direct Grant Schools	9,300	1·2
Independent Schools		
Recognized	15,300	2·0 (*a*)
Unrecognized	1,750	·2
Further Education (including sandwich courses)	26,600	3·4
Total	101,000	16·6
Total in the age-group	776,000	100·0

(*a*) The figure for boys only is 2·6 per cent. Data from statistics of the Department of Education.

What do these figures tell us about our society and its education? To begin with this main source of recruitment for the higher educational levels appeared, even in 1964, as a rather rare *élite*. So far as schools are concerned the relative strength of the Independent and Direct Grant Schools should be noticed. Together they contain over one-quarter of the total number of seventeen year olds still at school. Except for the free-place holders in Direct Grant Schools these are all pupils in the private and fee-paying sector of our educational system, whose social background is likely to give them an additional advantage in entering occupations of high prestige. In the recent past the strength of the private sector was even greater, and the trend to stay on at school longer in the fully maintained schools is shown in the increasing proportion from year to year as given in Table 4. Since 1948 this percentage has increased at such a rate that it had about doubled by 1961, whereas the percentage in the private schools has been very nearly constant. The numbers in further education in 1948 were only 1·0 per cent of the age-group. These were already doubled in ten years, and are still increasing rapidly. The increase in the total percentage for all forms of education at seventeen plus are shown in column two of Table 4. These figures throw into perspective the Crowther Committee's target of 50 per cent of the seventeen-year-old age-group being in full-time education by 1980.

TABLE 4

Percentages of the 17 year-old age-group in full-time education in different years (England and Wales).

Year	*% in maintained schools*	*% in all forms of education*
1948	4·2	7·7
1956	5·5	10·0
1957	6·0	10·8
1958	6·6	12·0
1959	7·0	12·5
1960	7·6	13·3
1961	8·2	14·4
1962	8·6	15·0
1963	9·0	15·6
1964	9·8	16·6

These figures obviously change from year to year and the tables should be brought up to date by the reader by reference to the most recent report of the Ministry of Education. The potential output of students can then be compared with the number of places in universities and other institutions of higher education, and with the demands of industry and the Government for scientific man-power. It has been clear for some years that very great pressure for accommodation is going to be put on the school sixth forms and the universities by 1965. This is in the first place due to the bulge in the birth-rate which reached a peak in the births of 1946–48. This means that whereas 546,000 persons reached the age of seventeen in 1958 the numbers reaching this age by 1965 will be over 820,000. This represents an increase of around 50 per cent, and thus due to the bulge in the birth-rate alone the sixth forms would be expected to be half as large again as those of 1958. But the trend to stay on, both before and after 1958, has been steady and if this trend continues at the same rate the sixth forms of 1965 and the following years may be more that double those of 1958. Our readers at those future dates will know which of the estimates is nearer the facts.[1]

TABLE 5

Percentages of total age-group of boys and girls still in full-time education at age 17 in 1964 compared with the same pupils at age 14 in 1961 (England and Wales).

Type of school	*1961 Age 17 % age-group*		*1958 Age 14 % age-group*	
Maintained Schools				
Grammar (*a*)	7·8		16·5	
Technical (*b*)	·5	9·8	3·0	24·0
Comprehensive	·6		4·5	
Secondary Modern (*c*)	·9		65·0	
Direct Grant Schools	1·2		2·2	
Independent, recognized	2·0 (*d*)		4·3	
Independent, unrecognized	·2		2·0	
Further Education	3·4		·7	
Total	16·6		98·2	

(*a*) Plus Grammar streams in bilateral and multilateral.
(*b*) Plus Technical streams in bilateral and multilateral.
(*c*) Plus all-age and Secondary Schools other than above.
(*d*) The figure for boys only is 2·6 per cent.
All calculations from data in Reports of the Department of Education.

[1] A table showing the possible size of the sixth form population related to 1958 = 100 on the two assumptions of either the birth rate increase alone, or the 'bulge' plus the 'trend' is given in the *Crowther Report*, p. 231.

Obviously the demand for university places will increase along with the increase in the size of the sixth forms. What kind of limit can or should be placed on this expansion? We need to examine in the first place, to what extent there are hidden resources of ability in our population.

THE WASTAGE OF ABILITY

By comparing the distribution of the same pupils in educational institutions in 1961 with the distribution, already given, at age seventeen in 1964, some further social facts are revealed. The figures are given in Table 5, where this comparison is made. It will be seen that those in fully maintained selective schools at age fourteen (which would include by this age any early transfers from Secondary Modern Schools), amounted to 24·0 per cent of all the fourteen-year-olds. Of these 16·5 per cent were in Grammar Schools (or Grammar streams in other schools), 3·0 per cent were in Technical Schools (or Technical streams), and 4·5 per cent in Comprehensive Schools. For the total in selective secondary education the 2·2 per cent in Direct Grant Schools should really be added, but many of these were fee-payers who were not selected through the 11+ examination. Those in independent schools were also selected, but on a completely different basis. Only 65·0 per cent were in Secondary Modern (and all-age) schools, and this figure should be specially noticed since it is often stated that three-quarters or more of the nation's children are educated in such schools. What is often forgotten is the numbers in Technical Schools and the strength of the private sector at this age when 6·3 per cent were in private schools, both recognized and unrecognized.

Since 1958 when all independent schools had to be registered and submit to inspection by the coming into force of Part III of the Education Act of 1944, an accurate picture of the number and distribution of private pupils in England and Wales has been obtained for the first time. What is surprising is that in some local authority areas the percentage of pupils in private day schools reaches even higher figures, topped by over 15 per cent of the school population in the county of Surrey.[1] It is true

[1] A very interesting section on independent schools, with a map showing the distribution of day pupils, is given in the Ministry's Report *Education in 1958*, H.M.S.O., pp. 21–28.

that those in unrecognized schools become an insignificant number by the age of seventeen, as the table shows.

Let us now consider what proportion of children, chosen on the grounds of ability for a prolonged selective education, in fact stayed on until age seventeen. If we take boys only, to give the highest results, we find that the recognized independent schools showed the highest proportion staying on to the sixth form with an average figure of over 62 per cent. The Direct Grant Schools also retained 62 per cent of their boys, and the maintained Grammar Schools 53 per cent,[1] the figures for girls in all cases being lower. It is a clear sign of the trend to stay on that the proportion of boys doing so in the Grammar Schools reached this figure of 53 per cent by 1964 when it was only 36 per cent in 1958. The percentage staying on to age seventeen has been steadily increasing for many years.[2] The high rate of leaving from Technical Schools was because sixth form work was not well developed except in a few of these schools, and pupils often moved on to further education. The effect of Comprehensive Schools on staying on cannot be judged at all until the new ones develop their full sixth forms.

The greatest drop out between the ages of fourteen to seventeen is thus seen to occur from the ordinary Grammar Schools, and this was the problem which was examined by the report on *Early Leaving*.[3] While the total situation has changed since this report its importance still lies in the attempts it made to look at the causes underlying early leaving, and in doing so the light it threw on the problems of selection and the influence of social factors on achievement at school. It was the first example of a modern sociological approach being adopted at the request of a Minister of Education. The report concludes that the most potent factor as a cause of early leaving was the child's home background.[4] The pupils were classified in five social groups according to the occupations of their fathers. The sample studied was about 10,000. Fewest left, in proportion, whose fathers were in professional and managerial occupations, and most left whose fathers were unskilled workers, with a regular increase of leaving going down the status level through clerical, skilled and semi-skilled manual occupations. Further the children of

[1] These figures for boys only are separately calculated and cannot be derived from Table 5.

[2] See Table 32, p. 227 in the *Crowther Report*.

[3] Report of the Central Advisory Council for Education (England) on *Early Leaving*, H.M.S.O., 1954.

[4] Ibid., Chap. IX, paras. 160–64.

professional and managerial fathers tended to improve in academic performance and promise during their school life, while the children of working-class fathers tended to deteriorate in these same respects, regardless of performance on entry, i.e. for children of similar measured intelligence at the time of selection.

The boys and girls were divided into three equal selection groups, representing their order of merit at 11+. Thus the top selection group contained the best third at 11+, and the bottom selection group the worst third of the sample. To compare the performance on entry with later performance at ages sixteen to eighteen the pupils were classified according to their academic record. Those could be said to have 'done well' if they had taken at least two Advanced level passes in the G.C.E., or had left after obtaining five or more passes at Ordinary level. Those could be said to have 'done badly' if they only gained from none to two passes at 'O' level, or if they did not complete the course for it. It might be expected that some in the top third selected at 11+ would do badly, but it seems surprising that a quarter of them did. At the same time some 31 per cent of the bottom selection group did well. A large number of pupils shifted their positions in the academic order between the age of eleven and sixteen or eighteen, and an analysis of these pupils' achievements at the beginning and end of their Grammar School life was made in relation to their different home backgrounds.[1]

It was found that the deterioration from the best selection group at eleven was most common among the children of the unskilled and semi-skilled workers, while only a few of the professional and managerial class children reversed their promise at entry. However the improvement which raised pupils from the bottom selection group to the highest academic categories was most common in children of professional and managerial fathers. With unskilled workers' children in the bottom selection group it was found that to get one success in the Grammar School six others were admitted who failed.

The fact of early leaving and its relation to social background was shown even more clearly by the National Service Survey undertaken for the *Crowther Report*.[2] This studied a random sample of nearly 9,000

[1] See *Early Leaving*, Table K, p. 18.

[2] Report of Central Advisory Council (England), 15 to 18 (*Crowther Report*), 1959. Vol. I, pp. 8–10 and p. 119 for general reference, or Vol. II, Part 2, for details of the survey.

men who began their National Service between 1956 and 1958. The sample was spread over different intakes, and turned out to correspond well with the national distribution, according with the 1951 Census, with respect of domicile, schools attended and parental occupation. The age at which each man left school was known, and the general fact emerged that it was still the exception for the children of manual workers to stay at school beyond the statutory leaving age, since 78 per cent, 85 per cent and 92 per cent respectively of the sons of skilled, semi-skilled and unskilled workers' children left school at fifteen, as against 25 per cent for the professional and managerial group. But those who left school so promptly did not all do so because they lacked ability, and the most important result of this survey was the revelation of the latent ability in the population which hitherto has not shown itself in educational achievement. This was discovered as follows:

On entry to the service each recruit was given a battery of five objective tests covering reasoning, mechanical, arithmetical and verbal abilities. From the sum of the scores in all the tests each man was assigned to one of six ability groups. Group I comprised the top 10 per cent, Group 2 the next 20 per cent, and so on, until Group 6 held the bottom 10 per cent. Thus ability Group 1 would represent the most intelligent tenth of the school population, and it was surprising to find that 42 per cent of them had left school at sixteen or under.[1] Thus none of these potentially most valuable students attempted a six-form course, for which they were all likely to be capable. Now if we look at the social composition of these leavers we find that the lower their social status, the higher proportion left, and it was three times as likely for the son of a skilled worker to leave as for the son of a professional man. The important thing to stress is that these were all men of the kind of ability which ought to gain a university degree or its equivalent, which a large number from this group who continued their education did in fact gain. When we look at ability Group 2, many of whom gained places in selective schools, we find that nearly two-thirds left at fifteen, as soon as the law allowed them to, and that up to 87 per cent had left by a year later. A social analysis of the group again showed that the greatest loss was among the sons of manual workers.

There seems no doubt at all that whichever way one looks at the figures of this report, whether one takes the chances of entering a selec-

[1] Op. cit., Vol. I, Table 4, p. 9, and Vol. II, Table 1a, p. 118.

tive school, the chances of staying there, or the chances of doing well academically, they are all weighted against the children of the lower status groups. Some wastage of ability is evident at all social levels, but the most serious loss is among the sons of manual workers. It is true that their mean intelligence, as measured by tests, is less than that of the higher status groups. But this social distribution of measured intelligence is not the only factor at work. It is among those who show intelligence and who fail that we count the obvious losses. They win places to selective schools, and then so many leave and still fail to develop their potential ability. There are social factors closely associated with home background and cultural patterns in our society which influence the educational achievement of school children. These are among the social facts of education.

Why did they leave? This question was investigated by several questionnaire and interview methods described in both *Early Leaving* and the *Crowther Report*.[1] The results were conflicting from a quantitative point of view and cannot be relied on. But a general qualitative picture shows three main groups of reasons. The first were vocational and financial. There was a particular job available, the leaver was attracted by the good pay or positively wanted to be earning, and fairly often money was short at home. The second set of reasons can be called cultural, and related to group customs. Many just wanted their independence, or their friends were leaving, or they left at what they reckoned to be the end of the normal course, perhaps thinking 'O' level examination results were all they needed. Large numbers came from an environment where it was a rare thing to stay on at school until age seventeen or eighteen. Thirdly it was surprising how many inadequacies were felt to exist either in the school or in the pupil. A large number would openly state that they disliked school, or that they were not interested in the work. For a few the restraints of school life were irksome. A good number found school work too difficult, and some of the others who blamed the school may have been among those whose academic promise was poor or had deteriorated. Most did not regret leaving early, but those who did regret it gave as their main reasons either wishing to change to a job requiring more education, or that lack of education made their job more difficult.

From the above conclusions it can be seen that not only the influence

[1] *Early Leaving*, pp. 88–94. *Crowther Report*, Vol. II, pp. 22–33, and pp. 134–7.

of the home but the influence of the school must be considered. Research in four London Grammar Schools has shown[1] that for boys of equal I.Q. on entry the working-class boys had on the average less good academic records as they moved up the school, than the middle-class boys. What seems specially significant is that the working-class boys received lower ratings from their teachers on personality characteristics associated with success in work and school affairs, in short on 'being likely to profit' from a Grammar School education. An unpublished thesis[2] gives some evidence of the different reasons why boys within the *same* social class decided to leave school at the age of sixteen while others decided to stay on for the sixth-form course. This work confirmed that leavers tended to have worse home conditions, and poorly educated parents whose attitudes favoured early entry to employment, sometimes, but not always, for financial reasons. It was also found that the influence on the boys of experiences at school was considerable. Those who left tended to be less involved in the school life and in out-of-class activities. They thought the curriculum unsuitable for their interests and were often bored with school work. In brief they were not assimilated into a community in which the traditions and values were foreign to them. Again it looks as though the influence of the teachers and the social organization of the school needs to be further examined. Jean Floud has suggested that much more investigation is needed of the social determinants of educability, and that a major factor will be found in the interaction of homes and schools.[3] She asks to what extent failure may come because recruits for a selective education fail, because of their background, 'to give the teacher what he wants'. Children will differ in the extent to which they are able to respond to the tacit value assumptions and cultural expectations of their teachers and the school *ethos*.

Some light has already been thrown on this problem by case studies of a number of young men and women from working-class homes who passed through Grammar Schools.[4] It appeared that in many cases a

[1] A. H. Halsey and L. Gardner, *Brit. J. Sociol.*, IV, No. 1, 1953.

[2] J. F. Porter, 'A Sociological Study of the Cause of Early Leaving from Grammar Schools', M.A. Thesis, London, 1957.

[3] Jean Floud, 'Social Class Factors in Educational Achievement' being Chap. 4 in *Ability and Educational Opportunity*, 1962, O.E.C.D. obtainable through H.M.S.O.

[4] Brian Jackson and Dennis Marsden: *Education and the Working-Class*, 1962.

degree of tension, amounting sometimes to acute anxiety, developed because of the differing standards of home and school life. The school, with the best intentions, exerted a pressure on many of them to reject their working-class background and attach themselves to new middle-class values. An attitude of rejection can have unfortunate consequences. The problem for the school is how to blend what is still socially relevant in the old middle-class culture with the vitality, intelligence and strength of character surging up from less privileged origins. It is a problem of adaptation on both sides. One can readily understand that among early leavers and poor performers there must have been some who were unable to tolerate the conflicts involved. It was also surprising to what extent the parents of these scholarship boys felt out of touch and unable to communicate with the schools their children attended.

THE SOCIAL DEMAND FOR EDUCATION

There is every reason to believe that the social demand for a longer education will continue to increase. We have noted the trend to stay in full-time education until the ages of seventeen or eighteen, and hence become potential candidates for higher education, and we have given evidence to show that we are still losing boys and girls of good ability in their struggle through our complex and class-stratified educational system. A greater appreciation of the value of a longer education is spreading throughout all levels of society. This is specially noticeable among working-class parents who are more than ever before willing, and even anxious, to let their children stay on beyond the statutory leaving age. The pressure on our system to respond and adapt to the demand is being felt in three major directions which will now be considered.

(a) *The Universities and Higher Education*

The modern university not only continues its traditional functions as a community of scholars and a centre for the advancement of knowledge and research, but has also become a source of recruitment for the leading positions of power and influence in society. With the continuing and large increase in the professional and managerial classes the universities come to have more and more sociological significance. They are finding themselves more closely linked with specialized occupational interests, and are called upon to examine their place and change the direction of their influence in a world becoming more geared to material production. In fact, along with the newer institutions of higher learning, they are now becoming a crucial factor in the development of our national economy. This is a great change from the traditional functions of a university.[1] Until well into this century the ancient universities were able to remain relatively aloof from the economic problems of society. Originally part of the religious rather than the economic life they became, with the secularization of knowledge, agencies for transmitting a traditional culture and conserving the status of certain *élites*. They tended to resist the growth of industrialism, or the opening of their doors to other than gentlemen. Cardinal Newman in his *Idea of a University* in 1873 thought of it primarily as a place for the teaching of the liberal studies, and considered knowledge as its own end, not carrying any attribute of utility along with it. T. H. Huxley associated the university with progress in culture and not with increase in wealth. Yet the very development of knowledge, which the universities brought about, in particular through scientific research, was one of the chief factors which has moulded the modern world, and created the actual conditions for technical expansion and the greater need for highly skilled man-power. One effect of this is the great increase in the percentage of students in the faculties of science and technology and the decrease in the percentage in the arts faculties during the past twenty years.

This changed function of our universities faces them with an overwhelming demand for expansion. Total numbers in British universities reached 100,000 for the first time in 1958 and had doubled in twenty years. The percentage of women over the period was unchanged at about 24 per cent. Estimates of future numbers have been revised by the University Grants Committee more than once in recent years, and in 1962 the number of places hoped for by the Government by 1966–7 was 150,000, which (if the target is reached) will be only just sufficient to cater for the birth-rate bulge alone, assuming that the percentage of the age group entering the universities remains at around 4 per cent as it then was. But clearly this proportion of the age group going to the

[1] A. H. Halsey: 'The Changing Functions of Universities in Advanced Industrial Societies', *Harvard Ednl. Review*, Spring, 1960, reprinted in *Education, Economy and Society*. Or for a general treatment H. C. Dent: *Universities in Transition*, 1961. See also *The Year Book of Education*, 1959.

university is bound to increase with the increase in the proportion staying on in the sixth forms. The planned numbers of 170,000 for 1973–4 also seemed very inadequate to meet the real needs of an advanced industrial society. We send fewer students to the universities per million of the population than most other developed countries. No great relief to this pressure for places will be gained from the smaller age groups after the peak of the bulge has passed, since a new birth-rate bulge, crowding the Junior Schools in 1963, will press upon the Secondary Schools from 1968 onwards.

Of the changing social composition of the universities only a few facts are accurately known. It is reported by Jean Floud[1] that for the period 1937–46 only 1·7 per cent of boys of working-class origins entered the universities compared with 8·5 per cent from other social classes. In spite of the post-war increase in actual numbers her estimate, based on the *Crowther Report*, is that the percentage of working-class entrants was unchanged by 1957, while for boys from other families it had more than doubled. Kelsall[2] studied the admissions to universities in 1955, and found that students whose fathers were manual workers formed 28–30 per cent of the total university population, but only 9 per cent of the student population of Cambridge, and 13 per cent at Oxford, while there were 21 per cent at London and over 30 per cent at Leeds and similar 'redbrick' institutions. He also showed that the 'manual proportion' of the top selection groups entering Grammar Schools was 66 per cent, but that these had been reduced to 36 per cent when they passed out of the sixth form to enter universities, although all of them were of suitable ability as candidates. Again this offers evidence that the chances of getting to a university are still weighted against even the highly intelligent working-class boy.

We need not fear that intellectual standards will fall for some time to come provided full use is made of the abilities of our population. For example 16 per cent of any age group are estimated to have an I.Q. of 115 and above (with a standard deviation of 15). Whatever one may think of intelligence tests there is no doubt that many degrees, even with honours, have been obtained by students with I.Q.'s lower than

[1] 'Social Class Factors in Educational Achievement', op. cit.

[2] K. R. Kelsall: 'Applications for Admission to the Universities', *Report*, 1957. Surveys in 1961 under the direction of Mark Abrams showed a slight increase in working-class students at Oxford and London.

115, and that any who score higher than this should certainly be considered as capable of becoming university graduates.

The main conclusion to be drawn is that we must face the possibility of many more willing and able students coming forward than the capacity of our higher educational institutions is at present planned to deal with. What has been said about the universities equally applies to the colleges of advanced technology, and the teachers' training colleges. If provision is made for training, and strictly on this condition, it means that there need not be any serious concern about finding the necessary number of scientists and technologists for the next stage of expansion which the Government thinks the economy needs. There will also be enough to expand the supply of teachers. But when these targets are reached do we again limit our output of specialists to that particular *élite*. Will our 18 plus selection mean the rejection of many who would be capable of a higher education? This raises the question of whether our educational system should be so closely tied to occupational needs. It is desirable for each individual to have the education which best suits his capacities, whatever his later work in life turns out to be. The development of such a genuinely educative society calls for the continuous adaptation of our educational institutions to meet the needs of its members.

(b) *More Secondary Education*

The trend to stay on at school is not only to be found in the Grammar and Comprehensive Schools, there is also demand for a longer school life in Secondary Modern Schools. There is already a voluntary raising of the school-leaving age, and hence the increase of extended courses for a fifth year (age fifteen-sixteen) with the possibility of taking the G.C.E. or other examination at the end of it. The *Crowther Report* recommended that 'even on the voluntary system, most authorities . . . ought to provide for nearly *half* the fifteen year olds to stay in school by 1965', since they considered that it is insufficient provision and 'not lack of desire for more education that makes so many leave school at 15'.[1] However according to the *Crowther Report* even this in the end would not be enough, and they make a strong case for raising the school-leaving age to sixteen. There are one or two things which should be said about this from a sociological point of view.

[1] *15 to 18*, pp. 67–8.

Even with the raising of the leaving age it is unlikely that more than half, at most, of the pupils would be prepared for an external examination for some time to come. Among the rest are two groups of pupils which would cause particular concern. The first consists of the backward and immature boys and girls, who may be physically as well as mentally below average. Also, states the *Report*,[1] 'There is another, and probably larger group, who are physically quite as well developed as any boys or girls of their age, and who are straining at the leash to get out into the world.' These are later referred to as 'these reluctant pupils', and many of them contribute to the juvenile delinquency rate which reaches its peak in the last year at school, and is reduced during the first year at work. Many of them would also be among the one-fifth of the boys and one-quarter of the girls who, in the Social Survey, gave as the main reason why they left at the earliest possible moment the plain fact that they disliked school. If these two groups of pupils are to be kept at school for a further year it is certain that the schools must be prepared to extend their function of providing a protective, moral and even therapeutic environment for the adolescent, which is what the *Report* clearly expects them to do. Much is already being done for the backward and immature, and a greater provision of suitable courses and teachers for them is urgent. But for an added responsibility to be successfully undertaken for the tougher group we need some assurance that we can get more of the right sort of teachers who can deal with, and interest, these 'reluctant pupils', for whom the school is not at present a sufficiently attractive place. It must be recognized that we face a teenage problem, the resolution of which depends very much on establishing the right relationships between adults and adolescents. It is thus a matter of extreme importance that the ordinary school should become a community which is congenial, helpful and useful in developing young people, no longer children, who are passing through what, in our society, is a difficult period of growth. Therefore we must feel as sure as possible that the necessary changes in provision will be ready before compelling this unwilling section of youth to remain at school. Otherwise they will be under conditions which might harden their resentment, and increase their sense of rebellion against a society which appears not to understand them, and has failed to enlist their loyalty or co-operation. No doubt this change in the nature and social climate of schools can

[1] Op. cit., p. 93.

happen, in time, and they will become places where the pupils will *want to stay*. This would be the best way to raise the leaving age.

The chief argument in the national interest for the compulsory raising of the leaving age is the wastage of talent.

The *Report* concludes, 'It is unlikely that this waste of talent can be remedied within a reasonable period without compulsion, because leaving at 15 is so deeply embedded in certain parts of the social structure.'[1] Are we sure this is so unlikely in view of the appreciation of the value of education which is spreading in our society? For the abler pupils the problem might easily be solved by persuasion. There is the inducement of better jobs, and devices such as additional maintenance grants where necessary. Those with special abilities and still missing a higher education are easily identified, and could be specially encouraged. The Advisory Council discussed the idea of attracting a voluntary staying-on, and nine members, including the chairman, gave a minority view that exceptions should be permitted. A longer education, even to seventeen, can be held to be ultimately desirable for the great majority of people, but it may yet prove that the voluntary principle is the best means of attaining this end.

(c) *Technical Education*

The demand for technical education has been increasing rapidly in the early 1960's. We refer here to the training of top and middle-grade technicians below the level of the technologists. These have, in the past, mostly been educated by part-time courses in which there has been a shortage of time, a heavy failure rate, and lack of breadth. There has also been a need for a closer integration between schools and the system of further education. For example there has often been a gap of one year between leaving school and entering a Technical College. These failings are being remedied by the reorganization proposed by the White Paper *Better Opportunities in Technical Education*, 1961. The essential qualification for the high level technician is the Ordinary National Certificate (O.N.C.), and this is a stepping-stone for the best to proceed to higher qualifications still. The O.N.C. course is of two years' duration, and the standard for direct entry at sixteen is four passes in the G.C.E. at 'O' level. However, boys leaving school at fifteen can now take a diagnostic General Course for two years, and move on to the

[1] Op. cit., p. 453.

O.N.C. course if they do well enough. These General Courses are on a broad basis to cover groups of subjects. Two already in operation are for engineering subjects and for applied sciences, and new ones are planned. They also serve as a method of diagnosis for entry to other courses for technicians at a lower level than the O.N.C. Another way up is for a craft apprentice to be switched on to any type of technicians' course if he shows the ability to make the jump. The craft courses for the City and Guilds certificates have been reformed on an ordinary and advanced level.

The part-time basis of all these courses has always been a difficulty, and arrangements are being made to give more time to a day-release scheme, often in the form of continuous periods known as 'block release'. Ultimately the development of sandwich courses for the sixteen to eighteen age range will be a still more satisfactory method, particularly if they are 'college based', which means that students are paid for by the local education authority while at college, and paid by their employers while at work. Forging a closer link between the schools and technical education is the most important aspect of these reforms, which come directly as a result of the failure of the system to keep pace with the changing needs of industry. It is the intention of the White Paper that at whatever age the student leaves school he should be able to continue his education in a Technical College without a break. Thus the modern school, or middle-school, can in one sector work towards the Technical College just as the sixth form works towards the university. The provision of a ladder through all the various grades of technical courses also provides a route for the boy of ability, even if he leaves school early, which can lead to the highest qualifications in this field. It is likely that this alternative road through a creative and practical education in highly skilled work will become a major highway of the future, leading to satisfying, well-rewarded and important positions in the occupational structure.

CHAPTER VII

Educational Opportunity and Social Policy

The Social Factors in Selection—Equality of Opportunity—What Should be Our Policy?

IT has been shown in the last chapter that the education system acts as an agency of selection within the social structure. This selection acts not only as a determinant of the type of schooling received by the pupil, but also of the type of occupation he is likely to enter and hence his status in the social hierarchy. We now turn to an examination of the process of selection itself. Ever since the state system of Secondary Schools began after the Act of 1902 the authorities have been faced with two problems which were, 'What proportion of children to take into a selective Secondary School?' and, 'On what basis to select?' It cannot be said that they are yet solved. The coming of the free place system in 1907 was intended to provide an educational ladder whereby children were enabled to compete for scholarships on equal terms, regardless of their social background or early disadvantages. The concept of equal educational opportunity came to mean the equal right to a Grammar School place for all who had the necessary ability. But how could such ability be defined and measured? The development of intelligence tests seemed to provide the answer. They were used as part of the scholarship examination in Northumberland[1] in the early 1920's, and their use gradually spread to all the educational authorities. Standardized tests of English and Arithmetic were added later. In the present selection procedures (early 1960's), with a few exceptions, the greatest weight is still attached to intelligence and standardized tests, with

[1] These were the well-known tests prepared by Godfrey Thompson. Tests devised by Cyril Burt were used in Bradford in 1919, and experimentally by the London County Council about the same time.

teachers' estimates and school records being given more or less weight in different areas.[1]

THE SOCIAL FACTORS IN SELECTION

Capacity, on the average, to score on intelligence tests improves with social level, so a higher proportion of middle-class children would be expected to win places in selective schools than the proportion of working-class children. This effect is due to what is known as the social distribution of measured intelligence, which is a statement of the observed fact that the mean intelligence quotients (I.Q.'s) of the social status groups decrease from that of the children of the professional and managerial class as the highest to that of the children of unskilled workers as the lowest. There may be up to twenty points of I.Q. between the two extremes, according to the sample, and a typical figure for the higher mean would be I.Q. 112 to 113 and for the lower mean would be I.Q. 97. The causes of this social distribution of measured intelligence are complex and will be referred to later. It means that if selection were based solely on intelligence tests there would be different 'class chances' of winning a place. According to the figures quoted by Vernon[2] it would appear that those children with an I.Q. of 113 and above, that is in the top 20 per cent, are assumed to be likely to win a Grammar School place (or in an equivalent maintained school). The chances of a child coming into this group are between 1 in 10 to 1 in 5 for manual workers' children (according to their grade), and 1 in 3 to 2 in 3 for clerical and professional workers' children. Although the chances of getting a place are less for the children of manual workers than for middle-class children, yet the total number of places won by the former will be greater because of their much greater numbers in the population. In fact there is a greater number of children of very high intelligence in the skilled working-class than in any other social class group in England to-day. Thus if measured intelligence were the only factor operating in winning a place one would expect about 60 per cent of the Grammar School population to come from the manual classes and about 40 per cent from the non-manual classes. The fact that many

[1] For the history and present position of intelligence tests in selection see P. E. Vernon (Ed.): *Secondary School Selection*, 1957.

[2] Op. cit., p. 109–10.

Grammar Schools to-day have such a proportion of up to 60 per cent, and sometimes more, of their pupils with a working-class background is a measure of the change which has come over what is still fundamentally a middle-class institution.

It is worth looking back to appreciate how different things were earlier this century, and to get some understanding of the social and educational changes involved. The first clear picture on a national scale of the influence of parental status on educational provision was given by Jean Floud in her chapter of the volume on *Social Mobility*.[1] She showed that the opportunity for a child to obtain the much-sought-for prize—a Grammar School education—depended in the past much more closely on the status of his or her father. This meant that the percentage of pupils entering a Grammar School (before 1944) had always been very high from the professional classes and decreased steadily through the status groups until it reached a very low percentage for the children of unskilled workers. The figures given in this research are not only of historical interest, but form a useful base against which to measure the extent of recent changes. At the end of the period under review (ending in 1949) the chances of a working-class boy obtaining a Grammar School education had certainly improved, and were two and a half times better than for those born twenty years earlier. Nevertheless only about 10 per cent of boys from the lower three status groups entered Grammar Schools, although these three categories made up about 70 per cent of the sample population. This was of course before the operation of the 1944 Act had begun to have any effect. However, intelligence tests were well established in the process of selection; but on the one hand the high proportion of fee-paying places strengthened the chances of the middle-class, and on the other hand many free or special places offered to the poorer children were refused owing to economic difficulties. The often quoted example of extreme inequality comes from the researches of Gray and Moshinsky[2] who showed that in 1933–4 for a sample of London children with unusually high I.Q.'s of 130 and above only a fifth to a third of them obtained secondary (grammar) education if their social origins were working-class, while nearly all the children of the professional and business classes at this level of ability entered state

[1] Ibid., Chap. 5, 'The Educational Experience of the Adult Population as at July 1949'.

[2] In Hogben, L. *Political Arithmetic*, 1938.

selective or independent schools. Another study of the social influences bearing on secondary education earlier this century is by Dr. F. Campbell.[1] He followed the varying fortunes of the London Grammar Schools. Before providing new school places the London County Council analysed the social status of the district in terms of occupations, potential fee-payers and rateable value. It was expected that the demand for secondary education was likely to be higher in the richer boroughs, and, to quote an example, in 1926 the percentage of the population attending Grammar Schools in Lewisham was ten times that in Shoreditch. Indeed it was population changes rather that enlightened policy which brought about the greatest influx of working-class pupils into the London schools. The professional classes began to move out of London and live in the suburbs, and at the same time the spread of commercial and business houses reduced the number of local residents so that the total population of the County of London declined. Thus there was both a decline of those best able to pay fees, and an increase of the school places available to the working-class. At the same time the suburban Grammar Schools still remained predominantly middle-class in social composition. There followed the strange situation that no new Grammar Schools were opened in London for twenty-five years after 1928. Thus it can be seen how the study of demography throws light on educational provision.

Both the earlier situation and the developments since the 1944 Act have been greatly clarified by the publication of the researches of Floud, Halsey and Martin.[2] This provides the history of the social distribution of educational opportunity in two contrasting areas. These were south-west Hertfordshire, suburban, with some clean light industry and a high degree of prosperity in all classes, and Middlesbrough, a centre of heavy and dirty industry, with a fluctuating economic history and a large working-class population. The historical part of the work confirms (with local details for the areas studied) the results of the social mobility survey already quoted, so far as the chances of a Grammar School education are concerned. It shows most clearly the conditions under which the terms of competition turned against the working-class

[1] F. Campbell: *Eleven Plus and All That: The Grammar School in a Changing Society*, 1956.

[2] J. E. Floud, A. H. Halsey and F. M. Martin: *Social Class and Educational Opportunity*, 1956.

boy, when, for example, in times of economic depression the middle and lower-middle classes began to win an increased proportion of the number of free-places. However, with all the places open to competition after the 1944 Act, and with an improvement in the standard of living, the position changed. For the years 1952–3 the measured intelligence of the entrants was known, and the minimum I.Q. necessary for winning a Grammar School place was 114·2 in S.W. Hertfordshire, and 114·8 in Middlesbrough. The question arises of how far all boys with I.Q.'s above this minimum succeeded in getting a place, regardless of the social status to which they belonged. The social distribution of intelligence also being known it was possible to estimate the number of boys from each social class who were above the required level of intelligence for entry, and to find that these numbers corresponded very closely to the actual number of places awarded. Thus, assuming this measure of ability is a fair and suitable one, equal opportunity of access to these Grammar Schools had been obtained for boys of all social classes. The figures only relate to the areas studied, but these are different and by no means untypical. Thus the authors are confident enough to write: 'We may reasonably conclude that in very many, if not most, parts of the country the chances of children at a given level of ability entering Grammar Schools are no longer dependent on their social origins.'[1]

This is a most important conclusion, and yet the problem of providing equality of opportunity still remains. By a curious irony of events, at the same time as selection based on equating ability with measured intelligence is becoming more efficient, doubts are being thrown on the value of intelligence tests for this purpose. We have already seen from the report on *Early Leaving* how great are the fluctuations of performance in the Grammar School itself by children on the same level of ability on entry.[2] Also accounts are frequently given of the academic successes of Secondary Modern children rejected at the 11 + examinations. Indeed psychologists are generally agreed that in spite of the favourable comparison of intelligence tests with any other methods of selection, any accurate classification of children, either by level or type of ability, is not possible at eleven years of age.[3] We are here only concerned with

[1] Op. cit., p. 139.

[2] Refer back to p. 114.

[3] See Vernon, op. cit., Chap. 10, for a summary of the results of a survey of the evidence.

pointing out some of the social factors involved. The first most obvious point to make is that there are wide differences between different Education Authorities in the percentage intake to selective schools, so that the minimum I.Q. required for entry will vary from place to place. Thus it cannot be said there is equal opportunity *between* different areas, although in a particular area a child may have as good a chance as any other of equal measured intelligence. But class chances also vary within the *same* locality from year to year according to such factors as the size, and social and intellectual composition of the age-group, the number of places available and changes in the conditions of the examination.[1] Further, it has been reported for some London schools that among boys with identical intelligence test scores a higher proportion of middle-class boys were assigned to Grammar Schools, and a higher proportion of working-class boys to Secondary Modern Schools.[2] This only refers to borderline cases, and it is probable that children of lower economic status did relatively less well in the tests of attainment which also formed part of the selection procedure.

It is, of course, likely that there are social factors which influence performance in the intelligence tests themselves and this involves the unsettled problem of 'culture-free' tests. We do not yet know the nature and precise effect of the factors which may mask, retard or prevent the development of intelligence in working-class or any other children. Lower status children may be handicapped by the very use of language itself. This possibility has been investigated by Bernstein.[3] His work suggests that success in learning, and more fundamentally the growth of intelligence, may be closely related to the type of language learnt from earliest years. The working-class child is more likely to be restricted to a 'public' language, which serves him for descriptive rather than analytic concepts, whereas the middle-class child who equally has the use of this 'public' language can also make use of a more complex 'formal' language which facilitates verbal elaboration and the possi-

[1] These facts are demonstrated for a particular locality in a paper by Floud and Halsey, *Brit. J. Sociol.*, VIII, 1957.

[2] Hilda Himmelweit, Chap. 6, in *Social Mobility in Britain*, op. cit., who reports a research by Halsey and Gardner.

[3] Basil Bernstein: 'Some Sociological Determinants of Perception', *Brit. J. Sociol.*, IX, June 1958, reprinted with additions as Chap. 24, *Education, Economy and Society*, op. cit. Also 'Social Structure, Language and Learning', *Educational Research*, VII, June 1961.

bility of more abstract thought. Bernstein found that working-class youth did better on non-verbal than on verbal intelligence tests, and this difference was not found for a middle-class group. The relation to success in school can be seen when one realizes that the 'formal' language is very much the language of academic education at the secondary level. This fits in with the theory of Nisbet[1] that the well-known inverse relation of intelligence and family size is partly due to the lesser development of language through the more limited contacts of children with their parents in large families.

Some further evidence that there are social and environmental factors in selection, concerned with home circumstances and parental attitudes, has been provided by Jean Floud and her collaborators.[2] By comparing the home environments of successful and unsuccessful candidates in the selection examination it was found that in S.W. Hertfordshire, where there are good material standards at all social levels, children of parents with higher incomes or better houses were not necessarily those who gained the most places. In Middlesbrough, on the other hand, purely material conditions still had a marked effect. But in both areas the successes were associated with certain attitudes, preferences and educational standards of the parents, and with a small sized family. One investigation in working-class homes requires special comment. The homes of the children of manual workers were subjected to special scrutiny and classified as 'wholly favourable' when material conditions and parental attitudes were both rated highly, and 'wholly unfavourable' when the opposite was true. Clearly, as might be expected a markedly higher number of Grammar School places were obtained by children from the 'wholly favourable' group. There were in between homes favourable in one aspect only. In S.W. Hertfordshire the children of parents whose attitudes were 'favourable' gained, in spite of their poorer material conditions, as many successes as the 'wholly favourable' group. On the other hand the materially good homes with 'poor' parental attitudes gained only slightly more places than the 'wholly unfavourable' group. The rating of 'favourable' attitudes depended on such factors as interest in, and visits to, the child's primary school, stated preference for a

[1] John Nisbet, 'Family Environment and Intelligence', *Eugenics Review*, XLV 1953, also reprinted in *Education, Economy and Society*.

[2] Op. cit., Chap. 6, 'Social Factors in Selection for Grammar Schools'. See also Chap. 5.

Grammar School, and the wish for a long school life and/or further education. In Middlesbrough the effect of poor economic conditions was still marked, and there were higher proportions of semi-skilled and unskilled workers, but even here favourable parental attitudes had considerable influence, but not so much as in Hertfordshire.

In another research Elizabeth Frazer[1] showed that factors in the home influenced progress at school in a way which was to some extent independent of intelligence. That is to say that while favourable factors at home were correlated positively with the intelligence scores of the children, they were correlated even more positively with school progress as estimated by a criterion based on examination results. The environmental factors which contributed most to success at school were partly economic, partly motivational and partly emotional. Large families were again found to be a handicap. The most important material factor was income per head, and when this was low the child's work appeared to be adversely affected by this fact. The highest correlation was the negative effect of an abnormal or emotionally disturbed home background which could disrupt the school performance of even intelligent children. Parents' attitudes were shown to be the strongest motivational factor and good attitudes were associated with success at school.

Measured intelligence is still the key factor in scholastic success, and none of the researches quoted can tell us how far a particular I.Q. is due to an inherited component and how far it is due to the influences of the environment. The conditions of growth and learning obviously affect all our abilities, both physical and mental, and in this sense any ability can be said to be acquired. But it is acquired on the basis of different constitutional or innate qualities in different individuals. However, the observed differences between social classes in measured intelligence *may* be caused almost entirely by environmental factors. That this is the more likely interpretation of the facts is argued by Halsey.[2] He throws no doubt on the existence of innate differences of intelligence, but argues that these could be equally distributed among the social classes at birth, and that the subsequent differences in mean I.Q. are due to the different circumstances in the upbringing of the children. Any direct test of this

[1] Elizabeth Frazer: *Home Environment and the School*, 1959.

[2] A. H. Halsey: 'Genetics, Social Structure and Intelligence', *Brit. J. Sociol.*, Vol. IX, No. 1, 1958. See also the reply by J. Conway, 'The Inheritance of Intelligence and its Social Implications', *Brit. J. Statist. Psychol.*, Vol. II, No. 2, 1958.

hypothesis is extremely difficult, and all the sociologist can do at present is to study the relations which exist, at different times, between educability, achievement and environment, and state his results as empirical facts. The explanation of these facts will be complex because of the number of variables which are involved. Sufficient is already known to indicate that there are social factors influencing the educability and achievement of school children, which depend on membership of a particular social group within society. The evidence is strongest for the effects of home background on the length of school life and the scholastic progress of pupils over the age of eleven, as was shown in the report *Early Leaving* and the *Crowther Report*. But it is reasonable to infer that any social handicaps operating on the adolescent would already have affected his prospects in the Primary School, and thus had an influence at the point of selection. These social factors cannot be discovered only by the psychological investigations of individuals at any one time or place, but must be assessed in relation to the whole environment and past history of the child. They can be called the social facts of education, as distinct from, though related to, the individual psychological facts. Thus the measured intelligence of a pupil at a given time is a psychological fact peculiar to that individual (whatever may be the cause of it) whereas his chances of entry to the sixth form or a university is a social fact partly determined by the social status of his family group. That women tend to marry earlier than they used to is a social fact, and the statistics will show the chances of a woman being married at any given age, but that a particular young woman decides to marry is a fact about her individual behaviour. A social fact, in Durkheim's original use of the term, has its source not in the individual but in society, and it tends to bring pressure to bear upon the individual and influence his behaviour.[1] A person does not choose the social class into which he is born, and this may well exercise a constraining influence upon him if he struggles to change it. Children are not free to choose their own education in the first place, and it is certainly imposed upon them if they resist. We all of us struggle from time to time against the social facts which impinge upon our existence through the customs, habits, beliefs and ways of life in our society.

[1] See A. K. C. Ottaway: 'The Educational Sociology of Emile Durkheim', *Brit. J. Sociol.*, VI, No. 3, 1955, for the relevance of this topic to Durkheim's views on the social facts of education.

Social change always involves strain and adjustment to strain. The problems of social mobility in society at large must be expected to have their repercussions on the educational system.

EQUALITY OF OPPORTUNITY

We can now easily see that the concept of equality of educational opportunity, if it is taken to mean equal opportunity of access to the Grammar School or other selective school, has many drawbacks. It is useful to compare the concept of opportunity with that of chance. Equal opportunity to pass in a competitive test or win a prize of any kind in a game of skill can only mean giving every entrant a chance of success in accordance with his ability. Equal chances can only be given for equal abilities—unless the event is a pure lottery when the chances depend on the number of tickets held. The opportunity given is to have a fair chance of winning a place, provided you have the necessary ability, and regardless of irrelevant factors such as class, income, religion or early handicaps. The validity of the selection then entirely depends on the validity of the test. If we were satisfied with the efficiency of intelligence tests to predict future academic success then we might feel more happy about the present state of affairs. Nevertheless there are other objections. It is clear from the start that the majority of children will fail the test, so that for most of them equality of opportunity, in this context, is quite unreal. The only opportunity which is equal is the opportunity to put their names down to enter, but for many the chance of success is so remote that they do not even do this. It is rather like saying we all have an equal opportunity of buying a motor-car. This would only mean anything if we all had the minimum of money with which to buy one. Then we would have both an equal opportunity and an equal chance. So also opportunity to enter a Grammar School only means anything if the pupil is within reasonable range of the minimum I.Q. required. Now it is possible to imagine a state of affairs where everyone earned much more money, even enough for all to have the opportunity to buy a motor-car. But it is impossible for them all to be given enough intelligence for a higher education. The two things are different.

But let us return to the chances of entering a Grammar School. We have found that home background influences scholastic progress. Let us suppose that one boy at eleven years of age shows less ability than another, and let us assume that the cause of his lower ability is that social factors have been weighted against him more than against the other boy, so as to cause his chances of success to be less favourable than they *would otherwise have been.* Yet it is clear that at the time of the test all the influences which have determined the abilities of the boys have already happened. Also if he fails, he fails. He has had his opportunity of access to the Grammar School. We now have to face the question whether the existence of these adverse factors in a child's environment do not constitute inequality of opportunity of another kind, namely lack of opportunity to develop potential ability. A potential ability means an ability which can be fully developed if, and only if, certain conditions are fulfilled. In the example quoted if the apparently duller boy's home or other environment did not fulfil these necessary conditions, it would appear that he did not have the opportunity of developing his potential ability to the full. If some have suffered from the influences of their environment, then all that can be done for *them* is to try and improve their conditions in the future, and try to compensate in their present schools for the deficiencies of the past. But a more important task for the future is to study what changes in home, school and society can prevent the same deprivation and frustration happening to some children now being born. Consider a clever boy of fifteen who decides to leave school when he has the apparent opportunity to stay on. All the experiences which determined that decision have already happened. Many other boys just born, if they are brought up in similar conditions of home, school and society, will be just as likely to make the same decision. But the adverse social factors have been found to be due to parental attitudes, customs and traditions of different social status groups, economic conditions, the attitudes of school teachers, the social climate of schools and so on. It is a very difficult task to equalize social and cultural environments. This is why the social distribution of intelligence will remain for a long time with us. If the cause of the difference which it engenders is *inevitable*, and cannot be changed, then the opportunities can be said to be as equal as possible while the class-chances remain very different. It is impossible to equalize class-chances except in a classless society, but it seems possible and desirable, through certain realizable changes, to make them much more nearly equal. We can do least about those factors such as heredity and accident which are normally outside of our control. But let us consider by what means it may be possible to enable a child's success in school correspond more closely to his potential ability.

It might appear at first sight that changes in the educational system are easier to make than changes in the social and cultural background. Yet we know that each is dependent on the other, and that in the past education has tended to follow behind rather than take the lead in social change. It would seem that we know enough to say that our present educational and social systems have many defects if judged by their adequacy to develop every child's ability to the full. But it does not necessarily follow from our present knowledge which particular changes in the school system would be most effective in reducing the known inequalities and obvious wastage of ability. We could adopt yet a third sense of equality of opportunity and say that all can go to the same Secondary School regardless of everything, class, creed, colour, income —and ability. All would have an equal right of entry, a free ticket from eleven to eighteen, which is already true for the Primary School from five to eleven. This would be accepting the ideal of those Americans who say: 'It is the sacred right of the child to have a High School education.' Indeed by considering the variations in the chances of success due to the child's social class, the known difficulties of prognosis in the selection procedure, and the differential rate of academic progress within the schools, one might reasonably infer that some form of comprehensive education was the best solution. Our whole approach to the problem of educational opportunity has been based on the concept of a limited proportion of the population being capable of a higher education. This supposed supply of potentially able people has been referred to in such phrases as 'the pool of ability' with the implication that it can be exhausted or drained. Selection has been thought of in terms of giving a privileged education to the best of the pool. In the past the number of these has been consistently underestimated. But, more important, they are not of one kind, nor are they all with a high I.Q. In fact there is a whole range of human abilities both in degree and kind. Opportunities of different kinds to suit different individuals is what we need, and what we are at last beginning to get. Access to further education of all kinds will inevitably become more available if our society continues changing in its present direction. People will be educated in the way that fits them best. It will become less and less necessary to use the word 'equal' in connection with opportunity. There is no point in discussing whether the *right* opportunity for one person is 'equal' to the *right* opportunity for someone else. For a long time it is perfectly certain that our selection has not given the right opportunity to many thousands of children each year. There is more than one possible solution to the problem of selection, but whatever we do we must avoid preselection at the age of ten or eleven into separate types of education. This is not a means of achieving equality of opportunity in any sense at all.

This matter may be summed up as follows. We should no longer consider educational opportunity in the sense of opportunity to enter the Grammar School, or its equivalent. This is the wrong concept and an out-dated concept. This is opportunity which depends on possessing a particular kind of ability, and its fairness as a method of selection entirely depends on the prognostic value of the examination procedure. It is the kind of opportunity in which the chances of success are only for the minority and they cannot *possibly* be extended to all. We need to ensure that each child should have the opportunity to develop his own potential abilities and aptitudes, and to achieve the kind of education, and the position in life, for which he is best fitted. This kind of education can, in principle, be given to *all*. It is only a question of devoting human resources to the task. The maximum opportunity should be given to each person to acquire the highest operational intelligence of which he is capable. This is the opportunity to develop potential abilities over a period of time. At all stages in this cumulative process of development the conditions should be such that no child is handicapped unnecessarily by his social origins, nor rejected at a stage of education when the prediction of his future success in life is so manifestly uncertain. This is the sense in which equality of opportunity remains a really worth while and possible ideal.

WHAT SHOULD BE OUR POLICY?

(a) *Alternative Routes of Development*

There are several ways of solving the problems of selection. They all involve providing alternative routes to a higher education, and allowing for differentiation of training at some stage. This, indeed, is what is happening.

(i) First there is no doubt that the number of Comprehensive Schools will increase. Yet the full Comprehensive School from eleven to nineteen may not provide the best conditions for the development of *all* children. We do not yet know that it will be the best environment in which to nurture those children with the highest mental abilities and special talents. The size of a school alone can constitute problems of communication, and hinder the close relationship needed between the specialist teacher and his selected students, if they are to do their best work. Consideration of the special problems of the fifteen to nineteen age-groups leads one to ask whether it would not be better to carry on their education at this stage in a separate institution. This would have the additional advantage of being able to treat them as young adults, and no longer as school children. The plan, which originated in parts of Leicestershire, to have a Comprehensive School to the age of fourteen followed by transfer to the Grammar School was a move in this direction. It would be possible to have a scheme extending the common school to the age of fifteen or even sixteen, to be followed by Grammar and Technical Schools dealing with advanced courses only. This is the essence of a scheme proposed by Robin Pedley.[1] This is called the two-tier organization of secondary education. Moving on to the second stage could be left to the decision of the parents, as in Leicestershire, or some other system of selection could be adopted. We need some means of keeping clear the way forward for the best minds without in any way denying the right of everyone to the fullest opportunity. We have to combine the ideals of equality and the promotion of excellence.

(ii) With selection remaining early a method of correcting its errors is to have an end-on scheme of movement from the Secondary Modern School to the Grammar School sixth form. This is successfully worked by many authorities, and it means that pupils must stay in the Modern School and take their 'O' level G.C.E. as a result of which, if they do well enough, they will be able to rejoin their contemporaries in the Grammar School, who were separated from them at 11 +. This end-on scheme has advantages over earlier transfer. It enables the pupil to feel fully at home in one school community before moving on to the next, and it does not interrupt his course at an awkward time. It also prevents the Modern School from losing some of its best and most responsible members.

[1] Robin Pedley, *Comprehensive Education*, 1956.

(iii) The developments in technological and technical education have opened up many new routes to a longer education. At the higher level there are the Colleges of Advanced Technology and Regional Colleges which provide alternatives to the universities for entrants from schools, or take recruits direct from industry. Thus a boy who had left school early and gone into a good industrial firm might receive a first-class training through a sandwich course and get back into the main stream of higher education through a technological course or a university scholarship. At the lower levels moving on from Secondary Modern School to Technical College has been much facilitated by the improvements first announced in the White Paper of 1961.

These developments begin to give reality to the ideas of the *Crowther Report* (Chap. 35) described as 'The Alternative Road'. This is basically an alternative approach to knowledge, not primarily academic and yet not merely skill with the hands. It demands a creative practical education, where the word 'practical' is used in the sense of inventive and machine-minded. It is a training with broad scientific interest and not directly linked to any particular vocation. It demands new methods of teaching, which work from the concrete example to the general rule and place less stress on verbal concepts and more on understanding how something works. Young persons of ability whose minds fit better into this practical approach, and for whom the academic route is ineffective, have an increasing chance of continuing their education either in schools or in Technical Colleges up to the age of eighteen or beyond. Full-time courses are best, but for some a combination of employment with sandwich courses at the under eighteen stage is a suitable use of their talents.

(iv) New policies should be supported by teachers attempting to influence public opinion more directly. We should recommend the value of staying longer at school. We should emphasize to parents and to older pupils the importance of a good home background. We should attempt to make schools more attractive places to non-academic adolescents, and then the idea might grow among the young that school was not unpleasant and boring, and, in time, they would pass on this new attitude to their children. Let us share and transmit the new cultural pattern of happy school days. Finally we should encourage any political programme which plans to devote more resources to education, and which includes measures of social reform which are likely to improve bad home conditions, where these still exist. The financing of education has become a most important issue since the rising percentage of the national income which it requires makes it impossible for local authorities to meet the increased cost, which will have to be met in greater measure by the central government.

(b) *The Public Schools*

The English Public Schools represent the most obvious example of inequality of opportunity to be found in the whole of our social system. The Public Schools are fee-paying, independent, and socially selective. Most of the best are expensive boarding schools, but a few are day schools. In what follows we are not discussing Direct Grant Schools, nor all the schools qualifying by representation on the Headmaster's Conference, but the 100 or so 'top' schools through which the widespread reputation of the system has been established.[1]

The old pupils are distinguishable from other members of society by their social habits, and form a sub-culture within the upper and middle-classes to which they belong. They have a close relation to Oxford and Cambridge, and over 40 per cent of the students in those universities in 1955 came from *boarding* schools only, and more than half from all the Public Schools. The first criterion for entry is to be able to pay the fees. On the whole they cater for a wealthy class, but some poorer parents save, insure and make great sacrifices in order to enter their children. The statistically few scholarships available can only be gained, with rare exceptions, from attendance at Private Preparatory Schools catering for the same well-to-do middle-class.

An argument with regard to the right policy to adopt for the future of the Public Schools might be developed as follows.

(i) In our modern democracy every child should have the right to the best possible education for which he is suited. Assuming the Public Schools to be good schools educationally (and if *not* they should either be reformed or helped to disappear), they should be open to all who can profit by them. No school should be socially exclusive.

(ii) It follows that the chief qualification for entry should not be ability to pay. This implies some control over the buying and selling of education. It could be argued that a privileged education is not the kind of commodity, like a motor-car or a fur coat, which should be bought or

[1] For a good general account see Vivian Ogilvie, *The English Public School*, 1937.

sold at all (or alternatively that everyone should be enabled to buy it). However, the claim that parents who can afford it should be free to pay for the education they want for their child is a strong one. But there are restrictions, in the public interest, on what a man does with his money, and it can be recalled that people used to be able to buy commissions in the armed forces or seats in Parliament. The State has the right to define the conditions under which expenditure can be made, and this established principle could be applied to education by allowing schools to accept fee-payers provided they also accepted a representative quota of scholarship entrants from all social backgrounds. When maintained Grammar School fees were abolished in 1945 the freedom to pay for the education they wanted was denied to parents. At that level the principle of not being allowed to buy what was thought to be a better education for one's child was accepted. This in fact opened up the Grammar School to the working classes. If one person's child can go to a Grammar School on merit why not another's to a Public School on merit?

(iii) But, what kind of merit? This brings up again the whole vexed question of selection. On what grounds can the State justify such a large expenditure on one child and not on another? Who are 'specially fitted' for boarding schools? We must first decide that the special education of a selected group is compatible with our idea of democracy. If not, then we must reject the Public School idea altogether, since it *does* and inevitably *will* prepare an *élite* of some kind. If entry were thrown open it would still be accepted as a prize, or special privilege, to be won in a competition whether based on intellect, leadership, character or whatever, and even if it were decided by a lottery. Assuming we accept the Public Schools as good schools preparing a valuable though specialized product, then it should be possible to devise both a system of selection and finance.

(iv) But, as they are, are they really such good schools in relation to our present-day society? Much has been said of their virtues in character-training. The boy's character is developed in a closed, isolated, tribal, single-sexed community, where emphasis is exclusively on male friendships. A basic uniformity and conservatism, in the name of tradition, underlies the permitted eccentricities. It is no accident that too frequently the resulting personality is that of the unimaginative Englishman, lacking in emotional expression and full of deep feelings of aggression. They produce a type much admired in their own circle, and with an in-bred assumption of superiority. It is admitted that many admirable qualities of independence and loyalty, devotion to duty and public service, integrity and courage may also be developed; but there is always the risk of the less desirable character traits being encouraged by the very nature of a closed, authoritarian community.

Again, much has been said of their training for leadership. But many observers[1] think it is not the type of leadership suited to the modern world, whereas in the nineteenth century it was relevant to social needs. We do not need the separate training of a ruling class any more, as equality of opportunity permits the rise of leaders from any social class. In brief the social exclusiveness of the Public Schools is the worst of their disadvantages. They have a divisive influence in society, which tends to perpetuate and encourage class distinctions based on privilege and wealth.

(v) Integrating the Public Schools more closely with the national system, and throwing them more open, would be to destroy their special character, say the old Public School men. No doubt it would, but are they not in need of reform? It is true that our society would lose some of the benefits of the best in the old cultural tradition they represent. But this culture was only available to the few, and its loss may be one of the sacrifices which must be made for a new type of society. The value of the new, and more widespread, culture which is emerging can be even greater. This is not the place to suggest in detail a practical solution, but a general idea which is gathering support is to use them as Higher Grammar Schools for the fifteen to nineteen age range, converting the Direct Grant Schools to the same use, and creating new schools as necessary for the same purpose.[2] In time all the sixth formers in the country might, in this way, be given an equivalent education, as the second stage of a two-tier organization of secondary education. The present Public Schools could be maintained and financed by an Educational Trust attracting endowments and government aid. It would be possible still to allow private fee-payers, if this were desired, provided their numbers did not upset the socially representative nature of the intake.

[1] With regard to this and the following points see the comments of John Vaizey: chapter on 'Public Schools' in *The Establishment*, 1959, and C. A. R. Crosland, article in *Encounter*, No. 94, July 1961.

[2] John Vaizey, op. cit. has made this kind of proposal.

(c) *Social Facts and Value Judgments*

Finally in considering any educational policy we must be prepared to make explicit the value judgments upon which our actions and intentions are based. The analysis of social facts can tell us what is happening, and act as a check on the practical results of our policies. But we have to consider what ought to be done in the light of our broader social objectives and from our ideas of the kind of society we wish to live in. We must always be prepared to re-think our concept of the function of education in a developing society. It may be that our schools are too much under pressure from the needs of the national economy, and tied closer than they should be to particular ideas of academic success and occupational prestige. It may be that we are too ambitious for our children and try to decide too soon the way in which a child should go. Perhaps we should nourish his individual creativeness and interests, and then help him as he *leaves school* to find a further training, or an occupation, which suits the abilities he is then seen to have developed.

What is the *best* use of a child's abilities when at school? It is unfortunate that ability to pass an examination seems to be our only objective test. Being happy to stay at school longer—whatever you did—would perhaps be a better one. In a perfect State formal education would be freely open to all, at all levels, from the infant school to the university. There would be no selection but self-selection, and the criterion of success would be the willingness to stay on. Students would stop when they felt they could learn no more in that particular way, and seek other forms of learning through their vocation. This might be when they had reached their top academic performance or it might not. That some are more able than others would in any case show itself. There would still have to be some kind of examination at some time, but there *need be no intelligence tests*. The following quotation from E. M. Forster[1] catches the spirit of this Utopia.

'Most of us must get a job before thirty, or sponge on our relations, and many jobs can only be got by passing an exam. The pseudo-scholar often does well in examinations (real scholars are not much good), and even when he fails he appreciates their innate majesty. They are gateways to employment, they have power to ban and bless. . . . As long as learning is connected with earning, as long as certain jobs can

[1] *Aspects of the Novel*, p. 14.

only be reached through exams, so long must we take the examination system seriously. If another ladder to employment was contrived, much so-called education would disappear, and no one be a penny the stupider.'

A suitable ending to this chapter will be to repeat a paragraph which the author has written elsewhere.[1]

'In particular we need to examine the motives behind society's demands, and be aware of the assumptions being made. When the politician says, "We must make the best use of our man-power," we will note that "best" is a value word. When he continues, "We must double the productive power of the next generation," we will ask, "Why?" However desirable his ends it can be doubted whether the purpose of education is *only* to train skilled man-power for the national effort, or to meet the personnel needs of industry and commerce. From the point of view of economic efficiency it is easy to regard human ability as either a commodity or an investment. If the former one tries to get the most out of it before it is used up, and if the latter one expects a high return for one's money. If our politician adds to his imperative, "This is what we must do——" the hypothetical clause, "if we wish to keep Britain a great power", then we will ask, "What is the meaning of 'greatness' in a nation?" We have much evidence of the wastage of talent in our schools. We know it is a grave matter to waste potential scientists and technologists, but is it not as serious to waste potential artists and writers, and those specially sensitive to our historical traditions and cultural heritage? Clearly our future as a country depends on our productive capacity and the use we make of our citizens. But it would be a mistake to assume that all we need as human beings, or as hard working citizens, is the achievement of prosperity and a high standard of living, or even, in the last resort victory over our enemies. Sociological research, though it deals with the working of society itself, has its limitations. It can only tell us the best means of achieving the ends we desire. That is why changes in our educational and social structure must always be judged in relation to the principles of our moral and social philosophy.'

[1] A. K. C. Ottaway: 'Sociological Research and Educational Policy', *Researches and Studies*, No. 16, June 1957.

CHAPTER VIII

Social Interaction

The Concept of Social Role—Changes in Family Life—Outside Cultural Influences

We have seen how education depends on the culture and the sub-cultures of the society in which it takes place. We have put forward a theory to explain how the culture of a society comes to be what it is, and how it tends to change in relation to changing techniques and values. We have considered some of the social determinants of our own educational system during the past 100 years and taken a glimpse at the kind of society we now live in, and some of the problems it presents for the education of the next generation. We now turn to consider the methods by which our society transmits its culture patterns to the growing child. It is obvious that learning often takes place directly or indirectly in relation to another person or other people. What are the social situations which lead the individual to accept his culture?

The child grows through an enlarging circle of social interaction, which means that he becomes involved with more and more other people. Social interaction is the name given to any of the possible relations between persons in groups or between the groups themselves considered as social units. It is through social interaction that culture patterns are passed on.

The earliest social situation of the baby is with his mother. He then gradually becomes aware of all those who attend to him, and at some stage is said to 'know' his father, and to recognize the various relatives and friends who from time to time appear. He becomes a member of a family group, and it should be noted that there are many possible variations of this earliest group which can have different influences on the new member. There may already be another child or children—the word sibling is used to indicate either brother or sister. There may be one or more of the grandparents, or some other relative or friend of the parents, living in the household. There may be a nurse or maid or some other domestic helper not related to the family. The number of people living in the family household is obviously of considerable importance to the child's social contacts as he grows up. The tendency in our society is for the family group, in immediate contact with the child, to be very small.

As the young child learns to talk and to walk about on his own he makes friends and joins in play-groups either outside or inside the home. The family, and all groups in which the members have close and intimate relations, are known as *primary groups*. These groups are characterized by the frequency of what are sometimes called 'face-to-face' relationships, whereby the members all get to know each other well.

A wider circle of social interaction is entered when the child goes to school. This will probably be his first experience of a *secondary group* in which, as distinct from a primary group, he will not know all the members in close face-to-face association, although he will get to know his own class group in this way and other groups inside the school. Secondary groups also have some kind of permanent organization which persists while the membership changes. As the child gets older many other possibilities of group life open up before him. He may join informal gangs, hobby clubs, or social groups of a primary group character while still at the junior school stage, but it is in adolescence that organized youth clubs, sports clubs and neighbourhood groups of all kinds become of considerable importance to him.

All the time from quite early years the child belongs to the local community in which he is brought up, and is exposed in varying degrees to the outside cultural influences which operate upon him. We refer in particular to the cinema, the radio and the press, even when the press for him means only the 'comics'. These are national, and even international, influences, and they are now able to spread into the smallest village. Such influences on the child are largely a one-way process, but they are rightly included under the heading social interaction since they are susceptible to change and modification in response to the demands or criticism of the community. A summary of the main factors in social interaction is given in diagrammatic form in Figure IV.

THE CONCEPT OF SOCIAL ROLE

The general theory of the way in which the developing person learns to behave in his cultural group has been clarified by the terminology of 'status' and 'role' which is now employed by writers on this subject.[1]

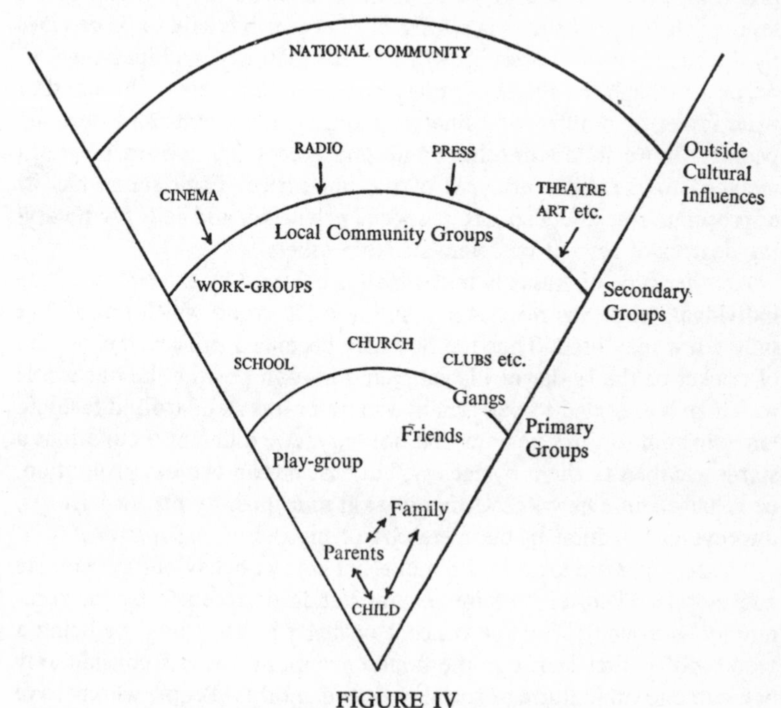

FIGURE IV
Diagram showing the enlarging circle of social interaction.

The term *status* means the position which the person occupies in his social group, and the term *role* indicates the behaviour which is expected of him as a person of that particular status. The roles the child has to

[1] See Ralph Linton: *The Study of Man*, Chap. VIII, and other writers on social anthropology.

play are of many different kinds, depending on the different statuses he occupies as he grows up. Some roles are of a general kind which a community assigns to all its members, for example those associated with sex and age. Little boys are expected to behave differently from little girls, and the expectation changes again as they become older. How often do we hear such statements as: 'You are a big boy now, and you are not expected to cry over little things like that', or 'You are a big girl now, and you are expected to be able to look after the baby.' Appropriate behaviour is also expected of the eldest and the youngest in the family. This type of status is a form of rank which is said to be *ascribed* by the society on the basis growth towards maturity, and it changes as we pass through the stages of young man or young woman, husband or wife, father or mother, and finally become grandparents and dear old people. Or we follow another route and accept the various positions assigned to the different types of the unmarried. Each status has its appropriate role and also has its special privileges, and calls forth varying degrees of respect or deference from others.

Another type of status is that which is *achieved* by the efforts of the individual, who thus reaches a position in his group which not all but only a few may hold. Thus the boy may become a prefect, the captain of cricket or the leader of his gang, and in each position he has a role which he is expected to perform in a more or less standardized fashion. On going out to work he finds that not only have different occupations a status ascribed to them by society, but that he can achieve promotion, or achieve some new knowledge or skill and thus, by his own efforts, improve his position in the hierarchy of his chosen occupation.

The social group also sets up models of correct behaviour in manners and morals. There are certain general standards accepted by the community as a whole, but the concept of being a 'good boy' or being a 'good girl' is first learnt in the family group, and varies considerably between one sub-culture or social class and another. People who behave as we do are said to be 'one of us', and there is great significance in the remark: 'I do not wish my children to mix with children like *that*.' Many parents make every effort to prevent their children getting in with 'bad' companions, as this will mean learning patterns of behaviour which are not approved of at home. It is a characteristic of our complex society that the customs associated with 'right' and 'wrong' behaviour known as the *mores*, show marked differences in different social groups.

This is partly due to the class stratification which still exists, and partly to the rapidly changing standards of valuation in our culture.

It should also be noted that appropriate forms of behaviour are also laid down to suit different social occasions, such as being at a wedding, or a formal meeting, or a party—and there are different kinds of party. The individual responds according to the situation, and to the role which he is called upon to play. So he becomes the bridegroom, or the best man, the chairman or the secretary, the host, the guest or the mixer of drinks.

The concept of social role can also be extended to group membership of all kinds. Even the small group has its local culture which assigns the behaviour expected of its members. Belonging to the group gives the feeling of 'we' as against the feeling of 'they' referring to those who belong to other groups. The term 'in-group' is sometimes used for the ones 'we' belong to, and the term 'out-group' for the various categories of 'they'. So a given person may at the same time be an Englishman, a resident of Leeds, a schoolmaster, a father of two, an active member of the N.U.T., a Buffalo, a church organist and the secretary of his Old Boys' Club, as well as belonging to a dozen other societies and associations. In each group, and according to his status, he will have a set of attitudes and a set of functions, which at times will overlap and at times be different. The same man may also dislike the French, be scornful of Cockneys, and have hated rivals among the Old Boys of a neighbouring school. These will all represent out-groups upon the members of which he has to some extent projected 'bad' qualities, which may not be rationally justified, but which serve to express an acquired group antagonism.

To return to the development of the growing child. In general it may be said that as his social interaction increases the child begins to learn his role in different groups, and to absorb the varied patterns of behaviour and attitude which are expected of him. His prestige and success in the group will depend on what the group values, and the extent to which he satisfies its requirements. The wishes and attitudes of the group are impressed upon the child by the degree of approval or disapproval which is given to his actions. Some system of rewards and punishments is the typical method of achieving conformity to the *mores*. Each group will have its various techniques of maintaining discipline, and of correcting those who break its rules. It is sufficient to point out here that the approval of the group is one of the strongest incentives to right behaviour, and being rejected by the group may act as a severe punishment.

The child may of course be a rebel and have a strong objection to conformity in a particular group. It may not be the right group for his interests and activities or he may have developed an emotional reaction against it. His happiness and perhaps his successful development may then depend on his leaving the disliked group, whenever this is possible, and joining another. The child who will not fit into *any* group has some more or less serious disturbance in his personality. This is not to say that rebels, as a general rule, are maladjusted in any bad sense. Some rebels become most valuable members of society. They may be specially gifted individuals who require all the encouragement possible to find a creative outlet for the energies which they have turned into opposition. Let us always remember that desirable changes in the culture may be initiated by those who do not exactly fit into it. To study in detail how and why some attitudes 'take' easily in an individual and others do not is an interesting problem for psychology.

It still remains true to say that the child learns the ways of his society, along with any desire to change them, by his growing concept of his role in social groups. The groups to which he can give his full loyalty, and in which he achieves status by his willing efforts, are of great significance to his development. We shall now apply this general theory to a selection of group situations.

Play-groups and Junior Groups

The play-group is a primary group and is usually of a transitory nature, the members quickly changing and coming together as the mood takes them. The activity of the game itself is usually the basis for the organization which need not persist when the game is finished. It is important to notice the highly imaginative nature of the play of children. A few will be bold robbers creeping behind the bushes, and a few others the pursuing cow-boys. One boy alone, possessing a peculiarly powerful model of an automatic rifle may represent a whole platoon of commandos. One thing to notice about these roles is the rapidity with which they change. Nevertheless social adjustment goes on for the child has to learn that he cannot always play the part which he wants, or that he must await his turn to be the most popular hero of the moment. More important still for the adult observer is to notice the kind of fantasy a given child most frequently employs. This can give a clue to his social development. For instance is he always the attacker or is he the one who withdraws in fear? It should also be noted with regard to sex roles that the play appropriate for boys is early differentiated from the play appropriate for girls. Boys are expected to play the 'tough' games and to adventure abroad, while girls are still playing with their dolls and anticipating their domestic roles.

More formalized groups will occur among pre-adolescents sometimes spontaneously organized by the children and sometimes stimulated by adults. Some may take the form of gangs but not usually of an anti-social nature at this age, though some may be. There are also types of secret society which may have a wave of popularity. These develop special rituals, passwords and codes, and may have elaborate initiation ceremonies and secret vows. Whatever form the group takes some social learning of the following kinds can be observed to take place:

(i) The struggle for leadership; the forms this takes and the shifting nature of this role.

(ii) The need for rules, and the training this gives in submitting the individual's wishes to the good of the group.

(iii) The expression of the child's need for some emotional response from his age mates.

(iv) The need to belong to a group is satisfied. The struggle to be accepted by the group is always present. According to the nature of the group the member may win approval by showing physical strength, by being good at a particular game, by making funny faces or performing as the group's clown or joker, by being more daring than others or being renowned for practical ingenuity.

(v) The opportunity given for co-operation and learning the team spirit.

(vi) The first experiences of inter-group opposition by rivalry with other groups, and possibly a conflict with the home over codes of behaviour learnt from the group. This latter reaction is more likely with the gang type of group which is mildly anti-social in its activities.

Adolescent Groups

It is in adolescence that the need develops for more organized groups which are conventionalized and have a more permanent purpose and tradition. There are many varieties of such groups from those organized by the boys and girls themselves to official Youth Clubs, connected with voluntary organizations, including the Churches, or under the control of the local state authority. The formal nature of the group is assured by the election or appointment of officers, committees and leaders of various activities, and the framing of a constitution and rules.[1] The Youth Club movement received fresh assistance and stimulus by State action after the Education Act of 1944, which recognized leisure time activities, for persons over compulsory school age as a *part of education* (clause 41b). In the same year the *McNair Report* recommended a great extension of the training of youth leaders. A new move forward began after the publication of the *Albemarle Report*, 1960, and a National College for the training of youth leaders was established at Leicester.

In whatever form it takes the value of social interaction to adolescents may be summarized by the following list of needs which group life may be expected to satisfy:

(i) The adolescent has a great need for social group experience, and to experiment with new relationships with others of his own age. It is a characteristic of adolescents to make close friendships, and to show strong loyalty to a group.

(ii) Some such group experiences can take place in family, school or work groups, but to all these groups he *must* belong. Voluntary membership of a group of a different kind fulfils other needs.

(iii) The need to mix with members of the opposite sex is not the least of these, but there are still some who prefer the single sexed club. Dances provide the commonest formal occasions for mixing the sexes.

(iv) A group or club of which a boy chooses to be a member can also be run by the members, and under such conditions serves as practice in democratic organization and procedure.

(v) As part of his growth towards maturity a young person learns to accept responsibility. This follows from accepting the status and the role which is assigned to him or achieved by him within his social group. Adolescents often seek definite tasks of social service, and value the opportunity to carry these out.

(vi) The adolescent needs adventure of a legitimate kind. Hence the popularity of groups for excursions, explorations and travel. Even a school or scout camp can provide its opportunities for adventure.

[1] For a general account see McAlister Brew: *Youth and Youth Groups*, 1957.

(vii) Adolescents learn a great deal from each other. Researches are tending to show that what is called the 'peer culture', in other words the community of the same age, has a very great influence on the individual. The standards of his group are often more readily accepted than the standards proposed by the adult. The discovery of the actual interests and opinions of adolescents is sometimes a surprise to adults when they turn out to be different from what the adults expected them to be. A recent research showed that in rating the value of incentives to good work and behaviour teachers thought that pupils responded best to rewards which showed adult approval, e.g. election to positions of authority, public praise or quiet appreciation by the teacher. These were the incentives which the pupils themselves rated lowest in effectiveness. In their opinion the most influential incentives were a favourable report for home, success in a test, and success in sport for their team or house.

The Social Role of Youth

The function of youth in society has been considered from a sociological point of view by Karl Mannheim in an excellent chapter of his *Diagnosis of Our Time.*[1] He points out that the co-operation of youth is all the more important in a changing and dynamic society. 'Youth belongs to those latent resources which every society has at its disposal and on the mobilization of which its vitality depends.' His general theory is that to make proper use of the energies of the young they must be given a more established function and integrated into the social life. Adolescents are in an 'outsider' position, on the fringe of society. They are the natural pioneers but the actions they take will depend on the use society makes of their energies. In other words they need to know the social roles which are appropriate to their status in the community. This is certainly a matter on which our society is still far too vague. On the one hand we treat our young people as still dependent and in need of protection, and on the other hand we call upon them to undertake responsibility. At one time we demand obedience, and at another we call for initiative. All this is closely related to the attitudes that adults expect towards authority, and some light on this problem is thrown by the concept of integrative behaviour which is discussed in Chapter IX.

[1] Chap. III. The Problem of Youth in Modern Society.

In many ways it can be said that as a society we are failing with our adolescents. This is not only shown by the increasing problem of delinquency, but by the exceptional stress and conflict to which young people are exposed and their uncertainty in the sphere of values. There has been much investigation and analysis of this problem.[1] It is not possible to summarize briefly all the factors involved. All we can say here is that the most recent research seems to point to the importance of the group culture in which the behaviour is learnt. 'Bad' or 'good' behaviour can only be understood in relation to the behaviour which is expected by the social group. So often we hear of delinquency being traced back to the influence of a 'bad' home. This means that this first intimate primary group, so essential for giving the necessary love and security to the child has broken down or is in hopeless conflict. Rejected or unhappy in the home the child seeks companionship elsewhere, and easily joins the anti-social or criminal gang if this opportunity comes his way. Such gangs show the intense power of small group loyalty, and are very difficult to deal with. What is certain is that it is impossible to take the individual from the bad home or gang and change him, in isolation, as an individual. All the evidence goes to show that his loyalty must be transferred to another group. The forces of group action are the most powerful means of re-education and reform. When a 'bad' culture makes a delinquent so a 'good' culture may cure him. He must learn to accept a different role, but a social role can only be played within a group. When his old group cannot be changed the difficulty with the delinquent is to find the new group towards which he will be willing to accept obligations and responsibilities.

It must be pointed out, however, that diagnosis, let alone cure, is by no means straightforward. The principal factors may still be found in individual reactions to emotional experiences relatively independent of the wider group culture. Again, when the causes of crime are traced back to the social environment, we are still left with the problem of why some individuals follow the bad example, while others reject it in apparently the same external circumstances. Society can help prevent the formation of delinquent gangs by providing sufficient *legitimate* opportunities for achieving success for the young, before they get confirmed in their

[1] T. R. Fyvel: *The Insecure Offenders*, 1961. Leslie Wilkins: *Delinquent Generations*, 1961, Home Office Report. Howard Jones: *Reluctant Rebels*, 1961.

feeling of unjust deprivation in a society which appears to them to have rejected them.[1]

Returning to the normal adolescent we can see many social factors which are tending to separate the generations, and to cause adults to find difficulty in understanding the teenagers.

(i) There has been a great increase in earnings of the young wage earners. Their spending power, in real terms, has about doubled in twenty years, and at a greater rate of expansion than that of adults.[2] This high spending power gains the prestige which in our society goes with the things that money can buy, and it dictates the nature and prosperity of those types of trade which are out to capture the teenage market.

(ii) As a result there has developed a teenage culture, shown by their own form of 'expressionism'. Some of their biggest spending is on clothes and shoes, and they have their own distinctive dress habits. There is a new type of casual, informal, gay, working-class elegance. They meet in coffee-bars and dance halls. They like 'pop' records, which are well reproduced, and have an enormous sale. Most take soft drinks, although the consumption of alcohol among them is increasing. The mass media glorify the teenagers, whose heroes are popular entertainers, games players and racing motorists.

(iii) New techniques of work in a rapidly changing technical age favour the young workers, who tend to lose respect for their fathers, and the older generation, who lack the modern 'know-how'.

(iv) The separation of home and work, especially with a distance to travel between the two, reduces the ties and influence of family life. Values are then obtained from the peer group or workmates rather than the parents. The young person is thus faced with conflicting roles. He still wishes to behave as a good son, while he is becoming conscious of a new loyalty to a teenage group with its own standards and a different way of life.

(v) Adult society has to some extent lost its nerve *vis-à-vis* the young. Adults who disapprove often feel guilty at the same time. Are we clear about what we, as a society, expect of our youth? If they are not given

[1] The psychology of the delinquent is often vividly illustrated in contemporary novels, such as Graham Green: *Brighton Rock*, Brendan Behan: *Borstal Boy*, Colin MacInnes: *Absolute Beginners*, Alan Sillitoe: *Saturday Night and Sunday Morning*, and *The Loneliness of a Long Distance Runner*.

[2] See Mark Abrams: *Teenage Consumer Spending*, 1961.

a clear social role to play how can we blame them for not being responsible in enacting it? Feeling insecure themselves adults hesitate to take the lead.

The energies of youth need to be integrated with the whole of society, and it is encumbent upon the teacher to try and bridge the gap in understanding which is liable to open before him. Authority which is imposed from above, which always claims to know what is right, is becoming more and more suspect. A change is taking place in attitudes to authority and morality; young people are asking for help in finding their own beliefs, and are less willing to accept them ready made. It is healthy for them to seek independence. They will accept the authority of the teacher who can communicate with them, who consults them, and offers them, freely, a share in responsibility.

CHANGES IN FAMILY LIFE

The family is the first and the most intimate group to which the child belongs. We are here concerned with the present-day nature of the family as a social unit, and not with the psychological reactions within it. We have already referred to the tendency in modern society for the family to become a small and intensive group. This is only one of the many changes which have taken place since the middle of the nineteenth century. No clearer result of the development of our industrial, urban and machine-run civilization can be seen than the changes it has caused in family life. The functions of the family have been classified in various ways. We have selected seven of its more important functions and each one will be examined to note the changes which are taking place.

(i) *Giving and receiving affection*

The value of the family circle as a source of love and security cannot be over-emphasized. This continues to be a major function of home life, and is the least changed. It is true there has been a great increase in the number of divorces. The census figures show that compared with 1931 there were over five times as many divorced people per thousand of the population in 1951. The fact that there were fewer divorces in the past does not necessarily mean that people were living more happily together. Affection may have gone and divorce not followed because of the social conventions and the stricter law of the time. We can say, however, that where lack of affection exists parents are showing it more openly to-day by seeking divorce. The relation between the parents and the child is inevitably changed by divorce, and the loss of love from one parent or the other can be of great seriousness to the child. But it is not true to say that the divorce is always more harmful to the children than the family group living together in constant discord and an atmosphere lacking in love. Once the family ties of affection are broken the harm has already begun.

(ii) *The function of reproduction*

Inevitably a family unit must accompany the birth of children. There has been a marked decline in the size of the family in England during the past 100 years. The birth-rate, which reached a peak of 35 per 1,000 in the 1870's, steadily dropped to 15 in the period 1933–9. It increased during the war years after 1940, and this gave rise to the first 'bulge' in the birth-rate. It fell back a little in the early 1950's and then began to rise again to cause a second 'bulge'. The net reproduction rate, and not the crude birth-rate, is the important figure. This measures whether the population is replacing itself. A reproduction rate of unity 1·0, indicates exact replacement and it was just above this figure for England in 1946. However it had dropped as far as ·75 in 1933, and if this rate had been maintained it would have meant the decline of the population by a quarter in a generation. For comparison let us remember the reproduction rate of approximately 1·5 in the Soviet Union, which means that the population is increasing by half as much again in each generation.

Until recently there had been a marked differential fertility in England, whereby the people with smaller incomes and less education were having more children than the better off. There is evidence that this is levelling up, which would be expected as the standard of living and education improves among the working classes. The motives behind the voluntary restriction in the size of family have great sociological interest, especially as it began among the wealthier classes. The decline of births spreading down the classes is thought to be in some way associated with our modern way of life, and the universal desire to maintain or achieve a high standard of living.[1] It cannot be unconnected with the emancipation of women, or with the desire of both parents to have more

[1] We have already pointed out the effect on the birth-rate of the cost of education and the desire to maintain or achieve social status, see p. 71.

freedom than the care of a large family allows. The question is clearly one involving many variables. The fact remains that opinion surveys show that for most people the size of an ideal family is considered to be two or three children, and the higher percentage favour two.

(iii) *Economic functions*

The family is now rarely the unit of production to supply its own needs. Agencies outside the home have gradually taken over more and more economic functions, such as the making of clothes and furnishings, laundering and baking, which used to go on in the home, and the growing of food in the garden. Even ordinary cooking has been partly replaced by the enormous increase of canned, preserved and frozen foodstuffs.

Employment has become separated from the family circle. Children to-day rarely see their father at work and may not even know any detail of his occupation. Indeed he may have so far to travel to work that they see very little of him at home. Nor are the boys so likely to be trained in the father's occupation, and they more often get employment away from their home town. The increasing mobility of labour has been a factor in breaking up the family group. While children do not earn so early and contribute to the family income, they tend to earn much more when they begin and can become self-supporting sooner.

Women have tended to take more paid employment outside the home, and this has changed the whole pattern of family life. The employment of girls and young unmarried women takes a helper from the home, and also gives much more freedom to the young woman who may want to live away from home before marriage. The absence of the mother from the home when there are young children is the most drastic change of all in the traditional pattern. It is true that in certain industries, such as textiles, this change began early in the nineteenth century, when work that had been undertaken at home was transferred to the factories. It is the increasing absence from home due to the rapid industrialization of this century, and stimulated by war-work for women, which is the important change. The employment of married women doubled in twenty years and reached a figure of over 4 million by 1961.

(iv) *The protective function*

The family used to take full responsibility for caring for its members in adversity. Now the state looks after health, unemployment, old age, and provides all forms of social security. This has brought untold benefits to the poorer classes, and has been of much positive value to the nation, but it is nevertheless a change to be recorded. The family still gives the protection of affection, which leads to the kind of emotional security which cannot so far be acquired in any other way.

(v) *Education*

Education is also being taken over more and more by the state. The tendency has been to raise the school-leaving age at one end and to lower the age of entry at the other. The discussion of this trend, and the frequent complaint that the responsibility for the children is being taken from the parents, is familiar enough to require no elaboration.

(vi) *Recreation and relaxation*

While the home used to provide the chief source of leisure occupations these have largely been transferred to outside agencies many of them commercial. Children and parents spend less of their leisure at home. The increase of sport, as a spectacle, the ease of transport, the cult of the outdoor life, the desire to travel, the vast growth of the entertainment industry, the increased spending power of the people, the independence of women and the greater freedom of youth, have all contributed to this change. The trend away from or towards the home tends to fluctuate with new inventions. The cinema takes people out, but television tends to keep them at home. But these small effects do not last and are not the main determining factors, which will depend on what enduring satisfactions the home can offer as children become more free to choose.

(vii) *Status and role in the family*

Each member of a family and kinship group usually has a clearly defined status and each status has its role. The English family has been based on the authority of the father dependent on male dominance and filial obedience to the parents. Various degrees of respect were accorded to the older members. All this is changing. Position in the family has become of less importance, except for the psychological effect of the order of birth among the children. There is less respect for the older members. Relatives are scattered and have less influence on each other.

The hierarchy of male dominance has been challenged and the father tends to exert less authority. (We have seen how in the United States the roles of father and mother have in some respects been reversed, pp. 30–32.) This is mainly the result of the changing status of women in the community. They have achieved full citizenship, entry to careers on almost an equal basis with men, economic independence, and social freedoms unheard of fifty years ago. They have also achieved the distinction of being one of the major problems of the modern world. Women in our society have become very uncertain of their proper role. While they are adept at changing roles too many changes are apt to be confusing. There are not only the varied psychological consequences of their wish to behave as men in some respects and as women in others, but conflicts arising from the real and practical choices which they have to make between marriage or a career, and between having children or having greater freedom and a better standard of living. Human relations within the family are thus in a stage of transition; people are uncertain what responsibilities are expected of them, and their attitudes reflect the role conflicts between male and female which also occur in the community around them.

All these changes indicate that there is to-day in England no stable pattern of family life. We have already referred to the sub-cultures within our society, each of which has different ways of bringing up children. Research into these different techniques of child-rearing is only just beginning, but our existing knowledge of the relations between culture and personality leads us to expect that it will yield significant results. In general the changes outlined can be said to have had both good and bad effects. On the one hand there is greater freedom for children to-day, and an increased democratization of the family, and on the other hand there is less parental control when it is needed, and less social interaction in the home. The school is often called upon to make up for the deficiencies in the home. Yet it is not of much use to blame the parents because they usually need help too, and may not know what to do. Many parents are neglectful not because they are bad characters, but because they do not realize the importance of spending more time with their children.

It is useless to deplore inevitable changes, and perhaps unwise to condemn any new pattern of family life which may be emerging until it is more clearly seen. More independence for children may well be a good thing, once basic security is assured, for the small family can lead to too intense an emotional bond when it remains isolated. Some more extensive grouping of families, if it were possible, with a wider spreading out of love and responsibility for children might be a better arrangement. We do not yet know what will suit our changing culture best. What we do see is a change from the patriarchal model to a marriage relationship thought of as an equal partnership; with different roles for the husband and wife but basic equality of status. Authoritarian methods in the family are also giving way to a more democratic pattern of behaviour. Many people are apprehensive about what is called the break-down of family life. This is to take a static conception of the family. We may be seeing necessary changes in the older pattern as family life becomes adapted to the new circumstances of our culture. This adaptation is a task which greater knowledge of what is really essential for good human relations will help us to perform successfully.

Parent-Teacher Relations

We cannot leave this topic of the family without referring to the importance of closer relations between the home and the school. Since the school is tending to share more and more in the functions of the family it becomes more necessary to provide frequent opportunities for contacts between parents and teachers. The child is, so to speak, sandwiched between the parents and the teachers, and all are involved in a complex of relationships. The early years in the home have already determined many attitudes and modes of behaviour before the child goes to school at all. The teacher must reckon that the child brings his parents to school with him, in the sense that their teaching is always present in his mind and conscience. The effects of a conflict between the teaching of the home and the school may be the root of a child's problem, and a cause of his difficulties over discipline. The teacher cannot avoid his position as a parent figure or substitute. A new situation which develops at home, a change in affection between the parents or towards the child, a change in the relation with his brother or sister, any of these can affect the child. A change of teacher also may reactivate a child's emotional experiences. It often happens that when a teacher comes to know the parents only a little he begins to understand more fully the meaning of the child's behaviour.

However difficult it may be in practice, teachers and parents should be *convinced* of the value of these contacts. This means meeting with the father too, although he may be available only in the evenings. The value of all this is accepted in theory, and lip service is paid to parent-teacher associations, but so often they do not really work in practice because teachers (apart from being overworked already), are not emotionally convinced inside themselves that it is worth the trouble. The best kind of co-operation comes if parents also know what goes on inside the school. Ideally the parent should be welcome in the school during its day-to-day life, and whenever 'open days' for visitors are possible these are appreciated by parents and are worth the complications to the school which they may cause. In any case demonstrations of various types of school work, and more important an *explanation* of the methods employed are possible as subjects for parents' meetings.

There are inevitable tensions between the roles of parents and teachers, and in the long run they can only be eased by better knowledge of each other's aims and expectations. It will be a great step forward in educational progress when methods are found to bring about closer relations between the home and the school, and to link both with the educative influences of the whole community.

OUTSIDE CULTURAL INFLUENCES

We have so far in this chapter discussed the influence of group membership in transmitting the culture of our society. The most important influences external to the small group, but which impinge on all members of the community in some way, are the mass media of communication. These consist of the cinema, the radio—especially television—and the reading of popular newspapers and magazines. All these media reflect the culture of the mass industrial society in which we live. They show the good and the bad. All the features of our life, the interests and tastes of the people, are being broadcast more and more widely for all to see and hear. By and large what the majority accept as suitable for their entertainment and for the occupation of their leisure is being given to them.

The power of the printed word is one of the oldest influences on the mind, and the capacity of the modern printing press and the almost universal literacy in England means that a great wealth of reading material is available to all. But what do people read? Only about half of the adult population read *books* at all. Of this half most read stories of detection and mystery, popular novels and light fiction, and only a few read serious fiction or non-fiction books at all frequently. But nearly everyone reads newspapers and magazines. Over 45 per cent read the *News of the World*, and the *Daily Express* and *Daily Mirror* are each said to be read by a quarter of the population. This can be compared with the 2·5 per cent who read *The Times*. It is claimed by *The Reader's Digest* that 60 million people read it throughout the world.

Among children the reading of comics is almost universal. It is quite common to find an average of up to three comics each per week read by children between nine and fifteen years of age. The popularity of *Beano*, *Dandy*, *Knock-Out*, *Eagle*, *Girl* and the rest is well known. Yet the fairly wide survey reported in *Out of School* showed that 50 per cent of children under fifteen had no library ticket. The increasing concern over the influence of comics is largely due to the spread of certain types, mostly from America and usually produced for adults, which often portray brutality, sadism, and sexual suggestiveness. There are also many other cheap magazines available with stories full of horror and violence. There is no doubt a need for much investigation into the influence of all this kind of literature, pictorial and otherwise, on children. The influence of mass-produced popular literature (and entertainment) on the standards and tastes of the working-class has been described in detail by Richard Hoggart in his book *The Uses of Literacy*.

The frequent discussion of the influence of the cinema on children may be taken as typical of the whole problem of the mass dissemination of cultural values and habits. A great deal of research has been devoted to this subject, but the essential question of what harm the cinema does remains unanswered. The problem is well put by the opening words of the Report of the Departmental Commitee on *Children and the Cinema*, 1950. 'Nine out of ten children of school age in Great Britain go to the cinema from time to time and more than half of them do so at least once a week. What children see there, what they think about it, and what effect it has upon them are matters about which those who desire the happiness and welfare of children are bound to ask questions. And it must be admitted that they await the answers with some anxiety.' Most people would admit that the cinema must have *some* influence, and the anxiety that its influence is often bad certainly exists. Yet it is extremely difficult to find any clear evidence of its effects, and easy for confident opinions to be expressed without any experimental basis. Some of the facts established by various researches (and they do not tell us much), may be listed briefly as follows:

(i) That children go to the cinema frequently. It is astonishing how many investigations spend time on establishing this obvious fact. Changes of attendance over a period of time have significance as measures of trends. For instance the attendance of children at the cinema increased up to the coming of television, and subsequently decreased.

(ii) That children have preference for certain kinds of films. As would be expected the most popular with boys under fifteen concern cow-boys and gangsters, detectives, animals and comedians. With girls the order of preference changes, and musical films with dancing and technicolor costume dramas come high on their list. Young children are not very conscious of the plot, and often see a film as a series of incidents. They tend to like murders and dislike 'silly love scenes'.

(iii) That children imitate the film stars. They copy their mannerisms, dress, hair styles, attitudes and methods of speech. Juniors re-enact scenes and impersonate characters in their play. Adolescents bring new social habits into their everyday lives, and find some guide to behaviour and conduct from observing the actors' behaviour in social situations. The children naturally have their favourite film stars.

(iv) That strong emotions are aroused by the films. This also would be expected, but the question is what kind of emotions and what results do they have? The most concrete evidence here is that children can be really frightened with bad symptoms resulting, e.g. nightmares, hating to be alone and fear of the dark. At the same time many like 'thrills' and appear to be unharmed by them. Much seems to depend on whether the child accepts the film just like a story and something that cannot happen in real life, or whether he fears it as something which could in fact happen to him. The child who is already full of fears is also likely to have them exaggerated by the cinema.

(v) It would appear that factual knowledge of some value can be learnt from the commercial films. While there is some doubt over how much children remember, the amount of information acquired over a period is fairly high, even if not always reliable.

(vi) Attendance at the cinema has *not* been shown to be a significant cause of delinquency. The memorandum of the Magistrates' Association to the Home Office Committee already referred to states the view that

'Investigations have never found any correlation between delinquency and attending the cinema; anti-social conduct arises from deeper causes than the imitation of things done on the screen; and emotional unhappiness is the most potent cause of juvenile delinquency.' There is other evidence that the kind of person who would be a delinquent anyway may get his ideas from the films. The magistrates even find them of positive value since as they say, 'the cinema keeps boys out of mischief, men out of public houses, and girls from the streets'.

As might be expected it is equally difficult to be definite about the effects of television. Two major investigations can be quoted, one for English and the other for American children, which agree in their main conclusions.[1] The final picture that emerges is that the influence of television is much less colourful and dramatic than popular opinion is inclined to suppose. One definite conclusion would appear to be that the time spent on viewing by the more intelligent child is less than by the duller child, and it has less effects on the brighter children, who in adolescence turn more easily to other interests. As would be expected the Westerns, detective series, crime and adventure playlets are among the most popular programmes. In spite of the admitted frequency of scenes of violence it cannot be shown that these have any substantial harmful effect on children. This means there is no way of *measuring* the effects, but it does not say they are good, and it might indicate that in life as it is now lived children's sensibilities are blunted by the many influences that lead them to accept a diet of horrors, assault and murder as normal in our society.

The main point we wish to make is that whatever the factual evidence may be about the influence of all the mass media, we still have to make a value judgment about the facts and decide what we consider good and what we consider bad. For example it is a fact that adolescents sometimes imitate the behaviour they see on the screen. As a result they tend to acquire new standards of dress and manners which may or may not be thought better than their previous ones. The fact that girls copy popular stars may tend to improve their looks or the reverse. Using make-up, looking smart and having fun are things which the mass media encourage. Some will think these good and some will think them bad. Again, urban middle-class values and a high standard of life are

[1] H. T. Himmelweit and A. N. Oppenheim: *Television and the Child*, 1958. Wilbur Schramm *et al*: *Television in the Lives of Our Children*, 1961.

predominant. People eat in expensive restaurants, have fast motor-cars, frequently change their clothes and are more handsome and richer than we are. This may be enjoyed as what is called 'escapism' or 'fantasy', but suppose it makes us discontented with our present conditions? Some may think this a good thing. Are we not right to look forward to a better life than we have to-day in our miserable drab cities?

We must not forget as well that a large number of documentary, informative and broadly cultural programmes are produced. In increasing measure television—both I.T.V. as well as B.B.C.—brings us closer to the triumphs of science and the lives of the great throughout history, and introduces us to the famous themes of literature and drama. No doubt from the point of view of the well-educated minority the level of popular taste in entertainment is rather poor. Yet the continued existence of the Third Programme (and Network Three) is evidence of the wish to cater for a minority and not be at the mercy of majority tastes. At the same time it is clear that television and the cinema have their bad sides, and the frequent reflection of all that is worst in our western culture must have a cumulative effect on those who watch little else. They often show a way of life which, if imitated, would not be in accord with the kind of civilized society we are aiming at. In particular the worship of money, the acceptance of violence, and the distortion of the value and place of sex are thought by all educators to be undesirable.

One comfort is that communication is a two-way process, and that the sending of a message does not mean it is received. Wherever the teacher's voice comes from it is, luckily, still possible for us not to listen or look. Part of education in these days, and increasingly so in the future, is to learn which knobs to twist and which switches to turn on and off. Having turned on the ones you want, you still have to pay attention, and even to think, before memorable communication takes place. The function of the educator with regard to all mass media and outside cultural influences is therefore clear. He must encourage criticism and selection. Our children will grow up in society as it is, and its cultural patterns are there for all to see. Being aware is the first stage and being able to choose is the next. The difficulty of selection is the difficulty of the background values by which to select. Here the educator must do his best by providing criteria of knowledge, taste and feeling, and above all by expressing his own choice with honesty and keeping his own powers of criticism alive.

CHAPTER IX

The School as a Social Unit

Democracy in School Life—Shared Responsibility—The Social Climate of the School—The Use of Authority—The Roles of the Teacher

A SCHOOL carries on an organized life of its own as a social group within the wider society around it.[1] A school is sometimes referred to as a 'society' but from the sociological point of view this is misleading. It is better called a community, since its members have many things in common, but by no means share all the functions of a society. It is a community in the sense in which this was defined in Chapter I since the majority of its members are children who are not yet ready to be full members of society, and are at school partly for this very purpose of becoming socialized.

The *Spens Report* refers to the school as 'a social unit or society of a peculiar kind'. The full passage reads as follows: '. . . a typical school of the present day is to be regarded as not merely a 'place of learning' but as a social unit or society of a peculiar kind in which the older and younger members, the teachers and the taught, share a common life, subject to a constitution to which all are in their several ways consenting and co-operating parties. . . .'[2] This passage suggests that the school itself should have a social structure on the democratic model as the use of the words 'consenting and co-operating parties' would imply. The *Report* in fact devotes several sections to describing practical methods for the training of boys and girls for life in a free community by an education which 'encourages initiative and the shouldering of

[1] Some passages in this chapter are taken from an article by the author entitled 'Social Relations in the School', published in *Researches and Studies*, No. 4, May 1951. University of Leeds Institute of Education.

[2] *Secondary Education* (Spens Report), 1938, p. 147.

responsibility from the earliest years'. This part of the *Report* is entitled 'The School as a Society',[1] and makes the following definite suggestions which are summarized briefly as:

(i) That pupils themselves should take some share in making the school rules.

(ii) That a greater number of pupils, not only the prefects, should take a share in responsibility.

(iii) (a) That it is wrong for the staff to control too much, especially societies and clubs outside the class room. (b) That more minor organization should be left to the pupils, even if done more easily by the staff—indeed that more opportunity should be given to the pupils to learn through making their own mistakes.

(iv) That there should be closer relations between the school and the adult society outside.

This matter is also referred to in a more recent official publication which is the pamphlet *Citizens Growing Up*. There is a section on 'The School as a Community', in which the question is raised of how far a school can be organized on a democratic basis.[2] If the school is to be concerned with practical citizenship it must obviously be preparing active members for the kind of society in which the pupils will ultimately play their part.

There is a point of view which insists that the imitation by the school community of the outside society can be carried too far. Children are immature and dependent, and it is not possible nor proper, it is said, for them to attempt to frame the rules governing their own life. They have their own social life and it is enough preparation for the future that this should be a healthy one. In answer to this it would be granted that any complete form of self-government on the model of political democracy is impracticable, since it would involve electing their own teachers. What is required is a gradual process. In order to train the young in the ways of the adult society they should gradually be given more and more independence; they should experience more freedom and responsibility as they grow up. As John Dewey said: 'The only way to prepare for social life is to engage in social life.' A person cannot *suddenly* become a free adult. If it be granted that children are part of

[1] Chap. 4, Part V, pp. 197–205.

[2] Ministry of Education Pamphlet No. 16, 1949.

the non-social community this is not a reason for keeping them all the time under authoritarian rule. The continuous use of force towards children is not the best way to train them to treat others with kindness and respect.

DEMOCRACY IN SCHOOL LIFE

What can in practice be done in the school? The essence of democratic control is the sharing of power and influence by methods of delegation and consultation. Let us begin by considering how these methods can be made use of in the social organization of the school. It is possible to distinguish various areas of control which can be shared in different degrees between the staff and the pupils.

(i) *Staff Control*

General educational policy is clearly a matter for the staff, and the headmaster or headmistress will have the final word as representing the governors of the school or the local authority. Some of the rules will need to be made by the staff alone without any discussion with the pupils. Most punishment should be in the hands of the staff. Curriculum and teaching method are usually solely under staff control, but here certain forms of consultation and discussion with the pupils are possible.

(ii) *Consultation with the Pupils*

Consultation over curriculum can take place when there is a choice of courses, and the pupils' wishes can be considered. This becomes more and more possible in school work when a form of Dalton Plan or other individual assignment method is used, or as project methods are developed. Over rules and school organization there are systems whereby an advisory body of pupils is asked to make suggestions to the Head or to the Staff Meeting. Alternately a representative group of pupils may be consulted in advance over changes the Head wishes to make. School Councils which are purely *advisory* and have no executive powers would come under this heading.

(iii) *Committees of Equal Co-operation*

This name is given to all committees where staff and pupils meet, and under a certain constitution meet as equals for the purpose in hand.

Ordinary examples are house meetings, form meetings, etc., especially when concerned with the election of officers and their own internal business. This is the place where those school councils would fit where staff and pupils are both represented. There may also be special committees for such things as the school magazine, the library, or for entertainments, where staff and pupils co-operate on equal terms. The essence of this type of council or committee is that decisions can be made within certain defined limits, and these can only be reversed by a special veto of the Head, which might never in fact be used.

(iv) *Pupil Control*

This does not mean *absolute* control, but that the decisions of the pupils have the dominant influence, and in most cases are not challenged. The Prefect system is an example of pupil control, which is, however, really a form of delegated authority. Prefects will usually have some powers of punishment, and a certain sphere of control within which they can make their own decisions. The organization of school games, and the various out-of-school societies and clubs can be left almost entirely to the pupils, although this is often not done. Members of staff can of course be closely associated with these activities, but not in a position of control. With regard to school work there are certain projects and free choice periods where initiative can be invited from the pupils with the minimum of staff interference. This likewise applies to hobbies which are sometimes conducted in school hours.

The most interesting experiments in what is sometimes called school 'self-government' in recent years have been by different forms of school council. Some information is given in *Sixth Form Citizens* published for the Association for Education in Citizenship in 1949. In response to a questionnaire answered by eighty state schools, seventeen of them mentioned a school council. This indicates that experiments of this sort are becoming fairly frequent. We quote the following extract to illustrate one type of constitution operating in a mixed Grammar School:

> 'Training for democracy runs throughout the school and is not limited only to the VIth Form. Pupils are elected by their class mates for various offices. In each form there is a Form Committee presided over by the form teacher. Suggestions of wider interest are sent to the School Parliament which meets twice a term. This is composed of all

the prefects and sub-prefects, and one boy representative and one girl representative of each form. The School Parliament's decisions are considered at a subsequent Staff Meeting and are implemented if acceptable. If not acceptable the reasons are communicated to School Captains, who in turn pass them on to an Assembly of the whole school. . . . The prefects themselves are elected from members of the VIth Form by secret ballot. All pupils vote. Pupils in Forms I and II have 5 votes each, those in III and IV have 10 votes each, and the rest of the upper school 20 each. The staff have the right to exclude elected candidates if they appear to them to be unsuitable.' (p. 73.)

In this case the School Parliament apparently has no staff representatives, but the staff represent an 'Upper House' which can reject the proposals put forward by the parliament. The system of electing prefects is one that seems worth imitating. It seems a simple and obvious democratic procedure and with suitable controls few mistakes are liable to be made. The best kind of control is limiting the electorate to certain forms, or, as in the example given, weighting the voting powers in favour of the older pupils. By analogy with society outside it would be appropriate if, on reaching a certain form, the pupil would be enfranchised for the election of prefects, and gain this extra social responsibility. It is certain that at present in the large majority of schools the prefects are appointed by the staff or the headmaster alone.

The prefect system and the meetings which prefects and sub-prefects hold must in no way be confused with school councils. The function of the prefects is not necessarily a piece of democratic machinery at all. In fact the position of the prefect has often fallen into disrepute, and is in need of vital revision in some schools. They act too often as minor police or sergeant-majors saving the staff trouble, or worse still they degenerate into ushers with control of the traffic in the corridors and have no position of dignity or responsibility as a compensation. Sometimes prefects do no more than maintain link with authority and established law from above, setting up their own closed oligarchy. The whole system needs to be adapted to suit a more democratic atmosphere.

To return to the school council the earlier experiments in private progressive schools are described in *The Modern Schools Handbook*, 1936. There is also the example given by J. H. Simpson in *Sane Schooling*. In this case a general meeting of the whole school was held from time to time, and the officers and the many committees to run all the affairs of the school were elected. A particular feature of this experiment was the prominence given to the financial aspects of government. There was a school bank, and a school shop, and the games and entertainments committees dealt with large sums of money. Budgets of income and expenditure were therefore drawn up and presented to the school meeting, by the pupil officers responsible. After debate a levy of taxes was then proposed on the school population, to cover the expenditure for the period. The value of gaining some early idea of the social responsibility attached to the spending of money would seem to make further adaptations of this procedure worth trying.

So many different forms of school council are possible that we would sum up with a general account of the features common to most of them, and the advantages usually claimed for them.

Features of School Councils

(i) The council is representative of all or most age groups in the school. Perhaps the youngest will sometimes be left out. Too big an age range is a disadvantage, and to make the privilege of being represented a mark of reaching, say, Form III, is a good plan.

(ii) Representatives are elected in a secret ballot by forms, or whatever other grouping is decided.

(iii) Sometimes representatives of the staff, selected by the staff meeting, and possibly the headmaster, sit on the council. In other constitutions it is left to the pupils alone.

(iv) When members of staff sit on the council they are in a position of equal co-operation, with the same voting power and subject to the same rules as the pupil members.

(v) For success there must be genuine co-operation, and the powers of the council must be clearly defined. If apparent powers are given and then the council decisions repeatedly rejected the whole system will fail. It is most important that real freedom should be given even in a very limited sphere rather than a pretence of freedom which in practice cannot be exercised.

(vi) The council normally elects its own chairman and officers, and draws up its own rules of procedure.

(vii) Matters dealt with depend on the constitution and powers of the council. Advisory powers and executive powers are clearly distinguished. The free discussion of any affairs concerning the whole school, or any section of the school, is normally allowed, but decisions must depend on the powers allocated to the council. The making or changing of some rules is frequently permitted. Whether the council should deal with offenders or not is often a debated question. In general we feel that it should not.

(viii) Normally decisions of the council have to be accepted by a full staff meeting before being acted upon.

Advantages Claimed for School Councils[1]

(i) It is a preparation for government by discussion which is the method of our democracy. Common problems are thus tackled in the council by the methods of reason and tolerance.

(ii) It helps to get the right attitude to authority, namely that authority should be used for the benefit of all, after proper consultation with those concerned, and that all must exercise responsibility in supporting it.

(iii) Rules are more likely to be obeyed when representatives of the pupils help to frame them. Discussions are 'fed-back' through the school, and the views of the council representatives have a strong influence on public opinion.

(iv) It gives members from all levels of the community a chance to introduce new ideas. There is thus a two-way process of ideas; both up and down.

(v) It helps individual members who are potential leaders, rebels or big-talkers, and helps to diagnose who are which.

(vi) For members of the council self-discipline grows through the exercise of responsibility.

SHARED RESPONSIBILITY

Another feature of a democratic school community is that responsibility is learnt, in appropriate ways, by the younger as well as the older pupils. At all stages, and in work as well as in play, school children can be allowed a much fuller participation in the choice and organization of

[1] Undoubtedly the same results can be achieved and similar advantages gained by other methods. The School Council is only quoted as one of the methods which may help towards democracy in school life.

what they are doing than was possible in the schools of the past, where a more rigid control was the accepted method of teaching Responsibility grows from having a definite role to play in the group. It is through the role that he plays that the child's feeling of significance in the group grows, and if he does not feel significant he cannot feel responsible. It can only be learnt by practice. If the child starts by being given a task well within his powers he can then make progress by gradually taking on more difficult responsibilities.

Many schools plan a system of duties whereby as many pupils as possible, from the lowest forms upwards have some duty to perform for the whole community or some section of it wider than just their own form or class group. It is a common enough practice to give class-room duties and these should be regularly changed and kept alive by criticism and discussion at class meetings. The carrying out of a duty for the larger group is worth the trouble it takes in organizing, and the ingenuity required to think out the largest possible number of significant duties in a graded order of difficulty. Routine duties are the simplest and cover such matters as bells, distribution of milk, letters and papers, tidiness, waiting at meals, keeping simple records, e.g. temperature, arranging flowers, or changing round pictures. Responsibility for things comes next in difficulty. This includes care of equipment of any kind, for example for gardening, outdoor work, camp equipment or games. Storekeepers and their assistants can be appointed for lending out and checking in equipment for communal use. Care of the bicycle shed, of the gramophone or radio, of pets and aquaria, lead on to the more important departmental responsibilities. Each department of the school can have its boys or girls in charge of duties under supervision of the members of staff. For instance the library, the laboratories, the workshops, the printing-room, the nature-study room, the canteen, the school shop, the gymnasium, the school hall or the theatre. In these larger duties there should be always two or three assistants under training and to act as reserves. Carrying out a departmental duty is learning to be responsible *to* people. The responsibility *for* people is the highest of all, and is given in the most obvious way to the sub-prefects and prefects. The captains of houses, games, sports and athletics also have responsibilities for others in their group and team.

This kind of training for leadership and initiative can be extended into other fields outside the conventional ones of games and community discipline. The most useful opportunity for this is a fuller development of societies and clubs run by the pupils themselves. The children in a school need time that they can devote entirely to their own ends, and which allows them the maximum of self-activity not under the control or direct suggestion of an adult. This time will usually have to be taken from out-of-class hours, but some schools manage to arrange for societies and hobby clubs, etc., to meet for part of the time at least in school hours and then continue after school. Given the opportunity it is surprising how the junior as well as the senior groups will organize themselves and how leaders emerge.[1] The seriousness with which children engage in these activities, and the hard work they sometimes carry out on things which interest them can also be observed when more individual freedom is given in ordinary classes which, far from being a waste of time, gives rise to really self-directed work. This is one of the basic assumptions of modern teaching method. The whole distinction (In terms of the children's feelings) between work and play tends to disappear when children find out that they can do just as important things on their own initiative as under the control of the teacher.

This is not the place to discuss teaching method, but it can be seen that those so-called 'activity' methods which involve co-operation in groups have also an important influence on the social life of the school. Learning to work together, which in the old days would have been called 'cheating' or 'cribbing' has now become a virtue. This is an indication that changes are on the way in our culture, which is still largely individualistic and competitive. Team work has been praised and encouraged in games and in war, with remarkable success, but the spirit of the team in everyday work relations is only just beginning to be appreciated. There are many tasks where the feeling of belonging to a group and working together with others for a common purpose adds energy and incentive to the participants.

We would here make a brief reference to the discoveries in the field of group dynamics which have considerable relevance to education, and which are described more fully in the next chapter. Social psychology now begins to offer us some understanding of the motivations underlying the working together of people in groups, which can be used

[1] I remember the quite small child who said to me in a school I was visiting: 'I am the President of the Rat Catching Society. . . .' However insignificant he may have felt elsewhere he was responsible and secure in one social role at least.

with the objective of improving our work output and our human relations. The co-operation of groups depends on free discussion, which is another aspect of the democratic process. Discussion methods could be used much more at all levels in the school community, for instance between staff and staff as well as between staff and pupils, and between pupil groups under their own leadership. Discussion can sometimes achieve better communication of ideas, and more often better relations between people by the communication of feelings and decisions within the group. The group situation is basic to the school programme whether it be the class, the practical work group, the school club, the team, the prefects' meeting, the school council or the staff meeting. The essential condition for a successful group meeting of any kind is full participation by its members, and that is one of the most difficult things to achieve. All groups will experience their stages of tension and misunderstanding between the members. Only when tensions are to some extent resolved and inter-personal adjustments are made will full participation begin. Then co-operative action can take place. On the other hand obstacles may be encountered which are too strong for the group. The group is frustrated, energy is wasted, no co-operative activity follows, and participation may even cease. We are all familiar with these experiences both positive and negative when working with other people.

The organization of the school community, the sharing of responsibility, the teaching methods, and the co-operation of groups all depend on the personal relations between people, the attitudes towards discipline and the use of authority, which are the matters to which we now turn.

THE SOCIAL CLIMATE OF THE SCHOOL

People's relations within a social group create a kind of atmosphere which can be called the 'social climate'. A group may be felt to be a happy or an unhappy one. That is the impression it gives to strangers. The word 'morale' can be used, and there is a certain feeling when morale is good or poor. The problem is to study what lies behind the social climate of a school community, and try to discover some of the factors which go to make a happy school with high morale, and those which lead to failure to achieve good morale and cause unhappy social relationships.

Although many years have passed since the *Spens Report* it is still doubtful whether a *typical* school would be one in which 'the teachers and the taught share a common life' as 'consenting and co-operating parties'. Sharing a common life in a school implies certain kinds of relations, human relations, between people in a small community. Once we grant that part of a schools function is to prepare for social living the nature of these human relations becomes of critical importance. This is not the whole of education for citizenship but it is the vital part of it which is often neglected. Social living is not concerned so much with textbook facts as with behaviour. It is not something which is learnt by having courses in social studies, or current affairs, or economics, or even philosophy—though all of these may also be necessary in the education of citizens. Again it is not sufficient, though necessary, to make attempts at self-government, to extend responsibility to many more of the pupils, or to encourage clubs and societies and out-of-school activities. All these courses and devices have in various degrees been attempted, but even then the essential spirit of democratic social relations may be missing. Becoming a free man and a civilized person is learnt and taught by the way we behave towards other people.

What seems so extraordinary is the high degree of acceptance both in official and unofficial quarters of the importance of democratic social relations in the school, compared with the remarkably few practical measures that have actually been tried in the schools to bring about this state of affairs. How far the schools of Great Britain do in practice represent a democratic culture is a question which may reasonably be asked. Where there is an autocratic headmaster or headmistress there follows a rigid discipline and an authoritarian atmosphere. Learning is associated with fear; punishment with force; and an antagonism between pupils and staff (often said to be natural) is generally accepted. In many schools the headmaster still tends to occupy the position of an absolute ruler, and assistant teachers have little freedom to initiate schemes of their own or to participate freely in planning the life of the school. As between teachers and pupils the relation is essentially one of dominance and submission, and docility and order are the measures of good behaviour.

Yet this description is no more that of a *typical* school than that of the *Spens Report* previously quoted. It is more likely that the atmosphere of the typical school is somewhere in between; a position which is not necessarily comfortable as the following extract from an account of his own school by a sixth-form boy will show: 'The main fault at —— is that it sits on the fence between authoritarian and democratic government, trying to get the best of both systems but in reality incurring many of their disadvantages. Here the relationship between the rulers and the ruled is uncertain, and this gives rise to difficulties.'

Is it not true that this uncertainty in the use of authority is becoming a frequent feature in schools to-day? Related as it is to the problems of discipline it is a recurrent discussion in school staff rooms—and how often the staff is deeply divided on these questions. The staff room atmosphere is an interesting indicator of a school's morale. There may be strong differences of opinion not only on the question of discipline and freedom, but on new methods, or on the views of a new Head, and there is the ever-possible conflict of the younger members against the older. These differences are likely to be reflected in varying attitudes from classroom to classroom, and lack of a consistent approach towards the pupils' learning or behaviour. That there should be a variety of views freely and reasonably discussed is all to the good and is in line with democratic principles; but that is very different from the deep and bitter divergencies which are found in the very nature of the democratic use of authority itself and which are exacerbated by not being freely expressed.

What is certain is that there are great differences to be observed in the methods of exercising authority in different schools even close to each other in the same regional district. This has been well expressed by A. G. Hughes at the beginning of his book on *Education and the Democratic Ideal*, 1951, which is an admirable survey of the whole problem. After experience of school teaching, the Army, teacher training and administration, Dr. Hughes writes: 'These varied experiences have subjected me to the stimulus of vivid contrasts. The most vivid of all is the contrast between social climates, ranging for the most part from cold, impersonal authoritarianism to warm personal friendliness. These climates do not comprise the whole range; at one end I have seen (forty years ago) authoritarianism backed by corporal punishment as a part of the daily classroom routine, and at the other end I have often seen friendliness developing at its highest into a relationship of love. I have seen contrasting climates in different classrooms in one school, and in different schools in one area.'

Such evidence of contrasting methods lead us naturally to ask whether it is possible to discover some method of comparing social behaviour or social climate, to show in what ways it is associated with, or determined by, differences of treatment by an autocratic or democratic school staff. Some relevant research has been done by social psychologists which will now be described.

THE USE OF AUTHORITY

We have so far assumed that what we have called democratic social relations are the most desirable in our schools. It must be pointed out that this is nevertheless an *assumption*, but it is justified if we accept the social philosophy on which our concept of the democratic society is based, and if in fact the methods employed lead to the behaviour we desire. The practical test is to obtain some objective evidence of the kind of behaviour which results from the methods we call democratic, compared with the methods we callauthoritarian, or any other methods we choose to observe. We should still have to make the value judgment on which results we considered more desirable, but the first step is scientific and involves recording and classifying the behaviour under different conditions. Some objective investigations of this kind have been recorded. The now well-known researches of Ronald Lippitt and Ralph K. White in the United States supply a good illustration.[1]

This work was carried out with selected groups of boys in youth clubs, where the leaders artificially created different atmospheres which were classified as authoritarian, democratic, or *laissez-faire*. For details of the experimental methods of these lengthy studies reference must be made to the original papers. A few of the results with implications for the school situation can be summarized as follows. The autocratic leader determined the work to be done, and dictated the stages of work step by step. He decided each boy's task and with whom he should work. He gave orders, or disruptive commands, or non-constructive criticism, or showed other behaviour of this checking kind twelve times as much as the democratic leader. The democratic leader allowed the work to be determined wherever possible by group discussion. He gave encourage-

[1] R. Lippitt and R. K. White: 'The Social Climate of Children's Groups' in *Child Behaviour and Development*, Kounin and Wright, 1940. Also 'Leadership and Group Life' in *Readings in Social Psychology*, 1947.

ment and practical advice, and the further stages of the work were foreseen by the group right from the beginning. The members of the group were allowed to work with whom they pleased and to choose their own tasks. The leader made guiding suggestions and stimulated self-guidance (e.g. asking the boys' opinions on the work, etc.) about eight times as much as the autocratic leader. The groups' reactions were fully observed and recorded.

There were two types of reaction to the autocratic leader, the one aggressive and the other apathetic and submissive. Both types of reaction showed marked dependence on the leader and frequent demands for his help, and the aggressive groups showed a high degree of critical discontent, which was probably felt but not expressed by the apathetic groups, who got on with their work reasonably well when the leader was present. But little work was done by any of these groups when the leader was absent, and irritability and aggression between members of the group and towards outside members and groups was frequent. On the other hand the reactions of the democratically controlled groups were less dependent on the leader, so that they continued working well in his absence; they were more friendly and confiding, they made co-operative suggestions and talked freely about their work. Experiments were made in changing the atmosphere of certain groups after a time. The change from an autocratic to a freer atmosphere led in the first place to bursts of horseplay, and a 'blowing-off' of tensions. In the change from democracy to autocracy a friendly co-operative group became in a short time apathetic and without initiative. There is no need here to describe the differences in the *laissez-faire*, the two extremes have been chosen for illustration.

More important still for our purpose are some lengthy studies by H. H. Anderson and Helen M. Brewer, and others. These are reported in several papers and the main results are collected together in three volumes entitled *Studies in Teachers' Classroom Personalities.*[1] These researches were carried out in many schools and with several different classes from the kindergarten to children in early adolescence. Before giving some account of this work we would stress the extreme thoroughness of the researches and the very great care taken to ensure the validity of the observations, and to check the agreement between differ-

[1] Applied Psychology Monographs of the American Psychological Society, No. 6, 1945 and Nos. 8 and 11, 1946. Stanford University Press.

ent observers. The first aim of the investigators was to make certain that the behaviour, as analysed into different categories, could in fact be observed objectively. Only when they were assured of that did they attempt to draw conclusions on the relation between the actions of teachers and the reactions of the children.

The basic concept of the work of H. H. Anderson and his collaborators is the distinction between 'dominative' and 'integrative' behaviour. 'Dominative' behaviour is typified by autocratic methods and the attempt to dominate the will of others; while 'integrative' behaviour is typified by democratic methods of seeking to integrate differences into agreement by tolerance, consultation and discussion. These types of behaviour can of course be observed in all spheres of life, particularly in industry, business and politics, in the armed forces, and wherever people are in positions of authority over others. In giving a description of the opposing types of personality based on these types of behaviour we would stress that most people cannot be placed clearly into one category or the other, but possess elements of both.

A *dominative* personality may be recognized by possessing many of the following characteristics. He usually thinks he knows best, and wishes to make other people behave in his way without being able to admit the value of the other person's experience, desires or criticism. In positions of authority he tends to make decisions on his own without reference to the others who may be concerned. He is in fact jealous of the ideas of others, and may take a suggestion from a subordinate as implying criticism of himself, or seeming to reject the suggestion may later bring it forward as his own. He tends to use the technique of threats and blame, he gives imperative commands and orders on what should be done, and behaves aggressively when his will is resisted. Attempts to dominate usually interfere with other people's aims and desires, and are followed by the frustrating of somebody else. The dominative person therefore tends to cause conflict, and incites aggression, overt or hidden, in reply. He is normally in a position of working *against* other people.

The *integrative* person, on the other hand, is normally able to work *with* other people instead of against them. He realizes the value of other people's knowledge and experience, and is prepared to invite co-operation and to adapt his aims to the desires of others. In positions of authority he consults those under him whenever possible on matters which concern them, and is quick to recognize and praise good ideas which come from someone else. He is able to share responsibility with others and does not insist in keeping all the control in his own hands. He tends to use praise rather than blame, makes requests rather than gives orders, and is able to tolerate the disagreement of others. The socially integrative person is flexible, permissive, and adaptive. He invites participation, encourages initiative, and as a leader is able to co-ordinate the work of others and develop a happy and creative atmosphere among those who work with him.

For their investigations into the social relations of teachers and their classes Anderson and Brewer listed categories of behaviour with different degrees of domination and integration. A brief description of three of the main categories follows.

Domination with evidence of conflict

Conflict is defined as working against the wish of the child, who *shows* his intention does not correspond with the teacher's and he usually resists or objects. For example the teacher may order the child's activity, in conflict with him, by such familiar remarks as 'Sit still! Don't do that! Put those things away! How many times have I told you not to. . . .' All direct refusal, disapproval, blame or shame, warnings, threats and punishments, especially when no reason or explanation is given by the teacher which is acceptable to the child, come into this category.

Domination with evidence of working together

Working together is defined as the teacher and the child pursuing the same goal with a common purpose, and without imposition by the teacher. Acceptance under pressure from the teacher is not working together. When there is an element of domination remaining the teacher always decides, but the child's wishes are considered. That the teacher selects activity for the child on the basis of his interest is typical of this form of working together, but the teacher still plans all the work.

Integration with evidence of working together

Here co-operation is based on the child's expressed initiative, and he is allowed to contribute freely his suggestions and wishes. The child is accepted as a partner in the enterprise, which he often *shows* that he wanted. In spite of being 'wrong' the child's views are attended to, examined and tested. The teacher will help the child advance and solve his own problem, and gives approval and agreement to the spontaneous and self-initiated behaviour of the child, following whenever possible the child's expressed wish, suggestion or need.

Anderson and Brewer also worked out categories of child response to the attitudes and actions of the teachers. Thus during any period of observation in a classroom a check was made of each item of behaviour on the part of the teacher, and each item on the part of any child in the room.

Categories of child response

General

1. Nervous habits, fidgeting, etc.
2. Looking up or looking around, and not paying attention to his work.
3. Leaving his seat.
4. Playing about with 'foreign objects' not related to his work.
5. Resisting the orders of the teacher.
6. Talking to another child (at a time when this is not permitted).
7. Acts in an aggressive way towards another child, perhaps with threats or actual use of force.
8. Attacks the status of another child, e.g. by calling him names or suggesting his work is bad.
9. Conforming meekly to the teacher's domination.

Social contributions of the child

These are important and are examples of integrative behaviour by the child. Each one can be either voluntary or in response to an invitation by the teacher.

1. Telling an experience relating to the work, from happenings in school or out of school.
2. Bringing something to school to contribute to the lesson or project.
3. Making positive suggestions to help on the work.
4. The child offers his services, e.g. to take charge of a group activity, or to accept a particular responsibility.
5. Holding up his hand wishing to say something *not* in response to a question.
6. The child shows appreciation of the work of others in his group.

Results of these investigations

For the elaborate experimental details of these observations and the statistical evidence we must refer the reader to the original papers. The main conclusions are of very great interest for any study of the use of authority.

(1) The teachers observed differed very considerably in the extent of their dominative or integrative behaviour.

(2) When the number of dominative contacts exceeded the number of integrative contacts the teacher would be working more against the children than with them. Thus one teacher worked *against* the children three times as much as with them, while with the same age in a neighbouring room the teacher was working *with* the children twice as much as against.[1]

(3) These differences in teachers' attitudes show that children live in very different psychological environments even within the same school.

(4) Where the teacher showed *more* integrative behaviour and *less* dominative behaviour, the responses of the children were *more* often in the categories of making social contributions (i.e. co-operating in the work) and problem solving, and *less* often of the type of inattention, playing about, aggression to others and resisting orders. The opposite was also true. This indicates that dominative teacher behaviour tends to intensify conflict, while integrative teacher behaviour encourages integrative pupil behaviour.

(5) To show that the teacher's behaviour was the critical factor and not the chance selection of pupils in the class, the behaviour of the same classes and teachers in one investigation was tested in the following year. It was found that the more dominating teachers and the more integrative teachers were about the same with their new classes. But the class of the dominative teacher on moving up did not carry on their resisting behaviour but co-operated more with their new teacher who was less dominative than the previous one.

We have described these investigations in some detail because they illustrate the kind of research which provides objective evidence of the ways in which teachers' behaviour can differ, and the influence this can have on the class. In the light of these facts we are then able to know

[1] The ratio of integrative to dominative contacts was worked out for a considerable number of teachers and showed wide variations.

which methods to attempt in order to achieve the behaviour in children which we desire. The mental hygiene assumptions of our democratic culture suggest that what has been called integrative behaviour has a high value, whether on the part of the teacher or the child, while dominative behaviour, and conflict between teacher and child has a low value. Teachers who make a democratic approach to education are bound to assume that a school atmosphere of willing co-operation, harmony and self-initiative in work is more desirable than one which stifles spontaneity and intensifies conflict and misunderstanding. At the same time it must be noted that there are some situations in which the teacher must take definite and even autocratic action, and when conflict is inevitable. The democratic approach is *not* the *laissez-faire* approach, but requires real authority in the teacher which can nevertheless be exercised with the least possible use of dominative action. The teachers who on the whole work with the children rather than against them are most likely to achieve a happy social climate in their classrooms.

It must be remembered that these researches were carried out in America but it seems likely, from what we have said earlier, that similar investigations in this country would lead to similar conclusions. Research into the social relations in school communities in England is scanty and is badly needed. It would be very valuable if comparative studies of the social climate in different schools could be undertaken, but social research in education is difficult because it is new and techniques are not yet well developed.[1]

The attitude of authority and the attitudes towards authority are the critical variables in all social relations. The fact that the social climate of our schools still shows such marked contrasts indicates the range of behaviour which still remains between the extremes of the autocratic and the democratic use of authority.

THE ROLES OF THE TEACHER

The teacher, like any other member of society, plays many social roles in accordance with the different statuses he occupies both in his private and public life. But the nature of the teacher's occupation places him in the special position of having a complicated set of roles in con-

[1] A research into the social structure of Secondary Schools with special reference to staff relationships is being undertaken in a part of Yorkshire by T. Brennan.

nection with his occupation alone. He is, as it were, in between the world of youth and the adult world, trying to meet the claims of his pupils while reconciling them with the expectations of their parents, and relating both to the needs of society at large. He has on the one hand an academic role concerned with scholarship, and on the other hand he is a character-trainer concerned with the development of the child's whole personality. The teacher's principal roles can be listed briefly as follows.[1]

(i) *The teacher as an academic specialist*

This is the teacher's traditional role. He is expected to know his subject, and to be the acknowledged superior to his pupils in this respect. Nevertheless he must be prepared to face the fact that some of his pupils will be potentially, or actually, cleverer than he is, and any teacher should be willing to admit when he makes a mistake. In the higher forms of a school the importance of the teacher's expert knowledge becomes greater, and he should always spend some time in keeping up to date with the advances of knowledge in his special subjects. Otherwise he may lose both social and intellectual prestige, for example, among a group of intelligent sixth formers. There is a type of teacher who values very highly his standard of scholarship, and another type who sees himself in the role of an all-round educator. Each has his place in a school. At the same time one hopes that the specialists will avoid the charge of narrowness, and will see the point of the growing trend towards a broader education at school age.

(ii) *The teacher as a methodologist*

The teacher is also expected to be an expert in the methods of teaching and learning. He may exercise this role in different ways, and all that has been said in this chapter on the dominative and integrative attitudes of teachers is very relevant here. In watching a teacher in the classroom the observer will notice how far he encourages passive or active learning, how far the lesson is teacher-centred or pupil-centred, how much it is a lecture and how much a discussion.

There are different social conditions for successful learning, according to the nature and stage of the learning process. Learning in class takes

[1] This subject is treated in detail by O. A. Oeser (Ed.): *Teacher, Pupil and Task*, 1955.

place in a group situation. The teacher's general task is to establish that learning is the expected behaviour in the classroom, and is the principal goal of the group. If this pattern of activity is accepted then the child will be ready to assume that he will get satisfaction out of the process of learning, and that the result will fulfil one of his genuine needs. There are teaching methods which allow communication between pairs, or groups of pupils who work together, using the teacher for consultation as well as consulting the sources of information which he provides for them. These learning situations produce a different social climate in the classroom from those, also necessary at other times, in which the teacher stands in front of the class, does most of the talking, and uses a rapid question-and-answer technique. The choice of method is within the power of the teacher, and he should always be aware that in making his choice he is determining the nature of a social situation. His general objective is obtaining a relationship between the class and the task which is before them. His is the position of a mediator, and he may sometimes be more successful the more he withdraws himself from direct action, and permits the class to learn for themselves.

(iii) *The teacher as a character-trainer*

To be able to keep good discipline is a highly valued quality in a teacher. There are different methods of achieving this end, covering a range of sanctions from enforcing a strict code of punishment to the gentle but effective persuasion by personal influence. There is, of course, more in discipline than keeping order, and the objective is the development of a capacity for self-discipline. This brings out the function of a teacher as a counsellor or advisor. If the pupil is lacking in interest, or unwilling to make the effort to learn, the first concern of the teacher is to find the reason, and then to remove the obstacle to learning. Anti-social conduct must also have its cause, and the teacher will try to understand the pupil's motivation, and act with the intention of seeking a cure rather than imposing a standard punishment. There is indeed a therapeutic aspect to school education, which is growing in importance as we understand more about the roots of both delinquent and normal behaviour. A new concept of character-training is developing, unlike the sadistic hardening process of some schools, and with none of the taboo on tenderness. The teacher's understanding and insight into the growth of personality, and his grasp of the principles of mental health are essential to this new approach.[1] If this type of responsibility is to be added to the teacher's other roles, it demands powers of self-restraint, objectivity and self-knowledge, and a degree of maturity the development of which should be a primary aim of teacher training.

(iv) *The teacher as a member of a school staff*

He is a member of the teaching hierarchy both in his school, and in the general educational system. Each school has a formal structure of authority, from the headmaster downwards through varying degrees of seniority. The new assistant, who is also a beginner, will have to learn the role which is expected of him in his new situation. The formal structure is not necessarily rigid, and the ease of social relations between teachers of different seniority varies very much from school to school. Again, different schools within the general system vary in prestige, and this affects the position and morale of the teacher. He will also find himself involved in a set of roles in relation to different other adults who impinge upon his work. He is thus at the centre of conflicting expectations which may be expressed to him in turn by the headmaster and the parents, Her Majesty's Inspector, the Director of Education, the N.U.T. representative, members of political parties and anybody in the public at large. As parents make increasing claims upon the educational system so teachers are more likely than in the past to be exposed to the pressures of local opinion.

(v) *The teacher as a member of society*

The teacher will himself be a member of a particular sub-culture within society. He will have acquired certain standards of behaviour from his upbringing which will influence his classroom and staff-room relationships. There has in the past been some uncertainty over the social class of teachers.[2] With the growth of secondary education during this century a large numbers of teachers have come from working-class origins, and have thus achieved upward social mobility. Nevertheless the attraction of teaching appears to be slightly weaker to-day for working-class than for other children.[3] The Grammar School is tradi-

[1] W. D. Wall, (Ed.), *Education and Mental Health*, 1955, see in particular Chap. X for the teacher's function.

[2] See *The Year Book of Education*, 1953 on the social position of teachers.

[3] Jean Floud and W. Scott: 'Recruitment to Teaching in England and Wales', Chap. 37 in *Education, Economy and Society*, 1961.

tionally a middle-class institution, but the proportion of teachers entering it from professional and managerial families has declined markedly since the end of the last war, and more so for men than for women. Working-class entrants have also declined slightly, and as a result the intermediate or lower middle-class group now supply around 60 per cent of the teachers entering Grammar Schools. In other types of school the proportion of teachers from manual families is higher. However, since nearly all teachers are themselves products of a Grammar School the whole profession may be said to be slowly assimilating, or modifying, middle-class standards of life. It is expected of a teacher to set some standards of taste and values before his pupils, whether it be with regard to speech, dress, manners or choice of reading matter and television programmes. This is not to say there is no conflict over standards in these respects. Teachers often do not agree, but a pattern is beginning to emerge of a cultural community very different from one securely attached to the dying tradition of the past.

Whatever his personal views may be, the fact stands out that the teacher has a role as a representative of adult society. This is the ultimate source of his authority. He is responsible for the socialization of the young on behalf of the adult society for which they are being prepared. The way he uses his authority may vary, but whatever he does he cannot abdicate, and must accept his responsibilities. The pupils will react to him, as they will to all authority figures, in different ways, but while they are in his care it is his duty to be the moralist and the final arbiter of the rules.

CHAPTER X

Understanding Human Behaviour

How did we get like this?—How can we be changed?—Group Dynamics

EACH social science has as its object the study of some aspect of human behaviour. The subject matter is so complex that it requires this division of labour. Yet any particular human problem may need the combination of knowledge from several different areas of study for its elucidation, and, when possible, its solution. A tendency can also be observed for the border-line between some of the social sciences to become less and less distinct. There is even some confusion over what shall be called a separate study. Thus one writer on social anthropology can refuse to accept social psychology as a separate field of inquiry but asks for it to be merged into a unified subject of psychology, while a recent writer on social psychology includes, as part of his subject, extensive references to the work of social anthropologists. An historian has said that anthropology is 'history or nothing' much to the annoyance of the anthropologists. These difficulties are largely matters of terminology and are due to the rapid expansion of all these studies of society in recent years. But they also show that the subject matter itself is so related that its division into parts is not possible without distortion.

What appears to be happening is that a new and comprehensive study of man is beginning to emerge, which is capable of providing an integrated body of knowledge, drawing on the research techniques of its contributing disciplines. This integration of the various branches of psychology and psycho-therapy, with sociology, anthropology and some history, has been called by Karl Mannheim the science of human behaviour.[1] It is linked with the life sciences of biology and physiology which consider the nature of man as an animal, with geography through the environment, and with the arts through the works of beauty created by man. Such a comprehensive subject requires the collaboration of specialists of different kinds. A similar need for co-operation between workers in different fields is found to-day in the physical sciences, and only in this way can progress be made in the subjects which lie on the borderland of several different existing disciplines. This kind of collaboration has been called the 'multi-disciplined approach', and research of this nature is carried out by inter-professional teams.

Why should such a study of man be called a science? Just as physical science is an attempt to understand and control physical nature, so the science of human behaviour (or social science) is an attempt to understand and control human nature. The essence of this control is an ability to make predictions, and a scientific law is a rule by which we predict what is likely to happen. In all science such predictions can usually be made only within a defined degree of certainty. The idea that physical science follows exact and invariable causal laws, the faith in cause and effect of the nineteenth century, is being changed in the explanations given by modern scientists.[2] More importance is attached to statistical laws which show that when the result of a particular event cannot be determined, the result of a large number of such events may be known with a certain degree of probability. There are statistical laws in economics and psychology which differ from such laws in physics not in kind but in the degree of error to which they are susceptible. Economic laws

[1] Mannheim uses this phrase in *The Diagnosis of Our Time*, and explains it on p. 57. *In Freedom, Power and Democratic Planning*, 1951, he writes on p. 179: 'The last twenty years have seen an immense advance in various branches of psychology, sociology and history, whose integration might be called the *science of human behaviour*. Experimental psychology, psychoanalysis, and the various schools of general psychology, as well as the specialized branches of applied psychology—such as child psychology, educational psychology and criminology—all have contributed to an ever-widening knowledge of the variability of human behaviour. If we add to this our anthropological knowledge of primitive man and what sociologically informed historians reveal of human nature and conduct in different ages; if we observe the behaviour patterns of different classes of contemporary society—man's reactions to gradual and sudden changes such as crises, wars and revolutions—then we can no longer speak of ignorance concerning human behaviour.'

[2] See J. Bronowski: *The Common Sense of Science*, 1951, for a simple account of the change from the idea of cause to the idea of chance in science; especially Chap. VII.

depend upon the free choice of individuals, but the results of the choice on the average can be predicted. So, while it cannot be said *which* people will buy a tin of cocoa next week the manufacturers can estimate the total sales with some degree of accuracy, and they know that their sales can be correlated closely with other variables such as the percentage of unemployment. The more the choice of people is restricted the more certainty can be given to the prediction, and this is the basis of economic control and planning, and of national budgets in time of difficulty.

The whole range of public opinion surveys gives another example of a quantitative measure of people's opinions on which their actions may be based, and the extent of error on straightforward issues is shown to be small.

British Railways (Southern Region) would be very surprised if three or four times the expected number of people decided to go to Brighton next week-end, if they had forgotten some special event which was taking place. It is the possibility of 'special events', or the unknown variables that cause the uncertainty in human affairs.

We are not denying the existence of human free will, but only saying that it operates within certain limits. This does not reduce the importance of what each individual chooses to do. It has been said that statistics is the method of blinding ourselves to the significance of the individual in the mass, and this is a danger to be watched. The measurement of intelligence quotients is an example. No reasonable person doubts the validity of the results *on the average*, but suspicions are aroused by the possibility of the incorrect measurement of individuals. But there are safeguards when sufficient trouble is taken to check unlikely deviations.

When dealing with a single individual it is possible to make *some* predictions of future behaviour based on the evidence of his past history and the observed knowledge of his reactions. Without there being some valid conclusions to be drawn from the relation between different factors in the personality there could be no clinical treatment for psychological disorders.

It is still frequently said, however, that it is impossible to treat human affairs by the scientific method. This is not true in principle. The number of variables place great difficulties in the way of making accurate predictions, but the same methods of patient observation, classification and generalization are employed as in any recognized science.[1] We do not cease to call meteorology a science because of the uncertainty of weather forecasts. It is also important to remember that the same experiment exactly repeated (if there is such a thing) is not essential to the scientific method, and cannot be performed in astronomy or geology although predictions can be made and their truth tested in these sciences. The social sciences can carry out experiments which have their degrees of validity, even though the controlled variables cannot be maintained absolutely constant.

It has been our general point of view that education cannot be separated from the social process, and that it is concerned with the formation of human attitudes and interests within that process. The teacher is educating for life in an existing society, and must reckon with all the influences that bear upon the development of personality. Thus the teacher's interest in the science of human behaviour lies in its application to education. The sociology of education is itself a branch of the science of human behaviour, and derives its principles and its methods from the social sciences. The value of the sociological approach to the teacher is that it shows his work against the background of man's life in society. Few can be experts in several different subjects, but everyone can try to see where his special knowledge fits in the wider framework of man's knowledge about himself, and thus come to understand where he needs to know more. The objectives of the science of human behaviour are of two kinds. It aims to show us how we came to be as we are, and how we can be changed.

HOW DID WE GET LIKE THIS?

We must distinguish between the science of society as a whole, and

[1] Barbara Wootton: *Testament for Social Science*, 1950. This book makes a strong case for the use of the scientific method in the social sciences. The following quotation illustrates the above points: 'The raw material of the social and natural sciences is identical over a large area. Both are concerned with primary sense-impressions, but the social sciences also use comparable data from the world of psychological experience. Further, each of these two branches of science uses the same methods, formulating hypotheses, which, after empirical verification become laws of association between phenomena. Such associations do not always attain the rank of certainty even in the natural sciences; in both social and natural science the degree of their probability varies in different cases.' (p. 178)

the science of individual behaviour within society. The culture concept is a result of generalizations formed from the comparative study of different societies in their normal ways of life. It is as a result of such studies that a science of society is developing. We might ask in the first place: 'How does a particular culture come to be like that?' or, as it has been put: 'What makes custom customary?' Our theory of social and cultural change in Chapter III was an attempt to answer these questions. The culture at a given time is determined by the interaction of the dominant techniques and values of the society. The place of the individual was not forgotten; he is the inventor of the techniques and the propounder of the values. Next we ask: 'How did the individual come to be like that?' We have gained some idea in Chapter II of the extent to which the individual personality is influenced by the culture of his society. There is a continuous cycle of interaction as the individual is moulded by and at the same time attempts to mould his society. But this is not the whole story. We must focus a little more closely on the place of the individual in his culture.

The development of the study of personality is an example of our statement that a multi-disciplined approach is necessary for the proper understanding of a human problem. The study of personality, in its modern form, is hardly twenty years old, and nearly all the early books on it were published as psychology. For instance, G. W. Allport published one of the best of these in 1937, which is called *Personality: A Psychological Interpretation.* In this book Allport explains that he is not concerned with the factors *shaping* personality, but with the effects of such factors (whatever they may be, and he did not at that time consider them in detail), when interiorized in the individual. Thus he proceeds to show how psychology is beginning to give a picture of the individual's personality as it in fact is. This most important task of description and analysis was developed by numbers of workers, and thus we had the different temperamental types, the tests of personality traits, the attitude tests, the scales of introversion-extraversion, ascendance-submission, perseverance, social distance and so on. The personality as a whole was explored by methods of projecting the self into a planned situation, as in the Rorschach method of giving a verbal interpretation of ink-blots, or the Thematic Apperception Test by making up stories about different pictures. We mention a few typical approaches to show what we are speaking about, but the point we would make is that however necessary these descriptions of personality are they still do not answer our question of *how the person came to be like that*. These methods of diagnosis of the person as he is are still, quite rightly, a large part of personality study.

Yet all the time other trends were developing. This could be seen by the appearance at the same date as Allport's book of a work by J. S. Plant called *Personality and the Cultural Pattern*. The title shows the new approach. By 1947, ten years later, a book by Gardner Murphy on *Personality: A Biosocial Approach*, shows the change of emphasis which had taken place. Murphy goes into origins, and calls on anthropology, child psychology, and social psychology to help him. A year later another typical work is a collection of studies edited by Clyde Kluckholn and H. A. Murray with the more comprehensive title still of *Personality in Nature, Society and Culture*, which has contributions from anthropologists, psycho-analysts, psychiatrists and medical psychologists, and includes the field theory approach of Kurt Lewin.[1] What had happened is clear. Anthropology and psychoanalysis had joined hands and were producing a new theory of the relation of the individual to his society. No psychologist could avoid the influence of this approach. Human behaviour can be explained and, up to a point, predicted by studying the growth of the individual in his social environment. The subject of Human Relations is another development, and the names of the sub-divisions of social science which contribute towards the new understandings of man's life in society matter less and less, except for methodological distinctions.

Let us consider another combined approach. It is becoming well known and generally accepted that many people show mild symptoms of maladjustment which only differ in degree from those of a sufferer from a neurotic illness. In fact few people have perfect mental health any more than perfect physical health. We all suffer from anxieties and fears against which we build up means of defence and escape which maintain us in a more or less 'normal' condition of adjustment. Our present-day culture generates a great deal of real anxiety, and ordinary observation will show the stress and strain under which many people work. It is in this respect that Karen Horney, among others in a group sometimes described as Neo-Freudians, has added to our knowledge of

[1] Field theory considers the individual as a structured organism in an environmental field, and is as it were the psychological equivalent of the culture concept.

the relations between culture and neurosis.[1] Her work is recommended to teachers and educationists not only because of its lucid explanation of the elements of psychoanalytic theory, but also because by studying the maladjusted it throws light on the process of normal development. She points out that neuroses are generated not only by individual peculiarities but by the specific cultural conditions under which we live. Life at the present day intensifies just the fears, contradictions, and conflicts that all with a tendency to neurosis are trying to avoid. We are in the presence of an apparently inescapable danger, we feel helpless and insignificant; we are engaged in a competitive struggle to live and are called upon to love our neighbours; we have our needs stimulated on every side, but are frustrated when we try to satisfy them. It is interesting that the Neo-Freudians differ from Freud over the stress to be laid on the repression of sexuality, and in particular because Freud neglected the cultural and sociological factors and based his theories on biologically given drives without accepting their susceptibility to social conditioning. Karen Horney also suggests that the existence of hostility and anxiety does not depend solely on experiences in early childhood, but undergoes development for better or worse, through the adjustment to other people in growing towards maturity.

Nevertheless there is no doubt of the importance of the emotional experiences in the intimate group of the family. It is here that the foundation of the authoritarian or democratic character is laid. The attitudes of the parents and the acceptance or rejection by the children of the parents' standards will be critical factors. Our culture still tends to encourage the dominative character structure, because for so long we have expected to have to fight in a competitive world both in peace and in war. Power-seeking and money-making are both normally considered as desirable, and the boy who rejected both would risk disapproval. The moral struggle against wrong doing is also emphasized, and in the authoritarian home severe punishment follows moral lapses. Harmony in the group, for instance at school, is not regarded as the normal expectation in our society, and this often makes the encouragement of co-operation difficult. Here again we are up against cultural determination passed on directly to the children, and while the cycle remains unbroken the old passions will continue to rule.

[1] Karen Horney: *The Neurotic Personality of Our Time*, 1937, *Neurosis and Human Growth*, 1951, and other works.

In the midst of considering all these external influences one is continually puzzled by whether there is such a thing as the 'real self' and how it can be understood. How early does a personality become a personality? A set of individual characteristics, unique and different from others, can be seen in quite small babies. That social behaviour is acquired one can easily believe, but how much of the core of personality grows out of its own innate beginnings? That there is an inborn core of potentialities in some form or other can hardly be doubted, and its differentiation begins to show itself very early in infancy.

Nor must we forget the development of the person within himself. He cannot become isolated from social life, but he can withdraw at times and be alone. It is in this realm of seclusion that we find the value of religion and the arts in providing unique individual experience. The individual may want to share his experiences, but he will always feel them within himself in a way peculiar to himself. Emotional and spiritual growth depend a great deal on these inner experiences, and the result of the debates we carry on with ourselves. Each person is of course influenced by others, it is unavoidable, but only he himself can know what he really believes. These inward and subjective searchings are not susceptible to scientific inquiry, except by the observer looking into himself and reporting what he finds. It is only our overt behaviour which can be compared with others.

Another question must be asked. For how long can our personalities change? So long as we are able to learn and to adapt to new circumstances it would seem that part at least of the personality remains modifiable.

HOW CAN WE BE CHANGED?

By education the behaviour of children is always being changed. It is the belief that they can put desirable aims before children, in a way that the children can accept and sometimes improve upon, that sustains teachers in their efforts. But there is a tendency to put too much responsibility on education for changing society. One hears it said that if only the young were brought up differently then we could within a generation produce an outlook that could transform the world. There is a limit to what education can do, and the limit depends partly on ourselves as educators. If we would transform society we must first transform ourselves. Let us therefore understand our limitations and study our strategy.

Education uses techniques of influencing behaviour, and is a means of social control, but normally in the interests of the *existing* society. We can also put an ideal of a different society before the young and do our best to educate for it, but only if we ourselves want it. We must also co-operate with all the social forces which are on our side, and oppose those which are against us. If not sufficiently supported by society outside, our efforts in the school are doomed to failure. Let us not forget that education tends to follow social change and not to lead it. Granted all these conditions let us see what the school can do. As an example let us suppose that we want to introduce a democratic atmosphere into a school, in the sense in which it was described in the preceding chapter. What steps would have to be taken?

(i) We must examine the relations between the staff of the school. Dr. Hughes, whose views have been quoted before, is definite on this point and writes: 'unless the staff is itself a democratic community there is no hope of the school becoming one.'[1] He raises the question of how we can cure ourselves of authoritarian tendencies, and answers, not by will power; we must grow out of them. He then gives an interesting clue to a method worth trying, which is quite in line with the principles of group dynamics as we shall outline them later in this chapter. He suggests the use of free group discussion. Staff meetings should turn into informal staff conferences. 'Courteous, even charming, notes issued from the Head's office are no adequate substitute for face-to-face discussions in his study.' The discussion must be free; it is easy to say this but actually this is *the most difficult matter of all* as we shall see. We must also assume that the head is willing to try the experiment, and is himself capable of being a democratic leader. Under these conditions what might happen has been described by the present author elsewhere as follows: 'With regard to inter-staff relations their improvement depends to a high degree on the attitudes and actions of the headmaster or headmistress. Heads of schools could act as change agents and develop a co-operative staff group where one did not exist before. Suppose the headmaster's problem is to achieve the smooth acceptance of a new scheme of work such as introducing a new time-table or a rearrangement of subject choices for the new examination. His strategy of action

[1] *Education and the Democratic Ideal*, p. 34.

could be to act as a discussion leader, or as the chairman of a staff council, rather than make all the decisions himself beforehand. Headmasters could carry out a little action research of their own in studying the transition from authoritarianism to democracy. This is called action research because the persons taking part in it are themselves involved in the change which their work is bringing about. . . . There is evidence from experiments in industry that successful group methods can produce more harmonious relations between people working together in a factory. And it has been shown that the integration of groups of workers who get on well with the management can increase production. If in a factory why not in a school; among the adults at least? It may be that some factories are more democratically run than many of our schools.'[1]

If the headmaster is a rigid autocrat such methods cannot possibly be used. Or it may be that he is in theory democratic, and apparently willing to co-operate but tied by his nature which is not really open to change. Openness to change depends on not being afraid of losing status or control. Older people are frequently status-ridden, and this is a great obstacle to learning new ways of behaviour.

(ii) The next step, in general terms, is to transfer the democratic attitudes to relations with the pupils. The teachers will make use of integrative methods instead of dominative ones (see pp. 181–85) by working with the children whenever possible instead of against them, and by inviting their participation whenever a reasonable opportunity presents itself. The teacher still remains in a position of authority, but that does not mean that he uses dominative behaviour. The central problem of authority is the way it is used. The democratic use of authority achieves better results, and is a much happier and more inspiring method of working. The teacher's position becomes that of a group leader. The difficulty so often is that teachers have no other model to follow but the traditional autocratic one. The old model persists, and until the teacher has seen or experienced a *successful* situation of a different kind he feels insecure and unwilling to change.

(iii) The result of democratic attitudes will gradually be to change the expectation of the school classes and groups from antagonism to harmony. It will be expected that people will work amicably together and try to seek agreement. The members of the group would normally

[1] 'Social Relations in the School', in *Researches and Studies,* Leeds University Institute of Education, No. 4, May 1951.

feel happy and creative. This expectation of good relations should start as early as possible.

The social climate of the nursery and infant school is often the best of all, and if this were carried through the junior school it would be a good foundation for democratic relations in the secondary stage. By starting early we can help to 'secure for children a happy childhood and a better start in life',[1] and hope that the psychoanalysts are right and that the early attitudes will tend to remain in spite of the child meeting an adverse environment later on. Unfortunately the school may already start with a disadvantage, for the outstanding difficulty is to change the attitudes of the parents. One despairs of any short-term method of achieving this; hence the slowness of change.

(iv) A further result will be that the school staff will encourage criticism and free discussion among the pupils. We speak now in particular of the older ages, but there are appropriate types of free discussion at the junior stage. There seems no reason why, when the social climate is suitable, the methods of the school itself should not come under discussion. We have already put the case for school councils and various forms of democratic machinery (see pp. 169–76). In addition to this the open expression of ideas should become a feature of the school, and the inevitable differences and clash of opinion tolerated and turned to constructive use. This is entirely in accord with the democratic principle of freedom of speech and opinion, and the respect for minority views.

(v) We would go further still and say that the school should encourage those children who do not appear to be going to fit our society. Their vision may one day be better than ours. Change in the culture comes from those who do not fit. We speak of healthy and creative misfits, and do not refer to those who deviate in such a way as to be classed as markedly neurotic, or who are quite unprofitably rebellious. These need special treatment and must be regarded as ill. But let us watch for children with new ideas and special gifts. Gifted children often do not fit the cultural pattern, and they may be our future inventors and pioneers. It is the test of the democratic use of authority that it can accept differences, even when such differences challenge the authity itself. It is true that the school must beware of producing pioneer types who are too far out of step with society, though, if they are pre-

[1] Among the opening words of the White Paper on *Educational Reconstruction*, 1943.

pared and strong enough to meet a hostile world, even those with extreme views can become useful citizens. It is also true that very severe attempts to suppress the innovator may turn him into an enemy of society.

Such a picture of the democratic school community may not attract some of our readers. They may be reassured by the thought that it cannot happen in many schools until there is a considerable change in the attitudes of teachers. But they should ask themselves seriously whether they do not think such a change desirable, if carried out with common sense, and in no freakish spirit of progressiveness.

GROUP DYNAMICS

Recent investigations have shown latent powers for changing the attitudes and future actions of individuals by their participation in small groups, under certain conditions.[1] These methods have not only been employed for group therapy in the psychiatric sense, but for any form of group activity where the better co-operation of the members is the objective. We have already pointed out that the working together in small groups is a characteristic of education in schools (see p. 176), and we refer above to the possibilities of free discussion for changing the attitudes of members of a school staff. The small group is very frequently used in our society as a technique for consultation, framing policy or deciding executive action, and examples readily come to mind in industry and commerce, in administration through committees of all kinds, and in politics. All such groups have certain features in common when we examine them from the point of view of human relations.

The following account of some of the conditions for the successful working of small groups is not taken from any particular source, but represents the author's analysis as a result of his experience.

All groups begin with some *interest* in common. The members come together with a purpose, and their aim may be called *co-operation* of some kind, whether it be for learning, for better understanding of each

[1] For accounts of such investigations the reader is referred to W. J. H. Sprott: *Human Groups*, 1958, Chaps. 7–11. Josephine Klein: *Working with Groups*, 1961. J. E. Richardson: 'Group Dynamics and the School', *Brit. J. Educ. Studies*, IV, No. 2, 1956. A. K. C. Ottaway: 'Group Dynamics—Some Notes on an Experiment', *Case Conference*, Vol. 6, No. 7, Jan. 1960. Ruth Strang: *Group Work in Education*, 1958.

other, or for deciding on action to be taken. In order to achieve co-operation there must be successful *participation* by the group members. The essential condition for participation is that all the members should take part, and that no member should be excluded from the thought and action of the group. Participation is not the same as co-operation, because the members may so strongly disagree, while taking part, that no successful co-operation follows. The expectation of the group should be that they are seeking agreement, even though they should not expect to reach it easily, and not try to force a superficial agreement. We are not speaking of groups with a dominating leader and with members expected to conform. Our analysis refers only to attempts at democratic groups, where the aim is the integration of different purposes. It should be noted that when fully carried out this aim is something more than compromise. A compromise is an adjustment between opposing views, and is often a necessary stage towards co-operation, or the only form of co-operation which is possible under the circumstances. But the ideal of integrating different purposes is that the opponents between them create a new synthesis of ideas, and willingly accept the new purpose which emerges.

Participation involves expression, thinking and feeling. Expression in words immediately brings up the difficulty of the communication of ideas. People are often said 'not to talk the same language' and this is true, because while all are apparently speaking English, different people attach different meanings to the same words. Hence the importance of clarity of thought and the transmitting of the thought in words that other people understand.

By thinking in a group we mean what might perhaps be called group thinking, whereby each member is not merely concerned with his own thoughts but is trying to bring them into active relation with what the others are thinking. Whether there is agreement or disagreement there should be relevance of thought to the matter in hand.

The place of feeling in participation is the need for achieving the sort of atmosphere in the group in which people feel able and willing to take part. There should be what is called a 'permissive' atmosphere, where members feel they can express themselves freely, as opposed to a 'restrictive' atmosphere which stifles expression and holds up participation.

The progress of the group may be thought of in stages though it should be said at once that these are only separated for the sake of analysis, and that in practice the work of the group is continuous, with stages overlapping, becoming telescoped together, or repeating themselves in a different order. Nevertheless there can be seen a certain cycle of interaction which is represented diagrammatically in Figure V.

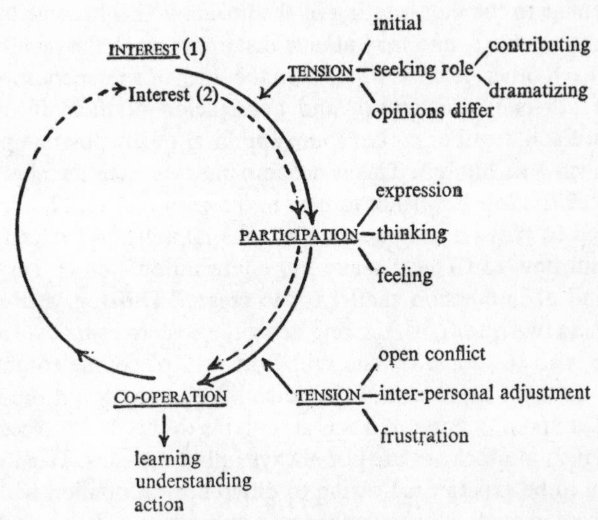

FIGURE V

Diagram showing the internal cycle of interaction within a small group. The circle can be thought of as the base of a spiral, and each time it goes round it covers new space. One never in fact comes back to the same stage in a group, since the situation has always changed.

The cycle of interest-participation-co-operation cannot be given a certain *time* in which it will take place. It may be repeated several times within one meeting of the group, or on the other hand several meetings may take place before any co-operation has been achieved. Each time successful co-operation is reached the group reaches a new level of interest, and participation continues in a new situation.

We wish to draw particular attention to the stages of *tension* within the group. Our analysis would run as follows:

Stage I. The members meet together with some common purpose. There is a chairman, director, or leader of some kind whatever he is called. All groups have a leader. If they begin without one they acquire one, or more than one, in the course of their proceedings. (We shall deal with the functions of the leader later.) An agenda has been drawn up or an announcement is made of the purpose of the group.

Tension I. There is a type of tension which develops while participation is beginning, and before it gets into full swing. There are *initial* tensions peculiar to the first meeting of the group, which become less with subsequent meetings, and may almost disappear when the members get to know each other. Such tensions take the form of an uncertainty of the status of others in the group, and a suspicion of them if they are strangers. Each member makes some appraisal of the possible purpose of others *vis-à-vis* himself. This is accompanied by each member beginning to seek the role he wishes to play in the group, or that he thinks he is expected to play. It may be that he asks himself: 'What can I contribute and how can I best make my contribution?' or he may think 'What kind of impression shall I try to create?' Different attitudes lie behind these two questions, the one being the wish to *contribute* and the other the wish to *dramatize* the self. Both will of course combine together in different degrees, and the person begins to try out the role he has decided upon, to find out if it is acceptable to the group. Needless to say these mental processes are not always fully conscious. Tensions will also begin to be experienced owing to differences of opinion within the group. These may often be unspoken and only felt to lie behind what the speaker is actually saying. Now the group is interacting and participation is beginning.

Stage II. This is the stage of full participation when people express themselves freely and show evidence of thinking and feeling. Before participation can lead to agreement and co-operation other and more difficult tensions will be experienced. While all appears to be going quite smoothly deeper differences of opinion will begin to show themselves.

Tension II. This is characterized by real, open conflicts developing and the group making its attempts to resolve them. For the group to reach agreement some degree of *inter-personal adjustment* has to take place. This means that members must face the fact of their personal disagreement, and must accept each other's views *as part of the group situation* even when they find they still cannot agree. It is when people know how, and when possible why, they disagree that a new synthesis of views is most likely to appear, or a minority view is included which is really respected.

If sufficient resolving of conflicts is not possible the obstacles developed at this stage may break up the group. The group can be frustrated, energy wasted, and participation may even cease.

Stage III. Finally co-operation begins and energy flows freely. Members of the group become orientated with their wills pulling together, and there is a feeling that a new source of energy has been tapped. The deliberations are led to a new level of interest and pressed on to the next occasion of disagreement and tension. Ultimately a successful group provides for all its members opportunity for (a) new learning and the enrichment of personality, (b) fuller understanding and better human relations, and (c) action in a common task.

The functions for the Leader

A great deal has been written about leadership, and it is not a concept that can be briefly defined. A recent view, which we accept, is that there is no quality of leadership in the abstract, but that there are different kinds of leadership according to the people who have to be led and the situation they find themselves in. There will nevertheless be some attributes which all leaders require. We are speaking now of the qualities needed by the leader of a small group, be it a committee, a staff meeting or a business conference, and the activity which has to be led is a mixture of thinking, feeling and talking. Some of these qualities may be of value in other situations while others may not. They can be listed as follows:

(i) The leader needs to be able to see the group in its dynamic situation, and be aware of the group processes we have just described.

(ii) He should be friendly and give a permissive feeling to the group, creating an atmosphere of spontaneity and confidence. He should be able to achieve good relations between himself and the group.

(iii) The leader must be felt to be a part of the group, one of them, but also in some way superior to the group, and therefore worthy of their respect. This is the real meaning of being accepted by the group as the leader. If the group reject him he cannot continue to lead them.

(iv) The honesty of the leader is essential. He must be fair-minded and seeking the truth, and not be tempted to deceive the group even when trying to persuade them.

(v) His main task is to develop participation and co-operation by overcoming the difficulties and tensions involved in the situation. He may be aided in this task by (a) a certain amount of planning the agenda beforehand, (b) by using the control expected of a good chairman, (c) by clear thinking, and preserving the logic of the discussion in spite of the emotional undercurrents which will be present.

(vi) His greatest asset will be to know the members of the group and be able to anticipate some of their behaviour. This will help the leader in dealing with the disruptive members of the group, and in encouraging those who are trying to bind the group together. There are often some members who tend to be aggressive and attack others or disapprove of the discussion. The leader should try never to lose patience or be over-assertive or aggressive himself, as this is a certain way of disrupting the group atmosphere.

(vii) The leader should be able to provide a 'feed-back' of information to the group. This means that he should, to some extent, interpret what has happened and explain to the group how they have reached a particular conflict or difficulty. If there is strong disagreement the whole group should be faced with the disagreement, because the conflict must be resolved in some way or other before progress can be made.

(viii) Finally the leader should always seek opportunities for passing on the responsibility to the group. It is wrong for the group to expect too much from the leader, and to rely upon him to do their thinking for them. There should be a gradual transition from the leader-centred group to self-reliance in all members of the group. Under some circumstances the leadership can be allowed to pass round to other members of the group. This is a sign that there is no over-reliance on one particular leader, and indicates a healthy condition in the group.

The above brief outline of the dynamics of groups has referred in particular to adult groups, since it was the re-education of the adult we had so strongly in mind when we asked: 'How can we be changed?' In educational groups where direct teaching takes place it must be realized that, while most of the above principles hold, the position of the leader is a different one. While the teacher often acts like a good group leader he is after all a professional teacher. This means he is not in a group of approximate equals so far as knowledge or experience are concerned. The class must clearly accept this distinction, but still should regard the teacher in a sense as one of them and engaged in a joint inquiry with them. It is still his task to encourage in his class the active wish to learn instead of passively to listen while they are told. As a matter of good teaching technique he needs to restrain himself as the leader and let the class do the thinking for themselves.

We believe that this last section on group dynamics is very relevant to the wider problems of our society. Leadership is needed more than ever in a modern democracy, but it is leadership of a new kind which is required. While we have stressed that the qualities of a leader depend on the situation he is in, the technique of successfully leading a small group has much in common with democratic leadership in general. It requires genuine authority and influence but not of an autocratic kind. The democratic leader, like the good teacher, does not restrict others unnecessarily, nor impose his own will in a dictatorial fashion, nor resist change. He invites co-operation and is unafraid and tolerant of disagreement, aiming always to transmute differences into a new form of agreement. He leads by persuasion and reason rather than by arbitrary command. He is not a power-seeker for its own sake, and uses what authority he has for the general welfare. Above all he preserves the ideals of those he leads, and is linked with them, and with their purposes, by the bonds of an affection unmixed with fear.

CHAPTER XI

Beyond Sociology: A Note on the Social Philosophy of Democracy

THROUGHOUT the major part of this book we have been speaking of education for a democratic society. We have thus made the basic assumption, or pre-supposition, that what we call democracy is the best way of life. The sociologist can record that this is an assumption that the majority of people in our society make, and can study its effects on the social system, but to justify it and consider its ultimate ends is outside his immediate province. To ask the question: Why do we believe in democracy?' is to enter the realm of social philosophy. Our first chapter ended with the suggestion that educators needed a set of beliefs on which to base their educational aims. It is not enough to educate for society as it is, we must also ask what its future ought to be, and direct our energies towards the realization of our ideal.

This takes us beyond the sociology of education, and we are not adding this final chapter in order to elaborate a whole philosophy of democracy. This would not only require another book, but it is a task that has already been performed by others more qualified to undertake it. Our intention is merely to try and clarify the issues involved, since it is impossible to write on sociology without touching on questions concerning the nature of man and the meaning of civilization.

In the first place we cannot avoid some responsibility for deciding in which direction we think our society ought to develop. Through education we are making a deliberate attempt to guide the development of children, and anyone who sets out to guide others must be following *some* theory, conscious or unconscious, of the direction in which they should go. There is really no such thing as allowing the child freedom to develop in his own way. Let us not be misunderstood. In one sense the child's freedom and his power of choice is his most precious possession, and the educator will always respect the uniqueness of each individual and his need to realize his potentialities to the full. This respect for the child's freedom will include his right to be different; and his ultimate responsibility to decide his own course of action. What we mean is that whatever we do, and we cannot do nothing, the child will inevitably be influenced by the prevailing culture of his society. It is our responsibility as full members of our society to take our share in deciding its aims, in the full knowledge that our choice will influence those we teach.

In the second place we shall find that in making our choice of values we can only get a limited amount of help from the social sciences as such. Once we assume that freedom and democracy are worth having, then the social sciences can give us some assistance in the means of carrying out our desired ends. It may be that we can plan for freedom, but we first have to decide what kind of freedom we desire. It may be that the science of human behaviour can give us some control over men's actions, but we have first to judge what results we wish to follow from the actions. It is one of the functions of science to provide the means for achieving what we desire, the results of scientific experiment may guide us in making our choice of ends, even when these are moral ends. The investigations of social science are certainly relevant to ethics, but this is a long way from saying that science can provide a complete foundation for ethical principles. We need to go beyond social science to decide on what values we should base our society and our education. Our knowledge of social processes, of psychology, and of the science of human behaviour may then be able to help us to achieve our aims in practice.

After these preliminary remarks on the need for a social philosophy, and the inadequacy of science to provide it let us get a little closer to our difficulties. It soon becomes clear that it is not enough to say that you regard freedom and democracy as ends in themselves. Apart from the extreme vagueness of the terms you are faced with the questions: 'Freedom for what?' and 'After full democracy is achieved what is the next ideal?' Freedom and democracy are only worth while if they are the means for achieving the kind of life that men ought to live. What is this kind of life?

The need is to find an ideal for the members of our democracy to follow. We shall suggest that our society should aim at becoming more and more civilized, according to the meaning of civilization which will now be described.

Civilization is a word which is very loosely used and our argument depends on its definition. We think it a mistake to define civilization in terms of material progress.[1] In its essence it concerns the quality of relations between people. The moral and spiritual test is better than the material one. Thus we do not base our definition on *civis*, a citizen, because of its association with living like a townsman, although, in fact, the attempt to live a peaceful life in community with others is the origin of being civilized. Living in a modern city is not a test of being civilized, and we would prefer to base our definition on the act of being civil. Civility in Dr. Johnson's dictionary is defined as 'the state of being civilized; freedom from barbarity.' Further the same word civilization is used for something which has happened, a dead civilization, and for something which is to come, the future civilization, so that it does not stand for something fixed but is a *process*,[2] which can be said to have a goal or ideal. We define civilization as a process towards civility.

Here we find our ideas running parallel with those of R. G. Collingwood who has fully worked out a meaning of society and of civilization in his book *The New Leviathan*. 'The essence of civilization', says Collingwood, 'is civility.' We will make a brief reference to his views without any claim to represent them exactly. We include it in the hope that it will draw the attention of students of education to Collingwood's work, which in our opinion deserves to be more widely known among educators. To begin by quoting a passage: 'Behaving civilly to a man means respecting his feelings: abstaining from . . . arousing in him any passion or desire which might diminish his self-respect; that is threaten his consciousness of freedom by making him feel that his power of choice is in danger of breaking down and the passion or desire likely to

[1] Cf. MacIver: 'By civilization, then, we mean the whole mechanism and organization which man has devised in his endeavour to control the conditions of his life. *Society*, p. 498. On the same page he gives the typewriter and the telephone as organs of civilization, and also various forms of social organization. This is precisely what we have described as techniques with the subdivision of social techniques. These are only means and we regard civilization as an end.

[2] Arnold Toynbee also thinks of civilization as a process. He writes: 'Civilization, as we know it, is a movement and not a condition, a voyage and not a harbour. No known civilization has ever reached the goal of civilization yet.' *Civilization on Trial*, p. 55.

take charge.'[1] He continues by pointing out that taking away a man's self-respect is equivalent to exercising force over him. He becomes a slave. So 'the ideal of civil behaviour in one's dealings with one's fellow men is the ideal of refraining from the use of force towards them'.[2] Becoming less addicted to the use of force is seen to be one of the chief aims of our civilization in its progress towards civility. Respecting the rule of law is the way of expressing this in democratic terms. But it is more than that; it is based on loving your neighbour as yourself, which is a moral quality, and is the essential principle of the democratic philosophy. Collingwood admits that some degree of force will always be necessary, because no society on earth can be perfect. The important thing is that we accept as a moral principle that reason and persuasion are better than force, and maintain that principle however much force may still have to be used in an imperfect world.[3] The less we use force the more we should reckon ourselves as civilized.

Also when men mean to reach agreement about the relations between themselves they treat each other with civility. So that when we believe that socially integrative behaviour is better than dominative behaviour (the contrast we have made in Chapter IX), we do so out of respect for the feelings of our fellow men, and from a desire to abstain from the use of force towards them.

The other important aim of our civilization concerns our relations with the natural world. This is the means whereby the members of a society become more able to get what necessaries or luxuries they demand by the intelligent exploitation of the natural world. The result is material progress, which as we have stated is not the final test of civilization. We will not make the mistake Disraeli referred to when he wrote of 'a society which has mistaken comfort for civilization', and he wrote of Europe not America. At the same time the value of material progress is not to be lightly disregarded. It is important to be well fed, well clothed, and have protection from the weather. It is important to reduce the amount of hard manual labour and to increase the amount of

[1] *The New Leviathan*, 1942, p. 291.

[2] Ibid., p. 292.

[3] Cf. Ortega y Gassett: 'Civilization is nothing else than the attempt to reduce force to the *ultima ratio*. . . . Direct action of the modern fascist and communist consists in proclaiming force as the *prima ratio*, or strictly *unica ratio*.' *The Revolt of the Masses*, 1930. New English Edn., 1951, p. 54.

comfort and material well being. It is our considerable success in controlling nature which has given us the means by which we can live in health, and have the leisure to enjoy the fruits of our art and culture. This is the way communities build up wealth and achieve vitality. And it also happens that the progress of science is brought about by the free interchange of knowledge between one person and another. The vast body of technical knowledge we possess was built up by agreement, and by being willing to teach others, that is to give a civil answer to a civil question. So Collingwood points out again that the essence of civilization, even on the material level, is civility.

It is now possible to gain a fuller understanding of the meaning of a free society. The free society is also an ideal state of affairs. It is wrong to say that our democracy is already a free society, but it is right to say that this is the ideal towards the realization of which we are striving. It should not be difficult to see that the free society is also the civilized society. The reason for wishing to become free is in order to become more civilized. Freedom is not an end in itself, nor is the free development of personality a satisfying aim unless it is guided by some ideal. By ideal we mean some idea in the mind of what ought to be. Freedom is one of the means, or conditions, for achieving the kind of life men ought to live. This is the life of civility, based on the respect and love of one's fellow men. (That the idea of freedom also includes the idea of discipline is another argument which does not affect anything we are saying about freedom.)

We do not here distinguish the aim of the individual from the aim of his society. A society becomes more free the more its members gain a consciousness of their freedom and their power of choice, and as they become ruled by the exercise of their own free will.

A free society is formed by the joint activity of free agents. For instance, if you are forced to join a society it is not, for you, a free society. Having social consciousness implies having a will by the activity of which you can agree with others about the ruling of your society. Ideally such a society would rule itself, but in reality it must give some of its members authority over others. This will involve the use of force by the authority. Why? Because a society is always accompanied by a non-social community. The community is everybody, adults and children, social and non-social persons, and the society is the socially conscious part of the community. Force is not necessary for those who freely accept the authority of their society, but it is necessary for children and immature members, and those who do not share full social consciousness or who break the law. This force will be exercised by permission of the joint will of the society's members through their appointed rulers. This is the safeguard against the arbitrary use of force which we already possess to a high degree in our own democratic society.

Living in such a society and civilization will also make men happier and more creative. Happiness alone is not enough, and it does not usually come when it is put as a chief object of desire. Happiness is a result of living rather than an aim. But creativeness, we suggest, is the other quality we desire which has a value equal to that of civility. If more creativeness is liberated by democracy this provides another good reason for believing in it.

We have already seen that creation in science depends on the free interchange of ideas and on civil relations between the collaborators. This is equally true of the arts. Science and art both require a certain degree of freedom in order to flourish. Some opposition may stimulate creation; but too much can kill it. We may be certain that there is enough to struggle against in the most peaceful life to challenge the creative spirit. The creative man is not always happy, but he loves his work and at times is the happiest of men, when he comes successfully through the efforts which may cause him pain.

We conclude that our democratic society, by aiming to become more and more free and civilized, can lead to an increase of civility and creativeness. These are its two chief values, and both are allied to love.

We will now ask the question: 'Do we also need a belief in absolute values?' It could be held that the values we have so far spoken of are not absolute in the sense of being outside of time and space. Suppose they are immanent in history, that is to say they have evolved and continue to evolve through the process of history. It is true that they are ideals held in the minds of men, but they could be held differently, or not at all, by other men at other times or in other places. It may become possible to provide convincing evidence that these values are good for man as we know him; meaning that to follow them is a way of preserving his civilization in peace and preventing its destruction. They could then be said to have universal validity for men on this earth, but does this make them eternal?

The case for absolute values as a necessary basis for a theory of education is put with great strength in the introduction to the *Norwood Report*. It says:

'We believe that education cannot stop short of recognizing the ideals of truth and beauty and goodness as final and binding for all times and in all places as ultimate values. . . . Further, we hold that the recognition of such values implies, for most people at least, a religious interpretation of life which for us must mean the Christian interpretation of life. We have no sympathy, therefore, with a theory of education which presupposes that its aim can be dictated by the provisional findings of special sciences, whether biological, psychological or sociological, that the function of education is to fit pupils to determine their outlook and conduct according to the changing needs and changing standards of the day. We agree wholeheartedly that scientific method and scientific planning can do much to help in the realization of the 'good life', and the education which does not avail itself of such aid denies itself one means to the realization of its ends. But our belief is that education from its own nature must be ultimately concerned with values which are independent of time or particular environment, though realizable under changing forms in both, and therefore that no programmes of education which concern themselves only with relative ends and the immediate adaptation of the individual to existing surroundings can be acceptable.'

There can be no doubt of the assumptions made in this passage. It assumes ultimate values independent of time and space, and does not accept social or ethical relativity, by which is meant the theory that social needs and ethical standards are relative to a particular environment. It is a religious interpretation of life, and would accept revelation as a source of knowledge in addition to reason and experience.

It is relevant in thinking of these problems to consider two different meanings which are given to the nature of man. For the sociologist, speaking only as a sociologist, the nature of man is what can be observed and inferred from man's behaviour in different parts of the world. All men have certain drives and needs in common which would be expected of members of the same species. Some values may therefore be universally valid for all societies because they serve the needs of man's basic nature. But in general human nature is variable and evolving.

To the christian human nature means something unchangeable, eternal, a spiritual reality, the perfection of which is in some way already decided or known to God. What is good for men at any time or place, because they are men, implies that present-day problems are changing forms of permanent problems. The different ways in which men understand values at different times and places are only changing forms of permanent values. Each age, then, has its own problems and values which it has to interpret in the light of the eternal verities. The argument is a strong one.

The Christian would add that it is under the inspiration of the Gospels that we have come to understand the dignity of man and to realize the democratic values. Christ taught the laws of brotherly love and the natural equality of all. The Christian would say with Henri Bergson that 'democracy is evangelical in essence . . . its motive power is love'.

And so it may be that the essential clue to why we believe in educating for a free society is only to be found in a religious approach to life. Education for civilization, yes, but it can still be asked: 'Civilization for what?' Shall we answer with Bishop Wilson, so often quoted by Matthew Arnold, 'That reason and the will of God may prevail'?

BIBLIOGRAPHY

PART I. THE SOCIOLOGY OF EDUCATION

GENERAL LIST

THE following references are arranged in chronological order and annotated to give some idea of the development of thought on the social aspects of education during this century. This list is only a selection of possible readings, and the works are chosen which best illustrate stages in the growth of new ideas on the sociology of education.

1899 DEWEY, JOHN. *The School and Society*. Chicago: University Press (2nd edition, 1915). Cambridge University Press. 1932. A pioneer book, much ahead of its time. John Dewey was one of the first thinkers to realize the influence of the rapid changes of the modern world on education, and to aim at reconciling the needs of the individual with the new needs of his society.

1903 DURKHEIM, EMILE. *Pédagogie et Sociologie. Revue de Métaphysique et de Morale*. Janvier, 1903. This paper was reprinted along with some other early lectures of Durkheim in a book entitled *Education et Sociologie*. Paris: Felix Alcan. 1922. Durkheim's work is of considerable historical interest. He stressed that since each society determines its own educational system, the methods and aims of education will vary according to the society in which they originate. Thus each society seeks to train the kind of human being it needs for its particular stage of civilization. In this respect he was in agreement with the views of modern social anthropologists. Translated as *Education and Sociology*, Free Press, 1956.

1908 SCOTT, COLIN A. *Social Education*. Boston: Ginn & Co. Not an important work, but it indicates the early development of the social point of view on education in the U.S.A. About this time courses in the social aspects of education began to be given in some American universities.

1916 DEWEY, JOHN. *Democracy and Education*. New York: Macmillan. This well-known work still remains of fundamental importance, and stimulated the developing study of educational sociology, which to begin with was mainly American. Dewey relates the social function of education to its aims and methods, as much in the day to day learning of the child as in the types of experience to be encouraged in a democratic society.

BIBLIOGRAPHY

1917 SMITH, W. R. *An Introduction to Educational Sociology*. Boston: Houghton Mifflin (revised edn. 1929). This was the first textbook on the social approach to use the name 'educational sociology'. It was quickly followed in the U.S.A. by others, such as the works of W. E. Chancellor, 1919, F. R. Clow, 1920 and David Snedden, 1922.

1921 ADAMSON, J. E. *The Individual and the Environment*. London: Longmans Green. An attempt to develop a theory of education in terms of adjustment to nature, society and the world of moral values. Book II treats of the relation of education to the political, national, religious and economic trends in the fabric of society, and while under the influence of Dewey, is written from the British point of view.

1923 CLARKE, F. *Essays in the Politics of Education*. Cape Town and Johannesburg. These essays suggest a social conception of education to some extent in opposition to Nunn's advocacy of the value of individuality, which was the dominant theory of education in England at the time. They are of interest as an early statement by a writer who was later to have a great influence on the development of the sociology of education.

1924 PETERS, CHARLES C. *Foundations of Educational Sociology*. New York: Macmillan (revised edn. 1930). Another textbook typical of a number of American works in the late 1920's and early 1930's such as those of Alvin Good and R. L. Finney.

1927 PAYNE, GEORGE E. and others founded the *Journal of Educational Sociology*. At this time writers had, for the most part, been applying the studies of pure sociology to education, with little integration of the two disciplines. Now a new trend to study educational problems from a sociological point of view can be seen, and is illustrated by George E. Payne's collection, *Readings in Educational Sociology*. Prentice Hall. 1932.

1932 WALLER, WILLARD. *The Sociology of Teaching*. New York: John Wiley. A good account of the relations between the school and the community with some interpretations of social life within the school. This book shows a new emphasis by beginning to examine the influence of the group life as a determinant of individual behaviour.

1932 RUSSELL, BERTRAND. *Education and the Social Order*. London: Allen & Unwin. Russell had already written *On Education* in 1926, dealing largely with individual development from early childhood. In the work here noted he discusses the difficulty of educating both the individual and the citizen, and examines how these aims can be reconciled.

1934 BENEDICT, RUTH. *Patterns of Culture*. New York: Houghton Mifflin. 1934. London: Routledge. 1935. Although not written ostensibly about education this book, along with other studies of social anthropologists, had an influence of outstanding importance on educational sociology. Two important books by Margaret Mead, her *Coming of Age in Samoa*, 1928, and *Growing Up in New Guinea*, 1930, had already appeared, and Ralph Linton's *Study of Man* was published in 1936. Educationists now gradually began to be aware of the extent to which the personality of the individual is influenced by the culture patterns of the society in which he grows up.

1935 HUBBACK, E. M. and SIMON, E. D. *Training for Citizenship*. Oxford University Press. By the initiative of these authors the Association for Education in Citizenship was founded in the same year. This Association has been responsible for producing, in the fifteen years which followed, a number of books and pamphlets of great value to the student of the social aspects of education. Education for citizenship became much more the concern of British statesmen and educators as totalitarian systems began to threaten our democratic way of life. Through this threat a fuller consciousness of the social functions of education began to develop.

1936 CLARKE, F. *et al. Review of Educational Thought*. London: Evans Bros These articles were reprinted from *The Year Book of Education*, 1936, and give an account of the growth of ideas leading to a turning point in English educational theory in the mid-1930's, when the sociological emphasis began to grow rapidly. Educators, along with other social theorists, were becoming very conscious of the changing nature of modern society and the importance of the new concept of 'culture patterns' as determinants of social growth.

1937 KILPATRICK, W. H. (Ed.). *The Teacher and Society*. New York: Appleton Century. This collection of articles was the First Year Book of the John Dewey Society, and illustrates the new sociological emphasis in American thinking, whereby education is studied in its interaction with with society and culture. This same trend can be noted by the devotion of a whole issue of the *Review of Educational Research*, Feb. 1937 to Educational Sociology. Subsequently research and literature on the social background of education and similar topics has been listed and commented upon every three years in the above *Review*, e.g. Feb. 1940, 1943, etc.

1940 CLARKE, F. *Education and Social Change*. London: Sheldon Press. A small book which has had a great influence. It is a concise statement of some of the historical determinants of English education, and a series of suggestions for the readaptation of the system to the social changes now accelerated by the onset of war.

1940 LEYBOURNE, G. and WHITE, K. *Education and Birthrate*. London: Jonathan Cape. This work is quoted as an excellent example of a quantitative social research studying the relations between the cost of education, and various social factors, with the willingness of parents to have children. The interpretations given throw much light on the attitudes of different social classes in England towards education.

1942 STEAD, H. G. *The Education of a Community*. University of London Press. A persuasive analysis of the challenge to the English education system to adapt to new social needs. While many chapters are arguments for reforms now achieved by the 1944 Education Act, the main sociological theme still illustrates contemporary problems.

1942 LESTER SMITH, W. O. *To Whom do Schools Belong?* Oxford: Basil Blackwell (revised 1945). A study of the ideas affecting the control of education in the historical development of the English system. The claims of the state are compared with the demands of other social forces, and the various aspects of the English compromise between the varied interests, whether private or public, traditional or progressive, are excellently described.

1943 MANNHEIM, KARL. *Diagnosis of Our Time.* London: Kegan Paul. The influence of Karl Mannheim as a writer and lecturer has been of the greatest importance in developing the sociology of education in the post-war period. His concepts of social techniques and the necessity of democratic planning were already put forward in his *Man and Society* first printed in English in 1940, but this is a much more difficult work than the one here quoted, which is the best introduction to Mannheim's ideas.

1944 INSTITUTE OF SOCIOLOGY, LE PLAY HOUSE. Report (Ed. E. M. Dymes.) *Sociology and Education.* Ledbury: Le Play House Press. An excellent collection of papers read at a Conference in 1943. Many of the other publications of Le Play House are of great value to the student of education, for example the reports *Synthesis in Education*, 1946, and *The School and Society*, 1949.

1944 WARNER, W. LLOYD, *et al. Who Shall Be Educated?* New York: Harper & Bros. London: Kegan Paul, 1946. A factual study of the relations between social status, social mobility, and education in the U.S.A., with some reflections on the implications for democracy.

1946 HARVARD REPORT. *General Education in a Free Society.* Harvard University Press. An exposition by a group of American educationists of the problems and conditions facing education for democracy. The extent to which education should be consciously used to produce a given type of citizen is a recurrent problem, which is again being debated in Britain as in the U.S.A. in terms of a developing democratic philosophy of education.

1947 BROWN, F. J. *Educational Sociology.* New York: Prentice Hall. A typical example of a sound, recent American textbook. Regards education as one of the fields of applied sociology. The interaction approach is used for the relations between individuals and groups, and between the school and other social groups.

1948 CLARKE, SIR F. *Freedom in the Educative Society.* University of London Press. This short book expresses in a condensed form some of the problems of relating education to culture in a society which is attempting, in Mannheim's terms, to 'plan for freedom'. It is one of a series edited by W. R. Niblett, all of which have some sociological emphasis. Note for example Marjorie Reeves: *Growing up in a Modern Society*, 1946 and W. R. Niblett: *Essential Education*, 1947.

1949 LESTER SMITH, W. O. *The Impact of Education on Society*. Oxford: Basil Blackwell. The three Joseph Payne Lectures of 1948. Deals with the relation of the schools to society in the past, present and future.

1949 RUSSELL, BERTRAND. *Authority and the Individual*. London: Allen & Unwin. In these first series of Reith Lectures Russell discusses how it is possible to combine individual initiative with the necessary degree of social cohesion to keep modern society together. He thus deals with social psychological and political problems which lie behind all educational effort.

1950 COOK, LLOYD A., and COOK, E. F. *A Sociological Approach to Education*. McGraw-Hill Book Co. Recommended as the best of recent American textbooks. It is a revision of *Community Backgrounds in Education*, 1938, which was also an excellent book of its time, but the present revision is much better. This work applies sociological knowledge and techniques to the whole educative process both in school and outside. The authors regard education as a group process, and see educational problems as essentially problems of society. They thus make use of the latest concepts from anthropology and social psychology, and include a chapter on 'Group Dynamics in the School'. Its great disadvantage for English readers is that it is written entirely from the point of view of living in the U.S.A.

1950 *The Year Book of Education*. Editors: J. A. Lauwerys and N. Hans. Published in association with the University of London Institute of Education by Evans Bros. The theme is the relation of education to occupational selection and social mobility in many different countries. The annual *Year Book of Education* has been a valuable reference book in comparative education since its beginning in 1932. Its post-war volumes, re-starting in 1948, have tended more and more towards a sociological treatment. Note the articles in the 1949 volume by F. Clarke, I. L. Kandel, S. Hessen and others. The 1952 volume is devoted entirely to the reform of education seen as a form of social change.

1951 HUGHES, A. G. *Education and the Democratic Ideal*. London: Longmans Green. This excellent book, based on lectures to teachers, is an up-to-date analysis of the problems of the use of authority in schools. The views expressed on the meaning of democratic methods, and their use in school communities, are both provocative and profound.

1954 GLASS, DAVID (Ed.). *Social Mobility in Britain*. Routledge and Kegan Paul. This volume gives the results of researches into the social origins, education and occupational achievements of a random sample of 10,000 adults in Britain. Thus for the first time some evidence was provided to show that education had become one of the main agents of occupational and thus social mobility during the first fifty years of this century. There are some chapters specially devoted to educational problems, namely Chap. 5, by Jean Floud; Chap. 6, by Hilda Himmelweit; Chap. 7, by F. M. Martin; and Chap. 10, by J. R. Hall and D. V. Glass.

BIBLIOGRAPHY

1954 *Early Leaving*. Report of the Central Advisory Council for Education (England). H.M.S.O. This report is notable for giving the first clear evidence, from a survey on a national scale, of the influence of social factors and home background on the length of school life, the educational achievements, and the scholastic promise of school children. The numbers of potential candidates for higher education lost through early leaving are estimated, and recommendations are made of steps which might be taken to encourage a higher proportion of pupils to remain in maintained Grammar Schools until the ages of seventeen or eighteen.

1956 FLOUD, J. E., HALSEY, A. H. and MARTIN, F. M. *Social Class and Educational Opportunity*. Heinemann. This is a report of intensive investigations, in two contrasting English localities, of the relations of secondary education to social structure. It outlines the history up to 1953 of the opportunity for gaining places in Grammar Schools in accordance with the social origins of the pupils. The chances of gaining a place, and of succeeding at school, are seen to have depended on many social factors, among the most potent being the home environment (including size of family), and the local conditions in the competition for places.

1959 *15 to 18* (*The Crowther Report*). Central Advisory Council for Education (England). Vols. I and II, H.M.S.O. This report is in effect a textbook of the empirical and quantitative aspects of educational sociology. Volume II consists of an account of the three social surveys specially undertaken to provide information for the committee. Throughout the report is a recognition of the influence of the social environment and the cultural pattern on educational performance, and there is confirmation of earlier researches on this subject. The importance of a prolonged full-time education, the loss of talent through early leaving, the need to raise the school-leaving age, the special value of the Grammar School sixth form, and the improvements foreseen in technical education are all fully discussed and many conclusions are reached.

1960 FLOUD, JEAN and HALSEY, A. H. *The Sociology of Education*. Vol. VII, No. 3, of *Current Sociology*. Basil Blackwell. This is described as a trend report, with special reference to the development of research in Western Europe and the U.S.A. It contains a most complete bibliography of thirty-four pages. The brief text begins to develop the views of the authors that the coming of industrialism gave rise to—or at least justified—the sociology of education in its modern form, and that the function of education is changing rapidly in relation to the more complex economic and social structure of the time.

1961 *The Year Book of Education*. Editors: J. A. Lauwerys and George F. Z. Bereday. Evans Bros. This still remains the most important annual volume on the sociology of education in its comparative and international aspects. The following past numbers have been of particular relevance: 1953 *The Status and Social Position of Teachers*; 1954 *Education and Technological Development*; 1956 *Education and Economics*; especially the editor's introduction; 1960 *Communication Media and the School.*

1961 HALSEY, A. H., FLOUD, JEAN and ANDERSON, C. ARNOLD (Eds.). *Education, Economy and Society*. The Free Press, Glencoe. This is a reader in the sociology of education containing reprints of thirty-eight papers mostly published between 1958 and 1961, and four published for the first time. This is particularly valuable for students in England, where there is a shortage of texts on the subject, and where new research is reported in a variety of different journals. The major theme of the book is the analysis of the changing functions of schools and universities under the conditions of rapid social change in advanced industrial countries. The relations of education to the national economy and the occupational structure are stressed, and there are also sections on the social factors in selection and academic achievement. The treatment is on the whole at an advanced level, but beginners in the subject can select the easier papers. The papers include comparative material from France and Germany as well as from Great Britain and the U.S.A.

GENERAL SOCIOLOGY

Recommended books for general background reading in sociology are:

GINSBERG, M. *Sociology*. Oxford University Press. 1934.

OGBURN, W. F. and NIMKOFF, M. E. *A Handbook of Sociology*. Kegan Paul. 1947.

SPROTT, W. J. H. *Science and Social Action*. Watts. 1954.

MACIVER, R. M. and PAGE, C. H. *Society*. London: Macmillan. 1950.

PART II. SPECIAL REFERENCES

The following lists of references are arranged under chapter headings, and consist of the works to which reference has been made in the text, with some additional works of relevance to the subject matter of the chapter.

CHAPTER I. THE SOCIOLOGY OF EDUCATION

CLARKE, SIR FRED. *Freedom in the Education Society*. University of London Press. 1948.

COLLINGWOOD, R. G. *The New Leviathan*. Oxford University Press. 1942.

DURKHEIM, EMILE. *Education and Sociology*. Translated Sherwood D. Fox. Free Press, Glencoe. 1956.

FLOUD, JEAN and HALSEY, A. H. *The Sociology of Education*. Vol. VII, No. 3 of *Current Sociology*. Basil Blackwell. 1958.

HALSEY, A. H., FLOUD, JEAN and ANDERSON, ARNOLD C. *Education, Economy and Society*. Free Press, Glencoe. 1961.

HALMOS, P. (Ed.). 'The Teaching of Sociology to Students of Education and Social Work.' *Sociological Review Monograph*, No. 4. Keele. 1961.

HAVIGHURST, R. J. and NEUGARTEN, B. L. *Society and Education*. Allyn and Bacon, 1957.

MANNHEIM, KARL. *Diagnosis of Our Time*. Kegan Paul. 1943.

OTTAWAY, A. K. C. 'The Aims and Scope of Educational Sociology.' *Educational Review*, Vol. 12, No. 3. June 1960.

CHAPTER II. THE CULTURE CONCEPT

ARNOLD, MATTHEW. *Culture and Anarchy*. Cambridge University Press. 1946.

BENEDICT, RUTH. *Patterns of Culture*. Routledge. 1935.

DAVIS, ALLISON. *Social Class Influences on Learning*. Harvard University Press. 1951.

ELIOT, T. S. *Notes Towards the Definition of Culture*. Faber. 1948.

GORER, GEOFFREY. *The Americans*, 1948 and *Exploring English Character*, 1955. Cresset Press.

KLUCKHOHN, CLYDE. *Mirror for Man*. Harrap. 1950.

LINTON, RALPH. *The Cultural Background of Personality*. Kegan Paul. 1947.

MAYS, J. B. *Growing Up in a City*. Liverpool University Press. 1954.

MEAD, MARGARET. *Gowing Up in New Guinea*. Pelican. 1942. *Coming of Age in Samoa*. Pelican. 1943.

ORWELL, G. *The English People*. Collins. 1947.

PEAR, T. H. *English Social Differences*. Allen and Unwin. 1955.

SPINLEY, B. M. *The Deprived and the Privileged*. Routledge and Kegan Paul, 1953.

SUTTIE, IAN D. *The Origins of Love and Hate*. Kegan Paul. 1935. Penguin Books. 1960.

WILLIAMS, RAYMOND. *Culture and Society*, 1958, and *The Long Revolution*, 1961. Chatto and Windus.

WINNICOTT, D. W. *The Child and the Family*. Tavistock Press. 1957.

YOUNG, MICHAEL and WILLMOTT, PETER. *Family and Kinship in East London*, 1957, and *Family and Class in a London Suburb*, 1960. Routledge and Kegan Paul.

ZWEIG, F. *The Worker in an Affluent Society*. Heinemann. 1962.

CHAPTER III. SOCIAL FORCES AND CULTURAL CHANGE

BRIGGS, ASA. *The Birth of Broadcasting*. Oxford University Press. 1962.

BUTTS, R. F. *A Cultural History of Western Education*. McGraw Hill. 1955.

BIBLIOGRAPHY

CLARKE, SIR FRED. *Freedom in the Educative Society*. University of London Press, 1948.

MACIVER, R. M. and PAGE, C. H. *Society*. Macmillan. 1950.

MANNHEIM, KARL. *Freedom, Power and Democratic Planning*. Routledge and Kegan Paul. 1952.

OGBURN, W. F. and NIMKOFF, M. E. *A Handbook of Sociology*. Kegan Paul. 1947.

CHAPTER IV. THE SOCIAL DETERMINANTS OF EDUCATION

DENT, H. C. *Education in Transition*. Kegan Paul, 1944.

FLEMING REPORT. *The Public Schools*. H.M.S.O. 1926.

HADOW REPORT. *Education of the Adolescent*. H.M.S.O. 1926.

LOWNDES, C. A. *The Silent Social Revolution*. 1937.

LESTER SMITH, W. O. *To Whom Do Schools Belong?* 1942, and *The Impact of Education on Society*, 1949. Blackwell.

MUMFORD, LEWIS. *Technics and Civilization*. Routledge. 1946.

NORWOOD REPORT. *Curriculum and Examinations in Secondary Schools*. H.M.S.O. 1943.

School and Life. Report of Central Advisory Council for Education. H.M.S.O. 1947.

SPENS REPORT. *Secondary Education*. H.M.S.O. 1938.

CHAPTER V. THE EDUCATIONAL NEEDS OF OUR FUTURE SOCIETY

ASHBY, SIR ERIC. *Technology and the Academics*. Macmillan. 1958.

DENT, H. C. *Change in English Education*. University of London Press. 1952.

DRUCKER, PETER F. *Landmarks of Tomorrow*. Harper. 1959.

FROMM, ERIC. *The Sane Society*. Routledge and Kegan Paul. 1956.

GEORGE, P. H. *Automation, Cybernetics and Society*. Leonard Hill. 1959.

HALMOS, PAUL. *Towards a Measure of Man*. Routledge and Kegan Paul. 1957.

MANNHEIM, KARL. *Man and Society*. Kegan Paul. 1940.

OLIVER, R. A. C. *General Studies in the G.C.E.* Northern Universities. Joint Matriculation Board. 1960.

ORWELL, GEORGE. *Nineteen Eighty Four*. Secker & Warburg. 1949.

Year Book of Education, 1961. *Concepts of Excellence in Education*. Evans Bros. 1961.

YOUNG, MICHAEL. *The Rise of the Meritocracy*. Thames & Hudson. 1958.

WIENER, NORBET. *The Human Use of Human Beings*. Eyre & Spottiswoode. 1951.

BIBLIOGRAPHY

CHAPTER VI. EDUCATION AND THE SOCIAL STRUCTURE

BANKS, OLIVE. *Parity and Prestige in English Secondary Education.* Routledge & Kegan Paul. 1955.

CROWTHER REPORT. *15 to 18.* Central Advisory Council for Education (England). H.M.S.O. 1959. Also *Early Leaving*. Report 1954.

DENT, H. C. *Universities in Transition.* Cohen & West. 1961.

FLOUD, JEAN. 'Social Class Factors in Educational Achievement.' Chap. 4 in *Ability and Educational Opportunity.* O.E.C.D. 1962. Obtainable H.M.S.O.

FLOUD, J. E. and HALSEY, A. H. 'Education and Occupation' in the *Year Book of Education.* Evan Bros. 1956.

FURNEAUX, W. D. *The Chosen Few.* Oxford University Press. 1961.

GLASS, D. V. (Ed.). *Social Mobility in Britain.* Routledge & Kegan Paul. 1954.

HALSEY, A. H. 'The Changing Functions of Universities in Advanced Industrial Societies.' *Harvard Educational Review.* Spring, 1960.

HALSEY, A. H., FLOUD, JEAN and ANDERSON, ARNOLD C. *Education, Economy and Society.* Glencoe, Free Press. 1961.

JACKSON, BRIAN and MARSDEN, DENNIS. *Education and the Working Class.* Routledge. 1962.

KELSALL, K. R. *An Enquiry into Admissions to the Universities.* Report for Association of Universities of British Commonwealth. 1957.

MACPHERSON, J. S. *Eleven Year Olds Grow Up.* University of London Press. 1958.

UNIVERSITY GRANTS COMMITTEE. *University Development* 1952/57. H.M.S.O. 1958.

VAIZEY, JOHN. *The Economics of Education.* Faber. 1962.

Year Book of Education. Education and Economics. 1956. *Higher Education.* 1959. Evans Bros.

CHAPTER VII. EDUCATIONAL OPPORTUNITY AND SOCIAL POLICY

BERNSTEIN, BASIL. 'Some Sociological Determinants of Perception'. *Brit. J. Sociol.* IX, June, 1958. 'Social Structure, Language and Learning.' *Educational Research*, VII, June 1961.

CAMPBELL, F. *Eleven Plus and All That: The Grammar School in a Changing Society.* Watts. 1956.

CROSLAND, C. A. R. 'Some Thoughts on English Education.' *Encounter*, No. 94. July 1961.

FLOUD, JEAN. 'Education and Social Class in the Welfare State', in *Looking Forward in Education.* Faber. 1955.

FLOUD, J. E., HALSEY, A. H. and MARTIN, F. M. *Social Class and Educational Opportunity*. Heinemann, 1956.

FLOUD, J. E. and HALSEY, A. H. 'Intelligence Tests, Social Class and Selection for Secondary Schools.' *Brit. J. Sociol.* VIII, No. 1. 1957.

FRAZER, ELIZABETH. *Home Environment and the School*. University of London Press. 1959.

HALSEY, A. H. 'Genetics, Social Structure and Intelligence.' *Brit. J. Sociol.*, IX, No. 1. 1958.

OGILVIE, VIVIAN. *The English Public School*. Batsford. 1937.

OTTAWAY, A. K. C. 'The Educational Sociology of Emile Durkheim.' *Brit. J. Sociol.*, VI, No. 3. 1955.

PEDLEY, ROBIN. *Comprehensive Education*. Gollanz. 1956.

TAYLOR, WILLIAM. *The English Secondary Modern School*. Faber. 1962.

VAIZEY, JOHN. 'The Public Schools', chapter in *The Establishment*. Ed. Hugh Thomas. 1959.

VERNON, P. E. (Ed.). *Secondary School Selection*. Methuen. 1957.

YATES, A. and PIDGEON, D. A. *Admission to Grammar Schools*. Newnes. 1957.

CHAPTER VIII. SOCIAL INTERACTION

ABRAMS, MARK. *Teenage Consumer Spending*. London Press Exchange. 1961.

BELL, N. W. and VOGEL, E. F. *A Modern Introduction to the Family*. Routledge & Kegan Paul. 1960.

BREW, MACALISTER J. *Youth and Youth Groups*. Faber. 1957.

Children and the Cinema. Report of Departmental Committee. H.M.S.O. 1960.

FYVEL, T. R. *The Insecure Offenders*. Chatto & Windus. 1961.

HIMMELWEIT, H. T. and OPPENHEIM, A. N. *Television and the Child*. Oxford University Press. 1958.

HOGGART, RICHARD. *The Uses of Literacy*. Chatto & Windus. 1957.

JONES, HOWARD. *Reluctant Rebels*. Tavistock. 1961.

Out of School. Report of Central Advisory Council for Education. H.M.S.O. 1948.

SCHRAMM *et al*. *Television in the Lives of Our Children*. Oxford University Press. 1961.

TANNER and INHELDER. *Discussions on Child Development*. Tavistock. 1960.

CHAPTER IX. THE SCHOOL AS A SOCIAL UNIT

ANDERSON, H. H. and BREWER, H. M. *Studies in Teachers' Classroom Personalities*. Applied Psychology Monographs, No. 6, 1945; No. 8 and No. 11, 1946. Stanford University Press.

Democracy in School Life. Report of Association for Education in Citizenship. Oxford University Press. 1947.
DURKHEIM, E. *Moral Education*. English Translation; Edited Everett K. Wilson, Free Press. 1961.
FLOUD, J. E. and SCOTT, W. 'The Social Origins of Teachers in England and Wales.' Chapter 37 in *Education, Economy and Society*. 1961.
HUGHES, A. G. *Education and Democratic Ideal*. Longmans. 1951.
LIPPITT, R. and WHITE, R. K. 'The Social Climate in Children's Groups.' In *Child Behaviour and Development*. Barker, Kounin and Wright. 1943.
MAYER, MARTIN. *The Schools*. Bodley Head. 1961.
MINISTRY OF EDUCATION. Pamphlet No. 16. *Citizens Growing Up*. 1949.
OESER, O. A. (Ed.). *Teacher, Pupil and Task*. Tavistock. 1955.
OTTAWAY, A. K. C. 'Social Relations in the School.' *Researches and Studies*, No. 4. May 1951.
SPENS REPORT. *Secondary Education*. H.M.S.O. 1938.
STEVENS, F. M. *The Living Tradition: The Social and Educational Assumptions of the Grammar School*. Hutchinson. 1960.
TROPP, ASHER. *The School Teachers*. Heinemann. 1957.
WALL, W. D. (Ed.). *Education and Mental Health*. Unesco/Harrap. 1955.
Year Book of Education, 1953. *The Status and Position of Teachers*. Evans Bros.

CHAPTER X. UNDERSTANDING HUMAN BEHAVIOUR

ALLPORT, G. W. *Personality*. Holt, reprinted 1955.
FROMM, ERIC. *The Fear of Freedom*. Kegan Paul. 1942.
GIBSON, QUENTIN. *The Logic of Social Enquiry*. Routledge & Kegan Paul. 1960.
HALMOS, PAUL (Ed.). *Papers on the Teaching of Personality Development*. Sociological Review Monographs 1 and 2, 1958–59. Keele.
HORNEY, KAREN. *The Neurotic Personality of Our Time*, 1937 and *Neurosis and Human Growth*, 1951. Kegan Paul.
Human Relations. Quarterly Journal published by the Tavistock Institute of Human Relations.
KLEIN, JOSEPHINE. *Working with Groups*. Hutchinson. 1961.
KLUCKHOHN, CLYDE and MURRAY, H. A. *Personality in Nature, Society Culture*. Cape. 1949.
LEWIN, KURT. *Resolving Social Conflicts*. Harper. 1948.
MANNHEIM, KARL. *Man and Society*. Kegan Paul. 1940.
MURPHY, GARDNER. *Personality: A Biosocial Approach*. Harper. 1947. *Human Potentialities*. Allen & Unwin. 1960.
OTTAWAY, A. K. C. 'Group Dynamics—Some Notes on an Experiment.' *Case Conference*, Vol. 6, No. 7. 1960.
PETERS, R. S. *The Concept of Motivation*. Routledge & Kegan Paul. 1958.

SPROTT, W. J. H. *Human Groups*. Penguin Books. 1958.
STRANG, RUTH. *Group Work in Education*. Harper. 1958.
WOOTTON, BARBARA. *Testament for Social Science*. Heinemann. 1951.

CHAPTER XI. BEYOND SOCIOLOGY

COLLINGWOOD, R. G. *The New Leviathan*. Oxford University Press. 1942.
RUSSELL, BERTRAND. *Authority and the Individual*. Allen & Unwin. 1949.

INDEX